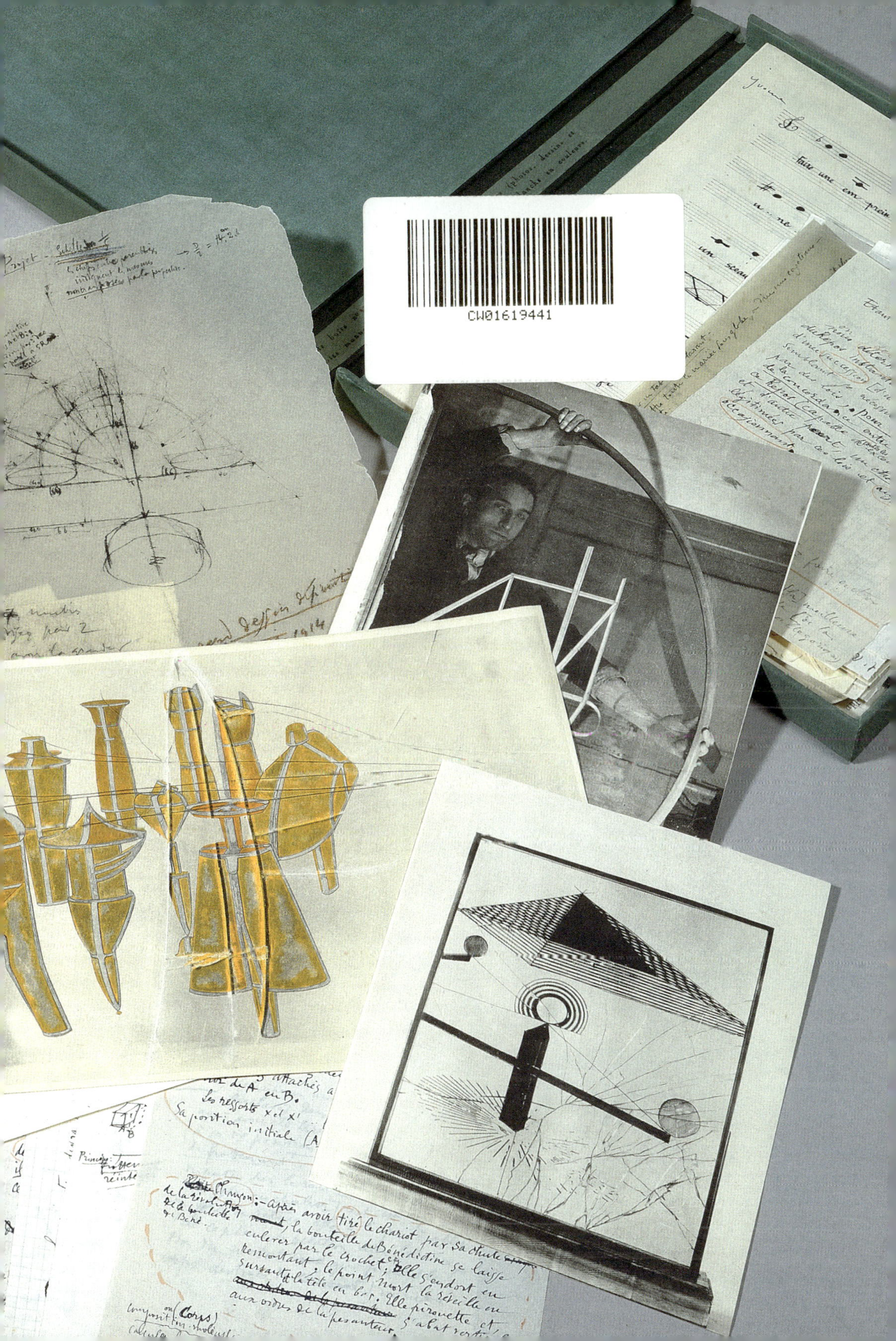

CHANCE

AESTHETICS

CHANCE

AESTHETICS

CHANCE

AESTHETICS

CHANCE

AESTHETICS

CHANCE

AESTHETICS

CHANCE

AESTHETICS

CHANCE

AESTHETICS

CHANCE

AESTHETICS

CHANCE

AESTHETICS

CHANCE

AESTHETICS

CHANCE

AESTHETICS

CHANCE

AESTHETICS

CHANCE

AESTHETICS

CHANCE

AESTHETICS

CHANCE

AESTHETICS

CHANCE

AESTHETICS

CHANCE

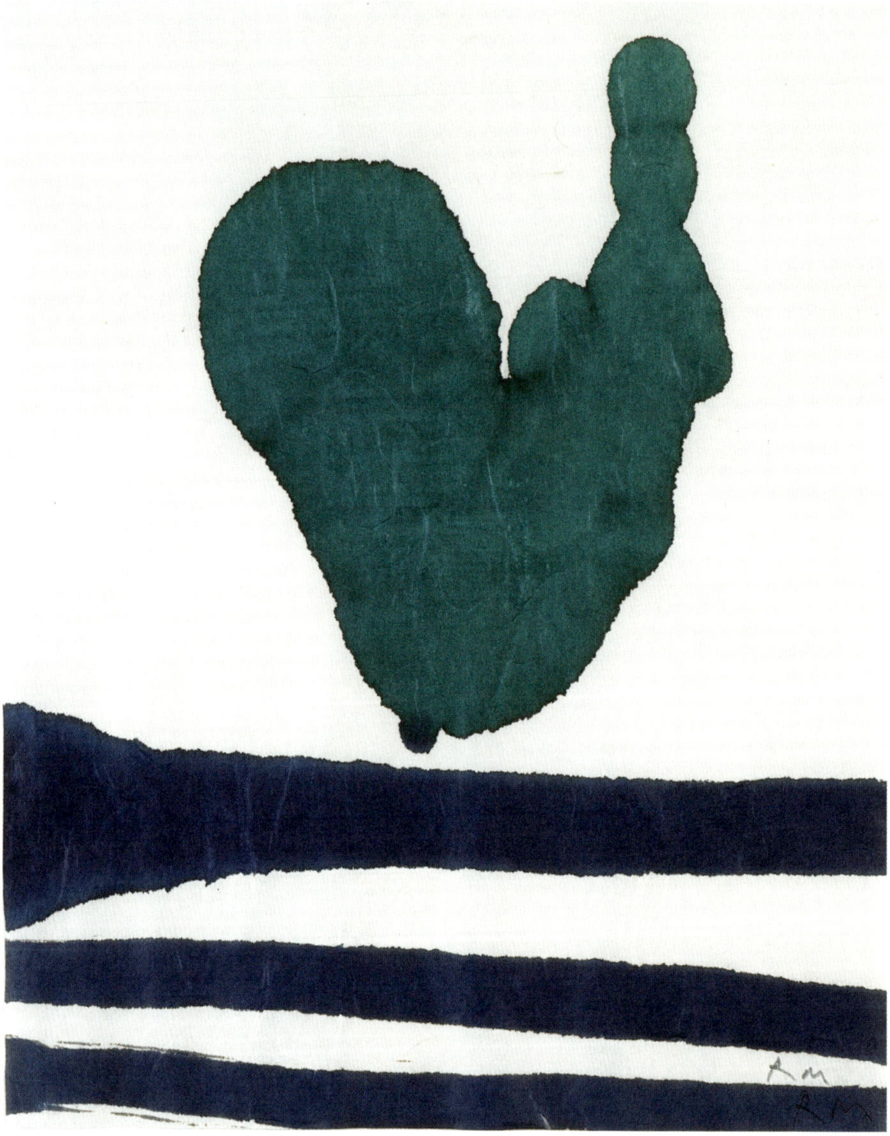

CHANCE AESTHETICS

Meredith Malone

essays by

Susan Laxton

Janine Mileaf

catalog entries by

Bradley Bailey

Emily Hage

Mildred Lane Kemper Art Museum / Washington University in St. Louis

MILDRED LANE KEMPER ART MUSEUM

This volume is published in conjunction with the exhibition *Chance Aesthetics*, organized by the Mildred Lane Kemper Art Museum at the Sam Fox School of Design & Visual Arts at Washington University in St. Louis, on view September 18, 2009, to January 4, 2010.

Support for *Chance Aesthetics* was provided by James M. Kemper, Jr.; the David Woods Kemper Memorial Foundation; the Hortense Lewin Art Fund; the National Endowment for the Arts; the Missouri Arts Council, a state agency; the Dedalus Foundation, Inc.; John and Anabeth Weil; the University Lane Foundation; the Regional Arts Commission; and members of the Mildred Lane Kemper Art Museum.

Published by
Mildred Lane Kemper Art Museum
Sam Fox School of Design & Visual Arts
Washington University in St. Louis
One Brookings Drive
St. Louis, Missouri 63130

Editor: Jane E. Neidhardt, St. Louis
Editorial assistant: Eileen G'Sell, St. Louis
Designer: Michael Worthington and Yasmin Khan, Counterspace, Los Angeles
Design assistant: Caelin White, Los Angeles
Printer: Shapco Printing, Inc., Minneapolis

Distributed by
The University of Chicago Press
11030 S. Langley Avenue
Chicago, IL 60628
Domestic:
Tel: 1-800-621-2736
Fax: 1-800-621-8476
International:
Tel: 1-773-702-7000
Fax: 1-773-702-7212

Library of Congress Control Number: 2009932496
ISBN: 978-0-936316-27-7

FRONT COVER:
Niki de Saint Phalle
Grand tir–séance Galerie J (detail), 30 June–12 July 1961
Plaster, paint, wire mesh, string, and plastic, 56 5/16 x 30 5/16"

END PAPER (FRONT):
Marcel Duchamp
La Mariée mise à nu par ses célibataires même (La Boîte verte) (The Bride Stripped Bare by Her Bachelors, Even [The Green Box]), 1934
Ninety-four facsimile documents in a green suede box, 13 1/16 x 11 1/8 x 1"

FRONTISPIECE:
Robert Motherwell
One work from the *Lyric Suite*, 1965
Ink on rice paper, 11 x 9"
© 2009 Dedalus Foundation, Inc. / Licensed by VAGA, New York, NY

END PAPER (BACK):
Daniel Spoerri
Topographie anécdotée du hasard (An Anecdoted Topography of Chance), published 1962
Artist's book, 7 1/4 x 5 5/16"

BACK COVER:
François Morellet
50 lignes au hasard (detail), 1967
Adhesive on Plexiglas, 45 11/16 x 45 11/16"

CONTENTS

ACKNOWLEDGMENTS

It was a great pleasure to organize *Chance Aesthetics* at the Mildred Lane Kemper Art Museum. Both the catalog and the exhibition were the topic of numerous conversations with friends, colleagues, and artists. For that I extend warm thanks to William Anastasi, Sharon Avery-Fahlström, Timothy Baum, Juliet Bellow, Elizabeth Childs, Anna Dezeuze, Natasha Ruiz-Gomez, Jon Hendricks, Jennifer Josten, Ellsworth Kelly, Sandi Knakal, Gregory Levine, Catharina Manchanda, Angela Miller, François Morellet, Alison Knowles, Christine Poggi, Tricia Paik, Judith Rodenbeck, Anne Rorimer, Alicia Walker, and Bert Winther-Tamaki. I also extend my gratitude to those who provided financial support and to each of the lenders to the exhibition—the dealers, institutions, and individuals listed on page 171—whose generosity allowed tremendous artworks to be seen here in St. Louis.

This unique catalog would not have been possible without the expertise of Jane Neidhardt, managing editor. She worked with exceptional dedication to see this book to completion, and her excellent questions, suggestions, and meticulous proofreading have guided it to its fullest potential. I am also grateful to Susan Laxton and Janine Mileaf for their thoughtful and enriching essays reflecting their distinctive and sustained engagement with the topic of chance and modern art. Bradley Bailey and Emily Hage provided important contributions to the catalog, and I thank them both for their keen interest in the progress of the project and the insights they provided throughout its development. Michael Worthington and Yasmin Khan at Counterspace designed the catalog with intelligence and enthusiasm, and were a pleasure to work with.

On the staff of the Mildred Lane Kemper Art Museum I am especially grateful to director Sabine Eckmann, who has been an enthusiastic advocate since the exhibition's inception. Rachel Keith, chief registrar, negotiated the loans with consummate good humor and attention to detail. Eileen G'Sell, publications assistant, worked tirelessly organizing images and permissions for reproduction as well as lent a dexterous editorial hand. Karen K. Butler, assistant curator, was a source of indispensible comments and criticisms and generously contributed one of the entries to the catalog. Research assistants Nicole Keller and Ruxandra Marcu provided early support for the project and its dynamic schedule of public programs. Other staff members who have been instrumental include Kimberly Singer, manager of marketing and visitor services; Jan Hessel, facilities manager; Ron Weaver, exhibition preparator; and John Launius, security supervisor. The entire team worked diligently, and this exhibition would not have been possible without them.

Finally, I would like to express my gratitude to both Carmon Colangelo, dean of the Sam Fox School of Design & Visual Arts, and Mark Wrighton, chancellor of Washington University, for their unfailing commitment to this and all Museum projects.

INTRODUCTION

MEREDITH MALONE

Chance has been understood as both a liberating source of unforeseen possibilities and a threatening force capable of undermining human self-sufficiency and moral self-determination. As an indication of the world's instability and our uncertain position within it, chance has been a perennial concern in the visual arts as subject matter and theme.[1] In the early decades of the twentieth century, however, avant-garde artists began to enthusiastically adopt it as a decisive factor in the actual composition of an artwork. *Chance Aesthetics* explores chance as a key compositional principle of modernism from the beginning of the twentieth century through the early 1970s, a time of transition after high modernism and just before the advent of the first fully postmodern generation.[2] Defined as operating outside of the purview of the artist, chance and its many manifestations (accident, luck, randomness, and contingency), when incorporated into the creative process, speak directly to questions of aesthetic philosophy and sensibility. While artists have called on chance to fulfill a variety of aims—aggressive anti-art agendas, revolutionary attempts to bypass the conscious mind and transform the way reality is perceived, statements of free will, and radical programs meant to open the artwork to the random flow of everyday life, to name a few—its strategic appeal is similar throughout much avant-garde production. Undertaken as a stimulus to new forms of artistic invention, the deliberate implementation of accident and the openness to vagaries of interpretation advanced a challenge to longstanding assumptions concerning what might constitute a work of art as well as the role of the artist as autonomous creator. The artistic recourse to chance bypasses the idea of personal responsibility and individual investment in a work of art by redefining the notion of creativity as a form of production whose development is contingent rather than deliberate. What is ultimately at stake is artistic subjectivity, as questions of intentionality, rationality, and decision making are suspended but never completely negated.

In the context of this project, chance is understood as a relative concept defined by an intentional curbing of artistic agency, not as an absolute absence of cause. *Chance Aesthetics* takes the productive tension between chance and determinism as its point of departure, placing critical emphasis on artistic processes that cede an element of authorial intent to circumstance, whether through internal or external forces, mechanical procedures, or the intervention of other agents. Such processes include dropping cut paper onto a surface and gluing them down where they lay, dripping or flinging paint across a canvas, letting the progressive decay of organic materials determine a composition, or tossing coins to arrive at formal selections, among others. The over sixty works presented in the *Chance Aesthetics* exhibition focus on the visual arts but also highlight certain expressions of poetry, performance, and sound art. Spanning numerous disciplines and mediums, the objects represent an equally diverse group of avant-garde artists, including such pioneering figures of chance-based composition as Marcel Duchamp, Jean Arp, André Breton, Jackson Pollock, and John Cage.

Previous exhibitions exploring the relationship between chance and art range in approach from ambitious historical overviews that reach, in some cases, as far back as the fifteenth century, to sweeping studies that move swiftly through the entire twentieth century.[3] *Chance Aesthetics* lays no claims to presenting a comprehensive survey of chance in modern art. Rather, this exhibition and its catalog offers a focused examination of the dynamic tension between chance and control, between the repudiation of accepted notions of autonomy and originality and the reassertion of authorship that lies at the heart of all artistic creation that employs chance. Through this unique approach, *Chance Aesthetics* attempts to advance fresh perspectives on an important and extensive subject in which critical discourse and artistic process are fascinatingly intertwined.

The exhibition is conceived in a thematic manner. Its three sections—"Collage, Assemblage, and the Found Object," "Automatism," and "Games and Systems of Random Ordering"—address central avant-garde strategies employed to subvert traditional genres and forms of expression such as painting and sculpture, as well as the bourgeois values and rationalist ideals they were understood to represent. While remaining necessarily fluid (several works can be understood as crossing multiple categories at once), these sections provide a framework through which individual movements—Dada, Surrealism, Abstract Expressionism, Nouveau Réalisme, Fluxus, and others—can be traversed in an effort to critically compare and contrast a variety of chance-based strategies and objectives as they were deployed, received, revised, and redeployed across diverse historical and cultural contexts.

A recurring pattern of abandoning and reclaiming agency becomes evident in all of the works discussed here, as artists exploit the possibilities of chance by tapping into its creative potential while inevitably intervening in its operations. "Proclaim as we might our liberation from causality and our dedication to anti-art," stated Dada artist Hans Richter retrospectively, "we could not help involving our whole selves, including our conscious sense of order, in the creative process.... Chance could never be liberated from the presence of the conscious artist. This was the reality in which we worked ... a situation of conflict."[4] As Richter's statement makes clear, it is hard to make chance an artistic program. Self-contradiction pervades its adherents' pronouncements. A balance must be struck between the ideal of pure, unmediated spontaneity and the need for a degree of critical self-awareness to avoid devolving into total arbitrariness and nihilism. To that effect, artists have established bounds so that some control, however loosely, can be maintained. This volume begins to unpack the fraught relationship between artistic intent and contingency as it reappears in different historical contexts at points throughout the twentieth century. It treats the category of chance critically and differentially by addressing three main factors: the process (or processes) chosen, the nature of the work produced, and the rhetoric employed to describe and theorize chance in both Western Europe and the United States.

Recognizing that the move to employ chance as a compositional factor did not occur in a vacuum, *Chance Aesthetics* also places significant emphasis on the relationship between artistic production and the sociocultural matrix in which it was made. Every age has its particular fascination with chance as origin, terminus, and possibility. In the early twentieth century, psychologists, philosophers, scientists, and artists alike were enthralled by the notion of chance as a possible key to a nondeterministic, acausal scheme for interpreting the universe. The pervasive preoccupation with randomness and contingency may be seen, argues artist and critic Jeremy Gilbert-Rolfe, as a product of overdetermination—as the logical consequence of attempts in the eighteenth and nineteenth centuries, through reason and mechanization, to diminish the role chance might play in everyday life.[5] In physics, it culminated in quantum theory and Werner Heisenberg's indeterminacy principle, which together toppled deterministic constructs of the physical universe.[6] In the realm of psychology, Carl Jung's theory of synchronicity (the experience of two or more causally unrelated events occurring together in a supposedly meaningful manner) and Sigmund Freud's notion of parapraxes (that slips of the tongue and other "accidental" gestures are actually involuntary clues to the sublimated life of the unconscious) became for many artists a source of inspiration. Accident began to appear as a serendipitous means of discovery. Modernist thinkers were also becoming increasingly aware of Eastern interpretations of experience as manifested in the Chinese *I Ching* (*Book of Changes*) and the Zen Buddhist nondeterministic understanding of the natural world.

With the rise of fascism in Europe in the 1930s, chance, accident, and play acquired a sharper political edge, as exemplified in Dutch historian Johan Huizinga's paean to play, *Homo Ludens: A Study of the Play-Element in Culture* (1938). In the immediate post-World War II period, many artists embraced an aesthetic of unmediated spontaneity as a means of grappling with a civilization traumatized by the Holocaust and nuclear devastation. The spontaneous gesture, considered a symbol of subjective experience, proved exceptionally appealing in a world understood by some existentialists as absurd. The 1950s and 1960s witnessed a confluence of unprecedented technological advancements, economic prosperity, and technocratic excesses resulting from the rise of corporate cultures of control. With the emergence of market research, risk management, game theory, and other forms of knowledge based on statistical surveys and probability, the random occurrence became the unpredictable exception that proved the predictable rule.[7] While statistical thinking may have theoretically robbed chance of its power, artists on both sides of the Atlantic mobilized randomness and indeterminacy as a counterpoint to the rapid standardization of experience attributable to increases in consumerism and functionalism. The emergence of a boundary-less postmodern culture in the late 1960s and 1970s inaugurated another major shift in assumptions about chance. As artists began to embrace all manner of representations and styles while querying notions of origin and authorship—a point of view crystallized by French theorist Roland Barthes in his landmark essay, "The Death of the Author" (1967)—chance was no longer readily conceived as a radical anti-convention capable of circumventing the status quo, but rather as one of many in a long line of modernist conventions.

***

In the first part of this volume, three essays draw connections across media and disciplines, linking the genesis and meaning of artistic production through chance to larger sociocultural, historical, and theoretical contexts. Janine Mileaf explores the link between the deterministic force of gravity and chance as manifested in practices of dripping, dropping, and scattering from Dada to Process art in the 1960s and 1970s. She interprets the enactment of falling in art and the seemingly random distribution of materials across horizontal planes as generative practices signifying the relinquishment of total control over processes of production in favor of unintended outcomes and contingent forms. Susan Laxton scrutinizes the Surrealist pursuit of automatism and its many structural paradoxes. Following the evolution from a preoccupation with supposedly unmediated practices, such as automatic drawing, decalcomania, and frottage, to the production of mechanical systems developed to guarantee chance outcomes, she unpacks the Surrealists' desire to demonstrate the inevitability of mediation in all experience, even as they insisted on "making strange" as a resistance to a society organized on the basis of a means–ends rationality. Finally, my own essay looks at the pronounced turn to chance-based procedures in art of the late 1950s and early 1960s in both Western Europe and the United States. Focusing on Nouveau Réalisme and Fluxus, I explore how the use of chance, and the stance of casual detachment it implies, is symptomatic of a broader reconfiguration of artistic practice and subjectivity in the face of both an increasingly administered culture and the stifling hegemony of high-modernist art.

The second half of the catalog loosely replicates the three-part structure of the exhibition. This section includes a series of short texts with contributions by art historians Bradley Bailey and Emily Hage that provide contextual information on the artists as well as specific interpretations of individual artworks. Whenever possible, artists' writings and excerpts from contemporary criticism have been included to further elucidate the diverse nature of the meanings assigned to chance and the divergent discourses used to describe and theorize its aesthetic application throughout the twentieth century.

NOTES

1. For an examination of chance in nineteenth-century art, see Dario Gamboni's foundational work in his essay, "'Fabrication of accidents': Factura and chance in nineteenth-century art," *Res: Journal of Anthropology and Aesthetics* 36 (Autumn 1999): 205–25, and his book *Potential Images: Ambiguity and Indeterminacy in Modern Art* (London: Reaktion Books, 2002).

2. There is no agreement among scholars of art history about the precise historical period to which the term "postmodernism" applies. Certainly there are works discussed here that display characteristically post-modern elements. While this project focuses on chance and modern art, this is not to say that chance is without relevance in postmodernism, but when applied outside of progressive modernist paradigms, its meaning and efficacy significantly alter so as to warrant another set of analytic criteria.

3. The importance of chance in the history of art has been widely recognized by artists, theorists, and art historians alike. Prominent examples of exhibitions that have addressed chance in modern art from a variety of perspectives include *Against Order: Chance and Art* (Philadelphia: Institute of Contemporary Art, 1970); *Chance and Change: A Century of the Avant-garde* (Auckland, New Zealand: Auckland City Art Gallery, 1985); *Art by Chance: Fortuitous Impressions* (Kansas City: Nelson-Atkins Museum of Art, 1989); *Zufall als Prinzip: Spielwelt, Methode und System in der Kunst des 20. Jahrhunderts* (Ludwigshafen: Wilhelm-Hack-Museum, 1992); and *Drawing on Chance: Selections from the Collection* (New York: Museum of Modern Art, 1995).

4. Hans Richter, *Dada: Art and Anti-Art* (New York: McGraw-Hill Book Company, 1965), 59.

5. Jeremy Gilbert-Rolfe, "Not By Chance Alone," *Chance: The Catalogue*, ed. Sarah Gavlak and Chris Kraus (Santa Monica: Smart Art Press, 1996), n.p.

6. German physicist Werner Heisenberg's publication of his principle of indeterminacy in 1927 revealed that any prediction is possible only on a statistical basis. Statistical thinking thus tamed chance by giving up the notion of universality in favor of a probabilistic model of natural law. See Ian Hacking, *The Taming of Chance* (Cambridge: Cambridge University Press, 1990), 2.

7. See Jackson Lears, *Something for Nothing: Luck in America* (New York: Viking, 2003), 21. Ian Hacking notes that the erosion of determinism at the end of the nineteenth century did not imply decay in knowledge or the creation of disorder; rather, a seeming paradox emerged—"the more the indeterminism, the more the control"—as chance became the loyal servant of the natural, biological, and social sciences. See Hacking, *Taming of Chance*, 2. See also Gerd Gigerenzer, et al., *The Empire of Chance: How Probability Changed Science and Everyday Life* (Cambridge: Cambridge University Press, 1989).

DROP, DRIP, SCATTER

CHANCE ARRANGEMENTS IN ART SINCE DAD

DROP, DRIP, SCATTER
CHANCE ARRANGEMENTS IN ART SINCE DAD
DROP, DRIP, SCATTER
CHANCE ARRANGEMENTS IN ART SINCE DAD
DROP, DRIP, SCATTER
CHANCE ARRANGEMENTS IN ART SINCE DAD
DROP, DRIP, SCATTER
CHANCE ARRANGEMENTS IN ART SINCE DAD
DROP, DRIP, SCATTER
CHANCE ARRANGEMENTS IN ART SINCE DAD
DROP, DRIP, SCATTER
CHANCE ARRANGEMENTS IN ART SINCE DAD
DROP, DRIP, SCATTER
CHANCE ARRANGEMENTS IN ART SINCE DAD
DROP, DRIP, SCATTER
CHANCE ARRANGEMENTS IN ART SINCE DAD
DROP, DRIP, SCATTER
CHANCE ARRANGEMENTS IN ART SINCE DAD
DROP, DRIP, SCATTER
CHANCE ARRANGEMENTS IN ART SINCE DAD
DROP, DRIP, SCATTER
CHANCE ARRANGEMENTS IN ART SINCE DAD
DROP, DRIP, SCATTER
CHANCE ARRANGEMENTS IN ART SINCE DAD
DROP, DRIP, SCATTER
CHANCE ARRANGEMENTS IN ART SINCE DAD
DROP, DRIP, SCATTER
CHANCE ARRANGEMENTS IN ART SINCE DAD
DROP, DRIP, SCATTER
CHANCE ARRANGEMENTS IN ART SINCE DAD
DROP, DRIP, SCATTER
CHANCE ARRANGEMENTS IN ART SINCE DAD
DROP, DRIP, SCATTER

Drop, Drip, Scatter: Chance Arrangements in Art since Dada

Janine Mileaf

The simplest game of chance—rolling dice—involves the launching of objects into the air followed by their collection upon a surface. Indeed, the very word "chance" derives from the Latin word for falling, suggesting the inseparability of chance from the operations of release and gravity. For players of chance games, the combinations of numbers indicated upon the surfaces of dice are paramount. Avant-garde artists who have taken up related engagements with gravity, however, more often focus on the spatial arrangements of dropped, scattered, or poured materials and things. Working with gravity, and against the conventional association of gravity with the inevitable or predetermined, artists have distributed materials across floors and over canvases in seemingly random arrangements. Such chance configurations work to imply the relinquishment of total control over the processes of production. Surrender of this type, which was first tested by the Dadaists, has been understood to signify a break with traditional readings of subjectivity in art. Artists' willingness to "let go" suggests a desire to downplay the significance of the self in their work. The generation of artists who took up scatter as a purposeful strategy in the 1960s and 1970s turned in part to the intellectual maneuvers of Marcel Duchamp, but more emphatically in this endeavor to the skeins of paint unfurled onto canvas by Jackson Pollock. The rhetoric surrounding Pollock at the time of his initial fame still claimed the importance of expressivity in art. Yet artists like Robert Morris quickly changed the terms of the discussion to align the seemingly disparate legacies of Duchamp and Pollock. Though still setting the two artists in opposition to each other, Morris, following the psychoanalyst Anton Ehrenzweig, theorized the aesthetic of gravity as a play between chance and determination, or scatter and containment. This very tension between the look of release and forms of control engenders the varying practices of chance aesthetics that are associated by enactments of falling.

In his notes for his opus *The Bride Stripped Bare by Her Bachelors, Even*, or *The Large Glass* (1915–23), Marcel Duchamp conceived of chance under the aegis of a "regime of gravity."[1] He played with the authority of happenstance, imagining a form of bureaucracy or order that would encompass both gravity and coincidence:

> — *Regime of gravity* —
> *Ministry* of coincidences.
> Department (or better):
> Regime of Coincidence
> Ministry of gravity.[2]

In this note, collected in 1934 with others in *The Green Box* [Cat., p. 126], we see Duchamp searching to name an office that would regulate or administer the inescapable pull to the earth in tandem with unexpected twists of fate. That Duchamp envisaged these two forces together under the direction of a kind of government office suggests that he saw them as at once coercive and liberating. The combination of gravity—which in and of itself is a kind of structure—with the uncontrollable effects of coincidence harkens directly to that primary form of chance—the throwing of dice, where the structure of number combinations can stand in for the

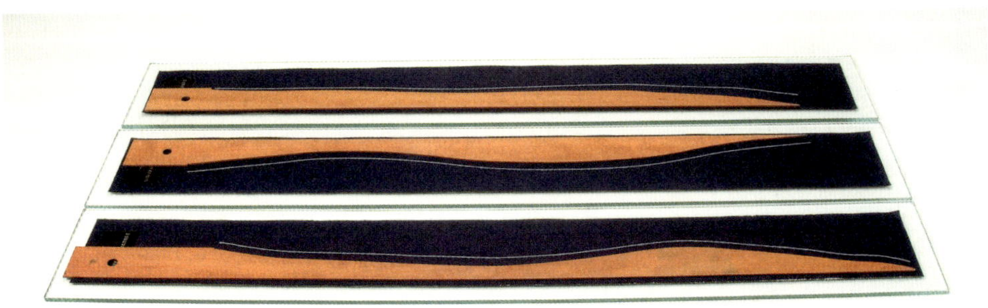

Fig. 1.
Marcel Duchamp
Three Standard Stoppages, 1964 (replica of 1913–14 original)
Thread on canvas attached to glass, wood sticks, enclosed in wood croquet case, 51 x 11 1/8 x 9" (case)

natural laws of gravity as they are paired with the unruly aspects of the fall. Whereas gravity has traditionally seemed to be something inevitable and determining, Duchamp posited it as an agent of surprise.

It is from this fundamental alliance between gravity and chance that Duchamp conceived his *Three Standard Stoppages* (1913–14) [Fig.1; Cat., p. 126], which he called a form of "canned chance."[3] In this work, Duchamp deformed the metric unit of measure through the aleatory operation of dropping. He released three one-meter threads from a height of one meter onto a surface. Each landed in a slightly different configuration, which Duchamp secured to a canvas. He then cut a new standard of measure out of wood in the pattern achieved through the fall of the thread. He explained in his note about this work that he included in his *Box of 1914*:

> *The Idea of Fabrication*
> —If a straight horizontal thread one meter long falls from a height of one meter onto a horizontal plane distorting itself *as it pleases* and creates a new shape of the measure of length.—
> —3 patterns obtained in more or less similar conditions: *considered in their relation to one another* they are an *approximate reconstitution* of the measure of length.
> The *3 standard stoppages* are the meter diminished.[4]

As in his rumination on a ministry of gravity, Duchamp here played with the structure of measurement against the presumed disorder of chance. The thread is afforded agency—finding form "as it pleases" and landing in an altered shape while maintaining its ostensible job of measurement.[5]

As Duchamp explained to Pierre Cabanne in 1967, he turned to chance for amusement, but also to escape the control and figuration of the "hand" in his art. "The idea of 'chance,' which many people were thinking about at the time, struck me too. The intention consisted above all in forgetting the hand, since, fundamentally, even your hand is chance."[6] Duchamp's assertion that the hand itself is indeterminate allowed him to incorporate all artistic activity under the edicts of chance. And yet, he continued to explain, there was a degree of pure chance that attracted him: "Pure chance interested me as a way of going against logical reality: to put something on a canvas, on a bit of paper, to associate the idea of a perpendicular thread a meter long falling from the height of one meter onto a horizontal plane, making its own deformation."[7] This description stresses the relationship between the upright force of figuration and the deformation of the horizontal plane—a space of illogic against that of "logical reality." Duchamp's *Stoppages* deny the artist's hand while also merging the possibilities of order and disorder—a standard of measure based on random curves disables the clean distinction between what can be assessed and what remains elusive.

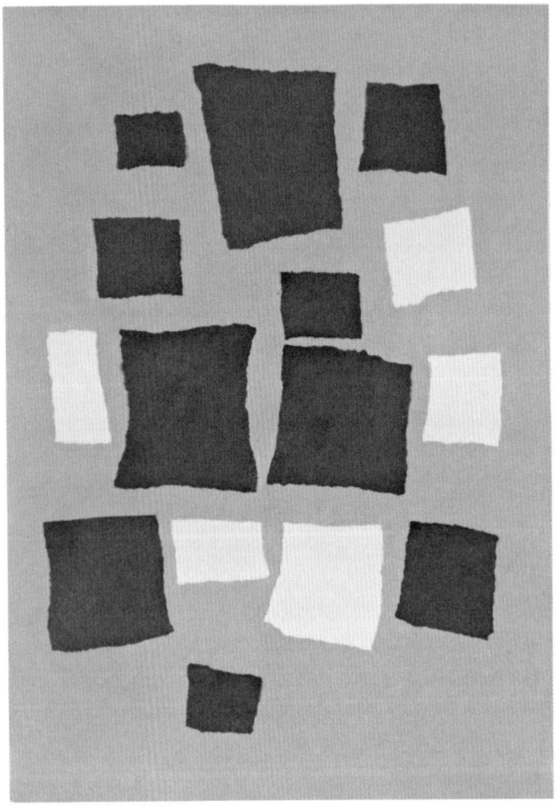

Fig. 2
Jean (Hans) Arp
Untitled (Collage with Squares Arranged according to the Laws of Chance), 1916–17
Torn-and-pasted paper and colored paper on paper, 19 1/8 x 13 5/8"

The construct of fallen material landing onto a plane of deformation echoes in the Dada collages of Jean Arp and Sophie Taeuber. These, too, are said to have depended upon the forces of gravity for their realization—although the precise degree to which this is true has been debated.[8] As in Arp's *Objets placés selon les lois du hasard III: Configuration symmetrique* (1931) [Cat., p. 78], a wooden construction in monochrome with oval forms adhered to an almost square support, Arp and Taeuber's paper collages from around 1916 secured somewhat irregular shapes upon a uniform surface, achieving the look of a skewed or exploded grid [Fig. 2]. Scholars such as T. J. Demos and Eric Robertson have noted the relative adherence of these arrangements to the overall structure of the grid, questioning the strict integrity of Arp's method. Yet, Demos argues that Arp's aims to "displace agency from artistic production" were achieved whether his chance effects were aided or not.[9] Furthermore, it was not Arp who codified his process as it has come down to us, but rather such Dada chroniclers as Georges Hugnet and Hans Richter. Presumably having spoken to Arp, Hugnet recorded the method as involving the shaking of paper scraps upon a piece of cardboard: "[Arp] also experimented with chance, putting on a piece of cardboard pieces of paper that he had cut out at random and then colored: he placed the scraps colored side down and then shook the cardboard; finally he would paste them to the cardboard just as they had fallen."[10] Hugnet's version of the story sees Arp as producing chance by holding tight to the surface of the image.

But it was Richter who put into place the possibly apocryphal story of the scraps of paper drifting through the air onto the floor—precisely adhering to the chance paradigm of falling and gravity. He described the process as a discovery rather than an intention. In other words, he posited two levels of chance—the first involves the falling of paper; the second relies on Arp's willingness to recognize the operation of falling as productive within his oeuvre:

> Dissatisfied with a drawing he had been working on for some time, Arp finally tore it up, and let the pieces flutter to the floor of his studio on the Zeltweg. Some time later he happened to notice these same scraps of paper as they lay on the floor, and was struck by the pattern they formed. It has the expressive power that he had tried in vain to achieve. How meaningful! How telling! Chance movements of his hand and of the fluttering scraps of paper had achieved what all his efforts had failed to achieve, namely *expression*. He accepted this challenge from chance as a decision of fate and carefully pasted the scraps down in the pattern which chance had determined.[11]

While the method of releasing materials onto the floor and then securing them into chance configurations in these collages is uncannily matched to Duchamp's process in the *Stoppages*, the similarities do not extend toward their interpretive matrices. That is, both Duchamp and Arp moved toward chance to avoid their own determinations, but according to Richter, Arp's method enabled fate to lead him to expressivity—"How meaningful!" Expression was never a goal of Duchamp.

If we focus on Arp's own memory of the genesis of these collages, we find that he did not stress the method of dropping paper, but rather conceived of chance as a synonym for spontaneity, or even abstraction. Chance is thus opposed to figuration—or the fixed idea for a composition—and approximates automatism. That is to say that in Arp's recollection, his method seems to prefigure a Surrealist form of automation in which the artist attempts to enable unconscious, or at least unpremeditated, processes. It is even unclear as to whether any dropping or falling took place:

> In 1915 Sophie Taeuber and I made in painting, embroidery and collage the first works derived from the simplest forms. These are probably the very first manifestations of this art. These pictures are Realities in themselves, without meaning or cerebral intention. We rejected everything that was copy or description, and allowed the Elementary and Spontaneous to react in full freedom. Since the disposition of planes, and the proportions and colors of these planes seemed to depend purely on chance, I declared that these works, like nature, were ordered "according to the law of chance," chance being for me merely a limited part of an unfathomable raison d'être, of an order inaccessible in its totality.[12]

In refusing to paint after motifs in nature, Arp claimed instead to align his work with the natural order, which he characterized as fortuitous, rather than deterministic. His image making seemed to be driven by a desire not only to avoid figuration but also to allow the elements to be arranged without any organizing principle.

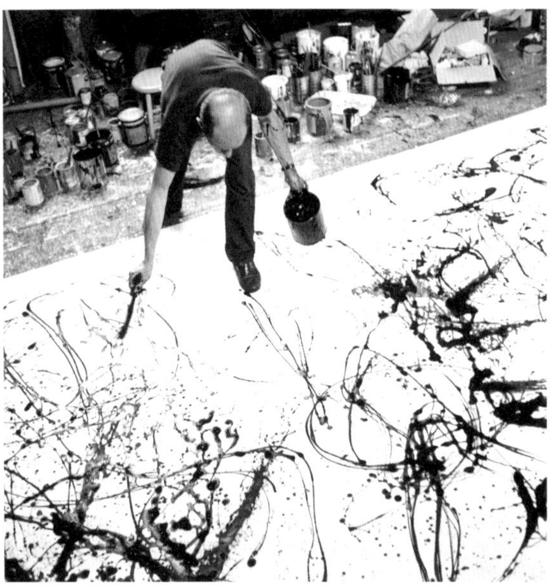

Fig. 3
Jackson Pollock, 1950
Photograph by Hans Namuth

Like Duchamp, who contrived his perpendicular strings to land upon the horizontal plane of deformation, Arp theorized the grid as a structure that enabled creativity by providing a format from which to depart: "The vertical and horizontal are the extreme signs available to man for touching the beyond and his inwardness."[13] This recognition of the alterity of the horizontal has been famously explored by Rosalind Krauss and Yve-Alain Bois, who argued for a reorientation of our understanding of certain strains of modernism toward this axis.[14] In their adaptation of Georges Bataille's notion of "formless," Krauss and Bois's theory highlights the ways in which horizontality escapes the hierarchical order of splits between mind and body, subject matter and the way things are made. They, like Robert Morris before them, link Duchamp's work with Jackson Pollock's painting practice by changing the parameters of interrogation from questions of form and content to those of operation or medium. Duchamp and Pollock may thus be brought together under the sign of gravity—and in this these artists further surrender to mechanisms of chance as generative of works of art and their signification. Pollock's rotation of his canvas from the wall to the studio floor became a paradigm for this unruly modernism [Fig. 3].

In more direct terms, we can see how Pollock's painting process deploys release, gravity, and the surface of the floor in ways that are surprisingly akin to his Dada predecessors. Like Arp, he used the fall of materials onto flat surfaces to arrive at an order that relates to nature only inasmuch as nature itself was understood to be ordered "according to the laws of chance." Pollock's abstraction in works like *Untitled* (c. 1950)[Fig. 4; Cat., p. 108] indicates the dance of movement above the receiving plane of the paper. While we are accustomed to imagining a drawing on the surface of a drafting table, and thus oriented toward the horizontal plane of landscape, Pollock, as is well known, conceived this graphic gesture of dripping liquid onto paper in the scale and format of painting, thus negating the valuation of the uprightness of the painter's practice. Krauss and Bois focus on the floor as the locus of this transposition: "The floor had become a production site that was set in direct opposition to the vertical axis of the easel of the artist's studio, or the wall of the bourgeois apartment, or the high-cultural ideals of the museum."[15] In this reading, Pollock may be seen to share Duchamp's impulse to escape painting, even as he has come to define it for midcentury America. He may further be understood against the reading of contemporaries like Harold Rosenberg, who, crediting the

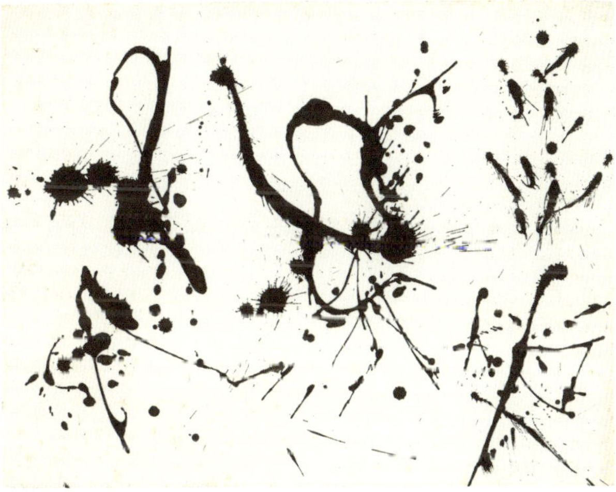

Fig. 4
Jackson Pollock
Untitled, c. 1950
Ink on paper, 18 7/8 x 24 3/4"

same automatic release of paint above rolled-out canvas, saw a vehicle for self-expression. As Rosenberg claimed: "The act-painting is of the same metaphysical substance as the artist's existence."[16] The comparison to Arp here is compelling—but not because both Richter and Rosenberg found in their subjects a journey toward expressivity. What Pollock and Arp share more insistently is the sense that automation of production—or rejection of control by the rational self—will arrive at satisfying conclusions in their work.

In theorizing the making of art, Robert Morris similarly conceived of an engagement with procedure in which the artist would tap into a structure of disorder. In doing so, he explicitly linked the operations of gravity and chance. As a writer and occasional curator as well as an artist, Morris worked to demarcate the boundaries of a new mode of sculptural production that stressed both materials and process. In December 1968, he organized an exhibition at gallerist Leo Castelli's warehouse where he mapped this terrain through the work of such artists as Eva Hesse, Richard Serra, and Bruce Nauman. It was there that Serra made his landmark *Splashing* (1968), which consisted of the chance landings of molten lead at the juncture between floorboards and wall.[17] A definitional example of a work involving release and gravity, *Splashing*, like Serra's related *Casting* (1969), literally recorded the shape and impact of its fall. The works exhibited in this show would come to define the Postminimalist tendencies eventually described as Process art.[18]

Morris declared the tenets of this new impulse in his watershed essay "Anti Form" (1968), which questioned the imperative of the right angle and the "well-built" and introduced interrogations of process. In his concluding thoughts, Morris turned to the indeterminacy of gravity and unstructured materials. In works where the artist refrains from intervening with the material, he argued, "considerations of gravity become as important as those of space."[19] He had in mind the type of undirected, yet engaged, automation that Arp discussed:

> The focus on matter and gravity as means results in forms that were not projected in advance. Considerations of ordering are necessarily casual and imprecise and unemphasized. Random piling, loose stacking, hanging, give passing form to the material. Chance is accepted and indeterminacy is implied, as replacing will result in another configuration. Disengagement with preconceived enduring forms and orders

> for things is a positive assertion. It is part of the work's refusal to continue estheticizing the form by dealing with it as a prescribed end.[20]

Morris's felt piece *Untitled* (1967–68) [Cat., p. 122] serves as an example of the kind of chance configurations he hoped to arrive at by abandoning the idea of a fixed end-product. Here, the weight of the unstructured material hanging off the wall allows the strips of felt to bend and fall apart from each other as they move toward the floor. Attached to the support of the wall, rather than falling through the air, Morris's felt pieces are ever in the process of becoming form.

In his essay "Some Notes on the Phenomenology of Making: The Search for the Motivated," Morris further theorized chance processes, introducing the rubrics of scatter and containment as matched against ideas about contingency and determinism.[21] It is in this essay, originally published in *Artforum* in 1970, that Morris articulated the legacies of Duchamp and Pollock as providing two possible models for chance operations in art. Duchamp, whose work he aligns with that of John Cage, provides a model for what he calls the "idealist" mode, where an "a priori system of mental logic" determines the results of the work. He does not cite *Three Standard Stoppages*, but we can see how the idea to use the three meter-length strings and drop them in space could be construed as an a priori system. Morris's notion that automation "serves to remove taste and the personal touch by co-opting forces, images, and processes to replace a step formerly taken in a directing or deciding way by the artist" has a distinctly Duchampian ring.[22] Both artists link taste to the hand and to the determining role of the artist.

The other model followed by those wishing to deploy the operations of chance, according to Morris, is an engagement with "materials / process" that he attributes to Pollock. Reiterating his conclusion in "Anti Form," Morris described how Pollock made paint interact with gravity:

> The work turned back toward the natural world through accident and gravity and moved the activity of making into a direct engagement with certain natural conditions. Of any artist in two dimensions it could be said that [Pollock], more than any others, acknowledged the conditions of both accident and necessity open to that interaction of body and materials as they exist in a three-dimensional world.[23]

While Morris precisely characterizes Pollock's painting in the terms that we have been discussing so far, he misses the opportunity to see how Duchamp's *Stoppages* might also be understood to engage with process, materials, and even the body. Following the rhetoric of the time (and Duchamp's own), Morris accepted Duchamp's oeuvre as fully intellectualized, but the corporealization that takes place through his deformation of the system of measure in the *Stoppages* also may be taken as bodily in the manner that interested Morris.[24]

In his essay "Phenomenology of Making," Morris further contributed a discussion about the contingency of art methods, addressing questions about the degree of will driving such seemingly automatic processes as the Pollockian drip. He turned to linguistics to ponder whether or not chance might be considered "motivated" or nonarbitrary in the manner of Ferdinand de Saussure.[25] In other words, he wondered if what seemed to be entirely arbitrary or fortuitous might not be driven by some unacknowledged logic. He noted the irony that the less ordered the work appears, the more it seems to imply direct access to the mental processes of the artist, thereby arguing that "ever more disjunctive art acts carry ever more ordered information regarding the systematic means of production."[26] To make his case, Morris turned in part to Anton Ehrenzweig, a psychologist of aesthetics who died in 1966, but whose influential text *The Hidden Order of Art* was published the following year.[27]

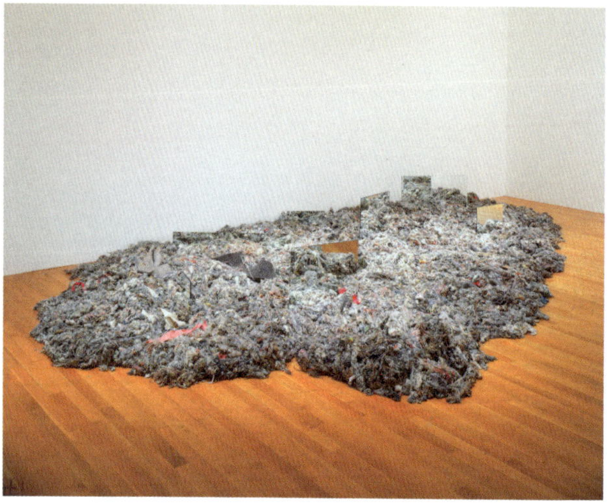

Fig. 5
Robert Morris
Untitled (Threadwaste), 1968
Felt, asphalt, mirrors, wood, copper tubing, steel cable, and lead, dimensions variable

Ehrenzweig, an Austrian who had emigrated to London in the 1930s and taught at Goldsmith's College, was recognized for his contributions on theories of creativity. His ideas about syncretism, or the active negotiation between primary (unconscious) and secondary (conscious) processes (in their psychoanalytic sense), are often cited, but rarely interrogated for their influence on artists of that generation.[28] Morris quotes Ehrenzweig on the resolution of the polarity posed between "'differentiation and dedifferentiation', or scattering (arbitrariness) and containment (motivation)" through rhythmic alternation.[29] Ehrenzweig posits creativity as the artist's ability to bridge the conscious and unconscious. In a Freudian vein, he understands the primary perceptual apparatus to be undifferentiated or unconscious—one that does not distinguish between self and other, nor seeks out the familiar through the differentiation of details. The secondary, or ego, processes focus on known images, seeking what is recognizable.

In terms of art, this suggests that the conscious mind looks for representation or figuration, whereas the unconscious mind is comfortable with more complex, even chaotic seeming, entities. Ehrenzweig proposes that the artist is able to make use of both forms of perception—switching between the two actively. This ability he names "syncretistic vision," or "scanning," a skill that differs from Surrealist automatism in that it is controlled or in a dialectic relationship with the secondary processes. Indeed, creative thought consists in the ability to actively draw up the primary processes—but in a conscious way. He calls this "dedifferentiation" to distinguish it from truly undifferentiated primary behaviors—of the child on the one hand and the psychotic on the other.[30] Thus, scatter, or the appearance of chaos, is linked to the "id" or unconscious, but it is the artist who has the capacity to avail himself of this seeming disorder: "The analysis of abstract gestalt elements is pitted against the syncretistic grasp of the total object, focusing on detail against complex scanning, fragmentation against wholeness, differentiation against dedifferentiation."[31] Thus, the hidden order of art is what Morris compares to the motivated sign—the look of chaos is merely a sign for the artist's direct access to his primary thought processes. Scatter, then, is privileged by Ehrenzweig as being closer to the generative order of the unconscious. As Morris wrote in his "Notes on Sculpture," Ehrenzweig's perceptual mode invites "randomness, heterogeneity of content, [and] indeterminacy," the very aleatory qualities being pursued in the new sculpture.[32]

The dialectic of containment and scatter was actualized in such works as Morris's *Untitled (Threadwaste)* (1968) [Fig. 5], where the gravitational pull on malleable, haphazardly arranged materials overtakes any sense of active falling. Here, it is the boundaries of the room, as well as the reflections of vertical insertions of mirror, that bind and limit the seemingly chaotic sprawl of felt, copper tubing, asphalt, and the eponymous industrial packing material. Morris's *Threadwaste* has been aligned with earlier works by Carl Andre and Richard Serra that coalesce around the aesthetic of scatter.[33] Andre was first with his *Spill (Scatter Piece)* (1966), which consisted of a canvas bag from which he released about 800 small, plastic tiles across the gallery floor.[34] Perhaps not coincidentally, the pieces that Andre used were blank tiles intended to be printed for mahjong, the ancient Chinese game of skill and chance.[35] This spill was followed by more complicated scatters that included ball bearings, pulley discs, and metal and plastic solids, and in later years by those of larger wooden blocks that were dispersed within natural or gallery settings. For Andre, the method of scattering limited his intervention in the work. While he selected the materials and site of the release, he could not control their dispersal. He wanted, instead, for the units or "particles" to combine according to their individual properties: "My first problem has been to find a set of particles, a set of units and then to combine them according to laws which are particular to each particle, rather than a law which is applied to the whole set, like blue, or riveting, or welding."[36]

In his scatter pieces, Andre was working against the order that characterizes much of the rest of his oeuvre.[37] Their look of randomness implies contingency—as if he had thrown the modernist grid off kilter in the manner of Taeuber and Arp. Andre explicitly sought a more flexible or incoherent organization through this method, explaining that "the particles are so small they don't make a coherent pattern. The small size dictates a less rigid form. The random spill makes the pattern."[38] And later, Andre even imagined that the scattered elements would continue to be shifted by means of "social entropy," or "foot traffic," suggesting that the scatter piece would never achieve a fixed organization, and would interact with the audience: "In fact, my Scatter Pieces were created as a solution to maintaining the coherence of many small elements. Social entropy is another force disturbing the coherence of my small sculptures. The normal flow of foot traffic in a busy museum or gallery is a sufficient cause of disorder in my small pieces...."[39] For Andre, then, the scatter or "nonstructural combinations of particulars" express the individual qualities of the dispersed units as well as the trace of audience presence, rather than the artist's willful design.

Serra's *Scatter Piece* (1967) [Fig. 6], on the other hand, more specifically engages with the rhetoric of both Pollock's legacy and Morris's anti-form. Included in the Castelli warehouse show along with *Splashing*, this configuration of strips of rubber and latex along with metal and wire was identified by an earlier reviewer as the tour de force of the exhibition. Philip Leider, who was then editor of *Artforum*, emphasized in his description of 1968 the "taut diagonal of wire suspended about six or eight inches off the gallery floor," noting that it gave "the impression that virtually any arrangement of the formless strips of latex would take on a compositional unity in relation to [it]."[40] Visible, but not prevalent in the installation photograph of the work, this wire was equally important to Serra, who described it as "an elevational counterpoint" that "created a relationship within a field that would otherwise have been undifferentiated."[41] The combination of taut rigidity and amorphous sprawl created a satisfying degree of conceptual tension. And, like Morris's *Threadwaste*, it defies gravity's connotations of inevitability or even fate. Lying on the floor, refusing the possibility of ever achieving a finished form—or end—these arrangements of amorphous and unfixed materials reiterate the surprising connection between gravity and chance first affirmed in Dada.

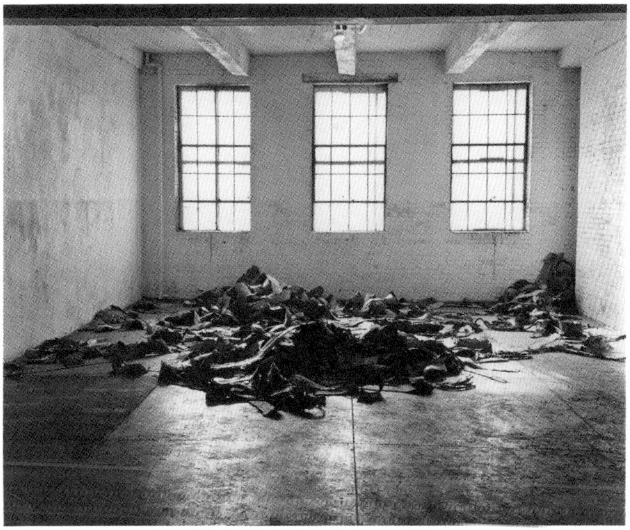

Fig. 6
Richard Serra
Scatter Piece, 1967
Rubber latex, 12 x 12'

Scatter Piece is furthermore one of the earliest of Serra's works that moved off the wall into the terrain of landscape, thereby avoiding a preoccupation with "relief." As he later explained: "I realized that open-field work had other potentials if it was not bound by the wall. The result of this consideration led me to open-field scatter pieces, tear pieces, splash pieces, and cut pieces. Here relief was no longer the issue."[42] The grouping of works to which Serra refers have long been associated with the "verb list" that he wrote from 1967 to 1968. As the list was first published in 1972, the words "to scatter" prominently top the second page, quickly followed by "to arrange," as if the idea of the contingency of scatter immediately conjured its opposite.[43] Serra has talked about how this list of "transitive verbs" was intended as "a way of applying various activities to unspecified materials," but it is worth mentioning that it also includes a number of qualities that could not be put into verb form.[44] Central among these is, not surprisingly, "of gravity."

The pitfalls of gravity's pull toward horizontality were not lost on Serra. In a text of 1970, he talked about the pictorial qualities of the "landscape mode":

> A recent problem with the lateral spread of materials, elements on the floor in the visual field, is the inability of this landscape mode to avoid arrangement qua figure-ground: the pictorial convention. The rationale for this investigation is a plea for perceptual wholeness or a willingness to allow the definition of the place to control the priority of relationships. In part this is a misinterpretation of Anton Ehrenzweig's concept of dedifferentiation.[45]

Both Benjamin Buchloh and Rosalind Krauss have quoted from this passage in influential essays about Serra's sculpture, but neither has questioned his reference to Ehrenzweig or answered the challenge Serra poses to prevailing adaptations of Ehrenzweig's concept of dedifferentiation.[46] Serra's direct reference to Ehrenzweig in the opening passage of this essay testifies to the psychologist's ubiquity and influence amid artists at the time. Yet for today's reader, the critique remains oblique. Serra credits a popularization of dedifferentiation—or polyphonic scattered attention—with a misguided desire for totalizing vision. In fact, Ehrenzweig actually favors the opposite. Rather than a unified view, dedifferentiation accepts the partial and incoherent view as meaningful.

Ehrenzweig argued that through dedifferentiation one could understand complex imagery, but only because, through recourse to the primary processes, one could ignore or suppress information that was not useful in arriving at an image. Someone who could only make recourse to the secondary ego processes would get caught up looking for recognizable details. Serra sees the call for a more totalizing vision as a corruption of this idea. And he argues further against allowing "place" to be a determining agent. Instead, he seeks to use the "state of suspended animation" to imply a "sense of presence" or time. For Serra, then, scatter was intended to reference the potential continuation of process, rather than a fixed pictorial expression. In wishing to avoid the restrictions of finished pictures, he is in line with artists since Duchamp and Arp who have turned to chance in order to make something other than figurative painting. The gravitational pull on unstructured materials lofting through the air, poured onto the floor, and strewn across surfaces has served to signal the embrace of unintended outcomes.

As a coda, I turn to *Mess* (2006) by Anne Wilson and Shawn Decker, which offers a twist on the aesthetics of falling and scatter. A single-projection looping video and sound installation, *Mess* responds to the generation of Process art that we have been considering. Using stop-motion animation, along with a jarring, industrial sound track, the video shows a pile of black threads and lace fragments as they accumulate on a white field and then disperse, only to build back up again. The growth and diminishment of the pile is achieved through the reversal of the animation sequence. At the beginning of the loop, small textile fragments precisely seem not to have fallen from anywhere. Instead, they give the sense of being spontaneously generated, growing up from the landscape, rather than dropping from above. But as the pile becomes denser and more loaded, the weight of the fragile scraps causes them to topple over and spread across the ground. Toward the climax of the growth segment of the video, the black threads attain a scale that is much grander than their size. It is not until the video begins to run in reverse, however, that we understand the pile to move against gravity: as fragments escape from the pile, they seem to be leaping into the air—a sense of reverse falling coalesces what was not apparent as the video ran in the opposite direction. The seemingly ambient and accidental noise of Decker's sound track, along with the found nature of many of Wilson's textiles, insert this finely crafted, and highly determined, animation into the realm of chance aesthetics. For even as the video must have been painstakingly constructed, it enables a sense of unending production that was a goal of those associated with scatter. Wilson and Decker ensure that their pile of scraps never disappears nor achieves final form by endlessly looping their video. For the Dada and Process artists, however, the deformations of chance were enough to guarantee that their works would resist the closure of completion, even as they enact the deterministic pull of gravity.

NOTES

I would like to thank Alan Baker, Kevin Konty, Jane Neidhardt, Meredith Malone, and Matthew Witkovsky for helpful discussions and comments about this essay.

1. For more on *The Large Glass*, in which Marcel Duchamp devised an idiosyncratic iconography for a frustrated love affair between a bride and her suitors through unconventional means of image making, see Richard Hamilton, "The Large Glass," in *Marcel Duchamp* ed. Anne d'Harnoncourt and Kynaston McShine (New York: Museum of Modern Art; Philadelphia: Philadelphia Museum of Art, 1973), 57–67.

2. Marcel Duchamp, "Note for *The Green Box*," translated and reprinted in *The Writings of Marcel Duchamp* ed. Michel Sanouillet and Elmer Peterson (New York: Da Capo Press, 1989), 33.

3. See Marcel Duchamp, "A Window onto Something Else," in *Dialogues with Marcel Duchamp*, ed. Pierre Cabanne, trans. Ron Padgett (New York: Viking Press, 1971), 47, in which Duchamp states: "My 'Three Standard Stoppages' is produced by three separate experiments, and the form of each one is slightly different. I keep the line, and I have a deformed meter. It's a 'canned meter,' so to speak, canned chance; it's amusing to can chance."

4. Marcel Duchamp, "Note for *The 1914 Box*," in *Writings of Marcel Duchamp*, 22.

5. David Joselit has convincingly argued that this opposition between the rigor of measure and the deformation of the curved line can be read as the conflation of gender oppositions as they are worked out in Duchamp's *The Large Glass*. See David Joselit, *Infinite Regress: Marcel Duchamp, 1910–1941* (Cambridge, MA: MIT Press, 1998), 29.

6. Duchamp, "A Window onto Something Else," 46–47.

7. Ibid.

8. These debates are reviewed in Eric Robertson, *Arp: Painter, Poet, Sculptor* (New Haven, CT: Yale University Press, 2006), 44–51; and Anne Umland and Adrian Sudhalter, eds., *Dada in the Collection of the Museum of Modern Art* (New York: Museum of Modern Art, 2008), 44–49.

9. T. J. Demos, "Zurich Dada: The Aesthetics of Exile," in *The Dada Seminars*, ed. Leah Dickerman and Matthew S. Witkovsky (Washington, DC: National Gallery of Art, 2005), 21–23.

10. Georges Hugnet, "The Dada Spirit in Painting" (1932), translated and reprinted in *The Dada Painters and Poets: An Anthology*, ed. Robert Motherwell (Boston: G.K. Hall, 1981), 134.

11. Hans Richter, *Dada: Art and Anti-Art* (London: Thames and Hudson, 1965), 51.

12. Jean (Hans) Arp, "Dadaland" (1938), translated by Ralph Manheim and reprinted in Arp, *On My Way: Poetry and Essays 1912–47* (New York: Wittenborn, Schultz, Inc., 1948), 40.

13. Jean (Hans) Arp, "Le langage intérieur" (1952), as quoted in Robertson, *Arp*, 44.

14. Yve-Alain Bois and Rosalind E. Krauss, *Formless: A User's Guide* (New York: Zone Books, 1997).

15. Ibid., 93.

16. Harold Rosenberg, "The American Action Painters," *ARTnews* 51, no. 8 (December 1952): 23.

17. An early review of the show already suggests that it would be a landmark. See Philip Leider, "'The Properties of Materials': In the Shadow of Robert Morris," *The New York Times*, December 22, 1968, D31. Leider interestingly mistook Serra's lead for "heavy silver paint," indicating how closely related were his sculpture practice and the look of flung paint. Other reviews by Max Kozloff and Grégoire Müller are reprinted in Richard Armstrong and Richard Marshall, eds., *The New Sculpture, 1965–76: Between Geometry and Gesture* (New York: Whitney Museum of American Art, 1990), 106–9. See also Martha Buskirk, *The Contingent Object of Contemporary Art* (Cambridge, MA: MIT Press, 2003), 132–33.

18. A second exhibition that helped to define this genre took place the following year at the Whitney Museum of American Art. See Marcia Tucker and James Monte, eds., *Anti-Illusion: Procedures / Materials* (New York: Whitney Museum of American Art, 1969).

19. Robert Morris, "Anti Form" (1968), reprinted in his *Continuous Project Altered Daily* (Cambridge, MA: MIT Press, 1993), 46.

20. Ibid.

21. Robert Morris, "Some Notes on the Phenomenology of Making: The Search for the Motivated" (1970), reprinted in *Continuous Project*, 71–93.

22. Ibid., 86–87.

23. Ibid., 77–78.

24. In recent years, there have been numerous revisions to the notion that Duchamp's oeuvre was purely intellectual. See Rosalind E. Krauss, *The Optical Unconscious* (Cambridge, MA: MIT Press, 1993); Amelia Jones, *Postmodernism and the En-Gendering of Marcel Duchamp* (Cambridge: Cambridge University Press, 1994); Joselit, *Infinite Regress*; and my forthcoming *'Please Touch': Dada and Surrealist Objects after the Readymade* (Hanover, NH: University Press of New England).

25. Ferdinand de Saussure's foundational *Course in General Linguistics*, originally published in French in 1916, has been variously translated and reprinted in numerous editions.

26. Morris, "Phenomenology of Making," 83.

27. Anton Ehrenzweig, *The Hidden Order of Art* (Berkeley: University of California Press, 1967).

28. A useful source of more information on Anton Ehrenzweig is Nicola Glover, "Ehrenzweig and the Hidden Order of Art," *Psychoanalytic Aesthetics: The British School*, www.human-nature.com/free-associations/glover/chap5.html.

29. Morris, "Phenomenology of Making," 81.

30. "I will speak of *un*differentiation when referring to the static structure of unconscious image making, of *de*differentiation when describing the dynamic process by which the ego scatters and represses surface imagery." Ehrenzweig, *Hidden Order of Art*, 19.

31. Ibid.

32. Robert Morris, "Notes on Sculpture, Part 4" (1969), reprinted in *Continuous Project*, 61.

33. Historically, Barry Le Va has been included in this grouping. See Robert Morris in *Robert Morris: The Mind / Body Problem*, ed. Rosalind E. Krauss (New York: Solomom R. Guggenheim Museum, 1994), 226. However, recent scholarship has emphasized the predetermined quality of Le Va's work, and his own preference for the term "distribution," to differentiate it from the group. See Pamela M. Lee, "The Archaeology of Scatter / The Logic of the Clue," in *Barry Le Va: Accumulated Vision*, ed. Ingrid Schaffner (Philadelphia: Institute of Contemporary Art, 2005), 22–35. In seeking to isolate Le Va from the "rebellion"

of scatter, Lee labels it a "debased version" of Process art (ibid., 24–28, 35).

34. See Eva Meyer-Hermann, ed., *Carl Andre, Sculptor 1996* (Stuttgart: Oktagon, 1996), 138. See also Mette Gieskes, "The Politics of System in the Art of Carl Andre, Sol LeWitt, and Vito Acconci, 1959–1975" (PhD diss., University of Texas at Austin, 2006).

35. See Carl Andre, interview with Ana Maria Torres, as quoted in Gieskes, "Politics of System," 84.

36. Carl Andre, "I want wood as wood and steel as steel..." (1970), reprinted in his *Cuts: Texts, 1959–2004* (Cambridge, MA: MIT Press, 2005), 142.

37. Andre experimented with the scatter method just before he developed his signature construct of gridded rugs of prefabricated metal plates, or "plains." The plains might be taken as counterpoints to Robert Morris's sense of deforming gravity in their straight-edged rigidity and absolute logic.

38. Carl Andre, as quoted in Dodie Gust, "Andre: Artist of Transportation," *The Aspen Times*, July 18, 1968, 3B, as cited in Gieskes, "Politics of System," 88.

39. Carl Andre, "Small Sculpture" (2000), reprinted in *Cuts*, 245.

40. Leider, "'The Property of Materials'," D31.

41. Richard Serra and Lizzie Borden, "About Drawing: An Interview" (1977), reprinted in Richard Serra, *Writings, Interviews* (Chicago: University of Chicago Press, 1994), 54.

42. Richard Serra, "Interview with Bernard Lamarche-Vadel" (1980), reprinted in *Writings, Interviews*, 114.

43. First published in Grégoire Müller, *The New Avant-Garde: Issues for the Art of the Seventies* (New York: Praeger Publishers, 1972), reprinted in *Writings, Interviews*, 3–4.

44. Serra, "About Drawing," 53.

45. Richard Serra, "Play It Again Sam" (1970), reprinted in *Writings, Interviews*, 7.

46. See Rosalind E. Krauss, *Richard Serra / Sculpture* (New York: Museum of Modern Art, 1986), 19; and Benjamin H. D. Buchloh, "Richard Serra's Early Work: Sculpture between Labor and Spectacle," in *Richard Serra Sculpture: Forty Years*, ed. Kynaston McShine and Lynne Cooke (New York: Museum of Modern Art, 2007), 54. Krauss does not quote the extended passage and therefore omits the reference to Ehrenzweig. Buchloh argues for a reformulation of the "phenomenology of gravity" with respect to Serra's sculptural response to Jackson Pollock. He wants to place it in a dialectic between the activities or "phenomenological inscription" of the artist's labor and the disembodiment caused by its dissemination as spectacle (see esp. 53–56).

THE GOOD FAIRY

AUTOMATISM

THE GOOD FAIRY

AUTOMATISM

THE GOOD FAIRY

AUTOMATISM

AUTOMATISM

THE GOOD FAIRY

AUTOMATISM

THE GOOD FAIRY

AUTOMATISM

THE GOOD FAIRY

AUTOMATISM

THE GOOD FAIRY

AUTOMATISM

THE GOOD FAIRY

AUTOMATISM

THE GOOD FAIRY

AUTOMATISM

THE GOOD FAIRY

AUTOMATISM

AUTOMATISM

THE GOOD FAIRY

AUTOMATISM

THE GOOD FAIRY

AUTOMATISM

THE GOOD FAIRY

AUTOMATISM

THE GOOD FAIRY

AUTOMATISM

THE GOOD FAIRY

AUTOMATISM

THE GOOD FAIRY

The Good Fairy Automatism

Susan Laxton

If the historical avant-gardes—at least in Peter Bürger's now famous formulation—are to be understood as having been focused on the politics of representation, intent on challenging the status quo at the institutional rather than merely formal level, how can we reconcile this commitment to political praxis with the Surrealists' repeated incorporation of the unstable and the spontaneous—of sheer, meaningless *play*—in their art practices? More specifically, how do we measure the effectiveness of the Surrealist "revolution" when Surrealists so often abandoned the work of art to chance? Bürger himself addressed this conundrum head-on in the 1970s in his *Theory of the Avant-Garde*, first by making clear that what the Surrealists meant to accomplish with their deployments of chance was a recovery of "the elements of the unpredictable in everyday life" as a resistance to the "restricted scope" of a society "organized on the basis of a means-ends rationality."[1]

For Bürger, this entailed a radical renouncing of specific goals in favor of a "pervasive openness to impressions," or "*disponibilité*," as André Breton put it—the effort to place oneself "in a state of grace with chance."[2] Bürger had in mind the extraordinary Surrealist practice of "objective chance," a dynamic rewriting of the subject / object relation wherein psychoanalytically derived procedures were used to activate the projection of the subject's unconscious desires onto the material field. The strolling Surrealist experienced these projections as the shock of inexplicable attraction, an unnamable recognition thought to be jolted directly out of the unconscious by a chance encounter with a figure, place, or object. Codified by Breton in his 1937 novel *Mad Love*, the experiences generated by objective chance occurred outside the usual boundaries of causality and conscious motivation, indeed relied on investing the aleatory and the coincidental with significance, and were best effected in marginal places that bore the signs of obsolescence, even superfluity—that is, "margins" understood as porous invisible frames around the city: interstitial spaces of freedom.[3] Like the neglected sites the Surrealists favored for their aimless quests, these encounters were as trivial as they were unlikely—unrelated, as Bürger observed, "to the preoccupations of the individual concerned."[4] This insistence that the most significant experiences occur at the margins of subjective attention, that they happen *automatically*, outside of conscious control, is central to the critical capacity of objective chance. And it keys with yet another practice that was then synonymous with Surrealism, a process that turned away from conscious invention to disclose the extraordinary latent in the commonplace: the practice of automatism.

Automatic writing, regarded as a transcription of pure thought, had been developed at the end of the nineteenth century by French psychiatrist Pierre Janet as a therapeutic means to elicit the spontaneous images of the subconscious. The patients, most often diagnosed as hysterical or neurasthenic, were brought to a state of distraction from their functional milieu in order to encourage their "automatic" impulses—actions produced without conscious intervention—to emerge either orally or graphically (as writing or drawing). Faith in the process was based on the belief that without the repressive presence of learned conventions, *anything imagined* would tend to be acted on spontaneously. Only conscious thought, Janet contended, and particularly an operation of consciousness that Janet named "the reality function," sublimates or represses these automatic responses, to the extent that when the utterances do emerge, they are unrecognizable to the speaking or writing subject—they are experienced, that is, as though encountered by chance.[5]

The process was officially established within the range of Surrealist practices with the publication in 1920 of André Breton and Philippe Soupault's *Magnetic Fields*, a collaborative text advanced as pure psychic utterances. As Soupault wrote in the preface:

> In the course of our research, we did indeed observe that the mind, once *freed of all critical pressures and school-bound habits,* offered *images* and not logical propositions; and that if we adopted what the psychiatrist Pierre Janet called a practice

of automatic writing, we produced texts in which we found ourselves describing a "universe" as yet unexplored.[6]

What is striking in Soupault's description is, of course, the assertion that significant images are produced only outside norms and conventions, but also this sense of these texts as "unexplored"—unprecedented words or images, signs experienced as "other," even to their own authors. Because the subject's hand in automatic writing or drawing was considered no more than a neutral recording device, employing automatic techniques served as a method of *guaranteeing* chance outcomes.

This extreme displacement of volition returns us to Peter Bürger and the critical capacity of chance in a functionalist culture, for Bürger sees the submission to chance as a form of opting out of means–ends rationality. "Paradoxically," he writes, "chance, which subjects man to the totally heteronomous, can thus seem a symbol of freedom."[7]

How does this disengagement from "specific goals" translate into art practices? What, in fact, is the equivalence of a "goal" in art production—proceeding, of course, in good faith from the premise that artists work not merely for material gain but are engaged with a set of practices that are meant to articulate the best intentions of their culture? Bürger argues convincingly that art's stated aim in the first decades of the twentieth century took the form of an acknowledgment by artists that officially sanctioned institutional practices had hardened into a set of conventions so rigid that art had become tautological—an end in itself—ceasing, in effect, to engage with the reality of social relations. In this scenario, paradoxically, the more artists actively sought to fill the very institutional requirements that defined their work as art (their goal), the less relevant these works became to material life. Bürger's formulation goes a long way toward explaining why so much art from Dada forward doesn't look like art (it seeks to avoid achieving institutionally mandated goals); why so much of it is intentionally ephemeral (it seeks to avoid entering the object-market and the museum); why so much of it looks like a mistake (it was made by "accident"—its final forms were unforeseeable).[8]

And in fact, in Bürger's theory, not all instances of chance-based art are equally critical: he qualified his opprobrium by breaking chance strategies into two types, the "direct" and the "mediated." Direct strategies completely obviate artistic decision making and permit chance alone to make the image. Bürger disparaged these as "arbitrary" avatars of "empty subjectivity" that at best can be interpreted later as mere freedom of expression (the work of Jackson Pollock is one example). "Mediated" chance, on the other hand, has for Bürger the advantage of generating an unforeseeable result that retains its *purposefulness* in spite of its purposelessness. These chance-based works emerge from machine-like art-generating systems in which the *means* are calculated to produce unpredictable outcomes. Because the systems are determined in advance by the artist, the objects and images they throw off cannot be attributed to nature alone, and their meaning is found in the *processes* by which they produce art, as opposed to inhering in the art objects themselves or in the lyrical subjectivity of their makers. These "constructions," as Bürger calls them, renounce "subjective imagination" as false consciousness by calling attention to—exacerbating, in fact—the pervasive and programmatic loss of individuality in modern life.[9]

Bürger's clearly defined categories, direct chance and mediated chance, would seem to have correlates in Surrealist art, with, for example, direct processes represented by "pure" automatic scrawl or by decalcomania, the process by which landscape-like images were produced by pressing ink between sheets of glossy paper and then pulling them apart to reveal arbitrary "non-compositions." Mediated chance, then, would take the form of the Surrealist parlor games, the most famous being the exquisite corpse game, an intensely regulated process that produced images that were at once oddly similar (being structured by the rules of the game) yet all unique (since those rules, through the forced intersubjectivity of the players involved, guaranteed chance results). Following Bürger's formulation, then, the "bad" politics of automatism's wild "transcriptions" and decalcomania's unmotivated imagery would merely affirm an ultimately false impression that human beings do have recourse to free will, and the corollary truism that art affords privileged access to this freedom. The Surrealist games, conversely, would be understood to be performing critically to reveal the otherwise sublimated conditions of modern reality.

As one of the first critics to attempt to grasp a politicized and historicized notion of avant-garde practices that would assess the critical capacities of advanced art both before and after World War II, Bürger's *Theory of the Avant-Garde* remains the most important statement acknowledging Surrealist chance-based processes without trivializing them or reducing their effects to nihilism or mere whimsy. Yet for an historian whose very definition of the historical avant-garde emerged from close analyses of the erratic and psychoanalytically inflected body of Surrealist literature, and particularly for one who was active during the expansion of poststructuralist theory into art historical practice, Bürger's organization of chance-based practices is rigid to the point that it risks being dismissed as formulaic and dogmatic in its judgments regarding the quality of works of art—judgments that effectively replace aesthetic criteria with political criteria, but with the same draconian pronouncements and inflexibility. In fact, Surrealist chance processes resist easy categorization into "direct" and "mediated" forms, with even the earliest attempts at automatic drawing admitting the inevitability of a kind of "secondary revision" that ultimately acknowledges representation as constitutional of subjectivity itself and mediation as the artist's inescapable condition, in life as in work.

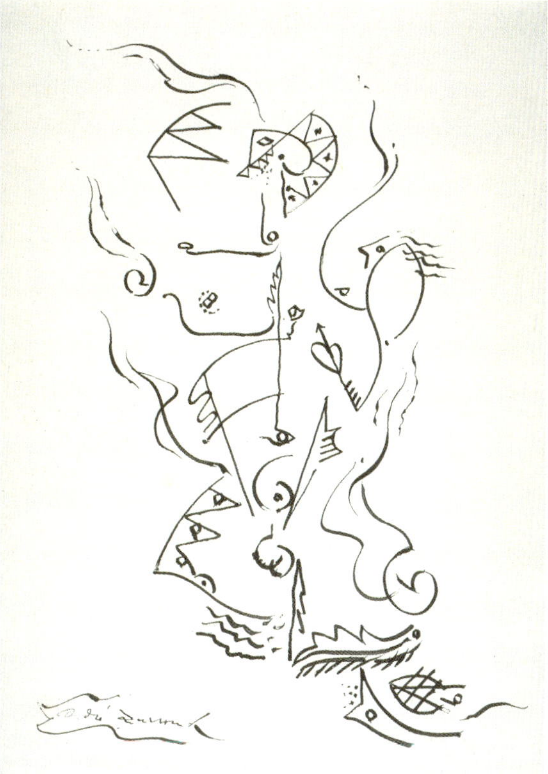

Fig. 1
André Masson
Untitled, 1926
Pen and black ink on off-white laid paper, 16 13/16 x 12 1/2"

The easy slide in Surrealist practice from automatic writing to drawing had been made as early as the trance sessions of the early 1920s, in which Robert Desnos combined writing, drawing, and speaking in hypnotic performances, and in the first Surrealist manifesto of 1924, Breton posited automatic sketches as the grounds for advancing the very possibility of Surrealist painting.[10] Accordingly, the first issues of *La Révolution surréaliste* were thick with automatic drawings by André Masson [Fig. 1; Cat., p. 100] who retrospectively described his method as bipartite:

> Materially: a little paper, a little ink.
> Psychically: make a void within yourself; the automatic drawing, having its source in the unconscious, must appear like an unpredictable birth. The first graphic apparitions on the paper are pure gesture, rhythm, incantation, and as a result: pure doodles. That is the first phase.
> In the second phase, the image (which was latent) reclaims

> its rights. Once the image has appeared, one should stop. This image is merely a vestige, a trace, a bit of debris. It follows that any break between the two phases must be avoided. If there was a pause, the first result would be total abstraction, and persisting too long in the second phase, something that was academic Surrealistically![11]

Masson's first phase seems to characterize automatic drawing as a primal utterance: a tapped impulse ("an unpredictable birth") that precedes figuration. He specifically cites those linear conventions that are associated with "naive" and "transcendent" marks identified with children, madmen, and ritual ("pure gesture, rhythm, incantation"), the underlying assumption being that drawing uniquely affords special access to fundamental mental processes—a passage past the rational that is denied to the consciously calculated use of mediums such as painting and sculpture. Yet Masson also describes an equally important second stage, in which the artist draws back into his inchoate calligraphy, an action that resonates with an apparent misprision of the psychic manipulations of secondary revision, in which figuration (specified as "latent") is recovered. Masson reclaims recognizable forms from what was originally a graphic notation devoid of any descriptive function much in the same way that Max Ernst, refracting Leonardo da Vinci's spotted wall through Sigmund Freud, would subsequently justify summoning dramatic motifs from the bumps and whorls that pressed through his frottage drawings and paintings [Fig. 2; Cat., p. 104].

Ernst's 1936 essay, "Beyond Painting," theorizes the importance of the aleatory and arbitrary as the *grounds* for the Surrealists' psychoanalytically driven images. He describes his hypnagogic *détournements*, or "turning around" of existing imagery, as a way of reproducing not what he saw in reality, but "only that which *saw itself in me*, a color, a pencil mark, a landscape foreign to the represented objects, the desert, a tempest, a geological cross section, a floor, a single straight line signifying the horizon...; thus I obtained a faithful fixed image of my hallucination and transformed into revealing dramas my most secret desires—from what had been before only some banal pages...."[12]

Ernst quotes Leonardo's words as the basis for his own frottage practices:

> It is not to be despised, in my opinion, if, after gazing fixedly at the spot on the wall, the coals in the grate, the clouds, the

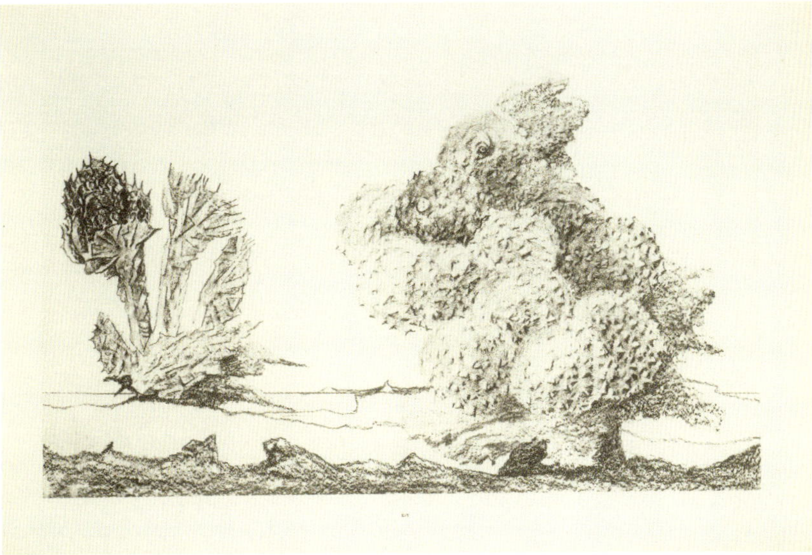

Fig. 2
Max Ernst
One work from
Histoire naturelle, 1926
Portfolio of photogravures,
19 5/8 x 12 3/4"

> flowing stream, if one remembers some of these aspects; and if you look at them carefully you will discover some quite admirable inventions. Of these the genius of the painter may take full advantage, to compose battles of animals and of men, of landscapes or monsters, of devils and other fantastic things which bring you honor. In these confused things genius becomes aware of new inventions....[13]

Leonardo specified a series of arbitrary starting points for art production—wall stains, clouds, glowing coals, a stream—that he described as "confused things," things unbounded or in constant flux, out of which other images would emerge once "all conscious mental guidance" was eliminated—a technique that Ernst had to have recognized as commensurate with the psychoanalytical mandates of automatism. In a modern variant of Leonardo's recommendations, Ernst ranged about for appropriately "unfixed" grounds—veined leaves, the brushstrokes on the surface of a painting, thread unwound from a spool—which, once covered with paper or canvas, were rubbed with a pencil or crayon, filling the field with the welter of arbitrarily motivated lines necessary to induce hypnagogic effects. His first experiment of this kind, encountered by accident as he gazed distractedly at his deeply grained floorboards, struck him with the power and "persistence" of "amorous memories" leaving behind their initial characteristics and taking on the aspect of what he called a "simulacrum" of memories recalled from the unconscious.[14]

It is important that for the Surrealists, both the initial, utterly random-appearing stage and the subsequent "emergence" of imagery from the tangle of lines were performed in a hallucinatory state, so that the iconography in the drawings, while recognizable as birds or breasts or hands, was alien and unforeseeable to its maker, and appeared as if by chance. Yet because those images were thought to have emerged specifically from the depths of an archive of repressed memory, they were paradoxically grasped not as the production of new images but, in the words of Rosalind Krauss, as vision's "ceaseless return to the already-known."[15]

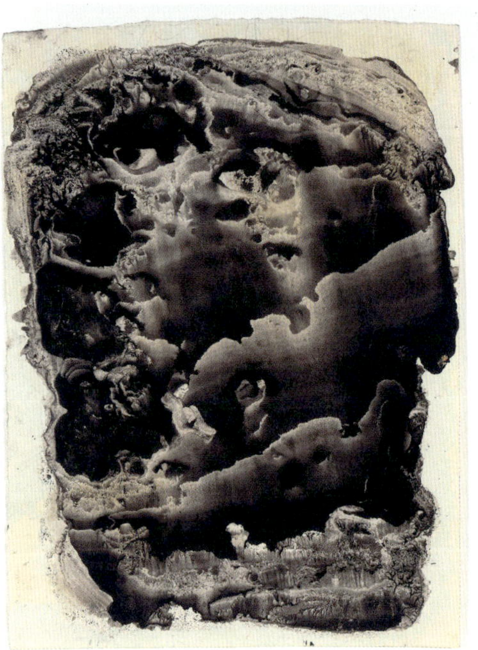

Fig. 3.
Marcel Jean
Untitled, c. 1936
Gouache on paper,
12 7/8 x 9 3/4"

In this way Surrealism, the very source of Bürger's theory of the avant-garde, itself rejects his dichotomy through the movement's early acknowledgment of the impossibility of withdrawing "original" material from the unconcious, since for the Surrealists even unconscious imagery is always already determined by signs of past experience. Breton himself affirmed this in his 1921 tribute to Ernst, where he naturalizes automatic production's "imitation of appearances" as an inevitable limit of the human imagination:

> Unfortunately human effort, which always varies the arrangement of existing elements, cannot be applied toward producing a single new element. A landscape in which nothing terrestrial figures is beyond the scope of our imagination....[16]

From this statement it is clear that Breton understood the Surrealist image not to be "original" in the sense that the word is conventionally applied to the work of art, but rather ready-made, poised in the psychic apparatus to be registered by a "blind instrument," as opposed to having been generated by an inventive subject.[17] But the "automatic" process of eliciting and transcribing those images must be initiated by first filling the field of vision with an expanse of utterly aleatory marks.

This aspect of late variants of automatic experimentation opens out Surrealist images enormously, radically unfixing them from stable meaning, and culminates in the development of the procedure that Oscar Dominguez called "decalcomania," in which Rorschach-like forms elicit subjective memory-images, but images that are not necessarily subsequently fixed in place, as they typically are in automatic drawing (although when Max Ernst adopted the procedure it did become the basis for figurative paintings), instead leaving the unmotivated field open for the next viewer's subjective projection [Fig. 3; Cat., p. 106].

The term "decalcomania," applied when the images were first published in the journal *Minotaure* in 1935, is a neologism derived by combining the French "*décalquer,*" to transfer, with "*manie,*" obsession or madness.[18] Use of the word "transference" is doubly evocative with regard to the images, at once drawing attention to the material process by which peaks and swirls of ink have been directly transferred from one sheet to the other through the mere physics of paper pulling on liquid without the mediation of the human hand, while also referencing the psychoanalytic meaning, or the projection of the viewer's inner landscape onto the visual field. But for André Breton, a single, particular kind of madness is indicated by the name; in a short passage describing the process he identified the images as "da Vinci's old paranoiac wall, brought to perfection."[19] Breton also referred to Salvador Dalí's "paranoiac-critical method," a mode of recognizing latent, *unintended* imagery coexisting within ordinary representations. Dalí demonstrated the method in 1931 in the third issue of *Le Surréalisme au service de la révolution* with an anthropological photograph he reconceived through a 90 degree rotation to resemble a primitivist head "in the style of Picasso" [Fig. 4].[20] By 1935, Dalí had codified the practice in his text *Conquest of the Irrational*, where he advanced it as a "systematic exploration of the irrational" developed as a "concrete" replacement for automatism, the results of which Dalí rejected as fatally open to literal psychoanalytic interpretation.[21]

Delusion trumps illusion in paranoiac-critical images. The success of the method depends greatly on the "paranoid" capacities of the viewer: the ease with which one perceives multiple and utterly unrelated figurations in a single image. In the case of the 1931 image, Dalí specified that the latent images contained in a single picture will vary according to the subjective "preoccupations" of the viewer, and that it is also possible,

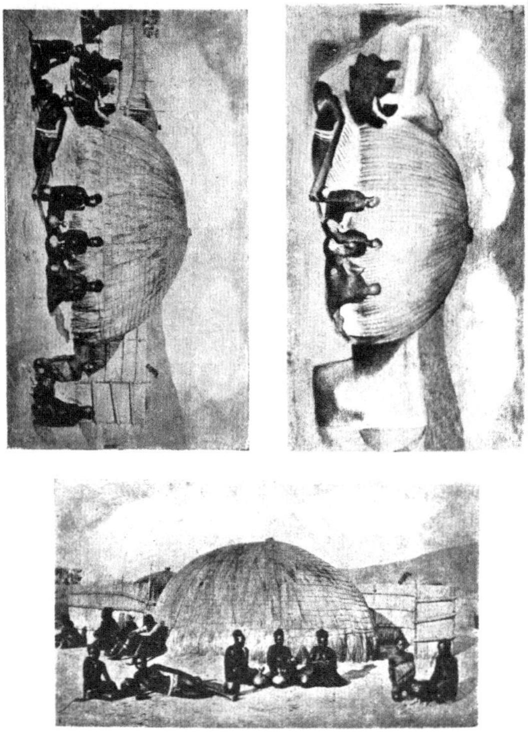

COMMUNICATION : Visage paranoïaque.

A la suite d'une étude, au cours de laquelle m'avait obsédé une longue réflexion sur les visages de Picasso et particulièrement ceux de l'époque noire, je cherche une adresse dans un tas de papiers et suis soudain frappé par la reproduction d'un visage que je crois de Picasso, visage absolument inconnu.

Tout à coup, ce visage s'efface et je me rends compte de l'illusion (?) L'analyse de l'image paranoïaque en question me vaut de retrouver, par une interprétation symbolique, toutes les idées qui avaient précédé la vision du visage.

André Breton avait interprété ce visage comme étant celui de Sade, ce qui correspondait à une toute particulière préoccupation de Breton quant à Sade.

Dans les cheveux du visage en question Breton voyait une perruque poudrée, alors que moi je voyais un fragment de toile non peinte, comme il est fréquent dans le style picassien.

Salvador DALI

Fig. 4
Salvador Dalí
Paranoiac visage, 1931
Illustration published in *Le Surréalisme au service de la révolution*, 1931

given the consistency of obsessions, for the meanings of different works to become interchangeable at the point of reception regardless of their authors' intentions. As such, the method permits vision itself (motivated by the unconscious) to enact a kind of *détournement* of the image-world in which it is possible, as Dalí wrote, to perceive that "such apparently dissimilar paintings as Leonardo's *Mona Lisa*, Millet's *Angelus*, Watteau's *Embarkation for Cythera* actually depict the very same subject matter, that is to say, exactly the same thing."[22] This is a cultivation of identity slippage that had been typical of early Surrealist practices, following on André Breton's exhortation to "free words" from their "dictionary definitions,"[23] and had been recently reactivated within the movement by Michel Leiris, whose interest in Raymond Roussel's arbitrary text-generating systems had spread to other Surrealists' practice. It is significant, for example, that in one of Dalí's rambling, associative passages in *Conquest of the Irrational*, the fragment "letters of white on the old billiard cushions and letters of white on the old mill-yard Russians" appears, a citation (itself *détourned*) from Roussel's then-recently published exposé *How I Wrote Certain of My Books*.[24]

The paranoid-critical method, operating at its best, opened vision onto a range of images that are never fixed into finite iconography, but rather remain radically open to as many readings as possible, in a demonstration of pure, meaningless proliferation that Dalí claimed was the "organizing and productive force of objective chance": the *systematic production of coincidence*. By the end of the 1920s, these methods for generating images that delivered an "automatism-effect" had overtaken the sessions of automatic transcription that characterized early Surrealist works. Of them, the longest lasting and most widely practiced was undoubtedly the game of exquisite corpse [Fig. 5; Cat., p. 128]. Unlike the vaguely defined paranoid-critical method, which depended on the special "skills" (or psychic instability) of the practitioner, the exquisite corpse game is very regulated, affording it a leveling quality that subjected the players to an extreme form of deskilling, but which guaranteed a kind of democracy in the play, answering Lautréamont's dictum: "Poetry will be made by all."[25] The players pass sheets of pleated paper to be marked successively by each, beginning at the top, with each player drawing a "head." It can be in profile or it can be frontal, the features can be displaced or hidden, it can be two heads, a wig, a snail, a wheel, a musical instrument, a hot air balloon, four sticks of dynamite, but the player must be careful to extend the drawing ever so slightly below the fold—to move a little outside the apportioned section. This will be the starting point for the next player's drawing (typically of a torso), for the marked sections are then folded back and hidden before passing the paper along to one's neighbor. Now each player has a page marked and hidden by somebody else, and must draw on the next blank section, using the remaindered ends of the previous drawing as a starting point. Thus a certain degree of autonomy is preserved for the "head," but this does not hold for the "body" of the work, which becomes increasingly variously—and unforeseeably—determined as play continues until the final leg of the game, when the figure is bunched behind the last marked field. When everyone has put down their pencils, the sheets are unfolded and "one judges the viability of the monster thus produced."[26]

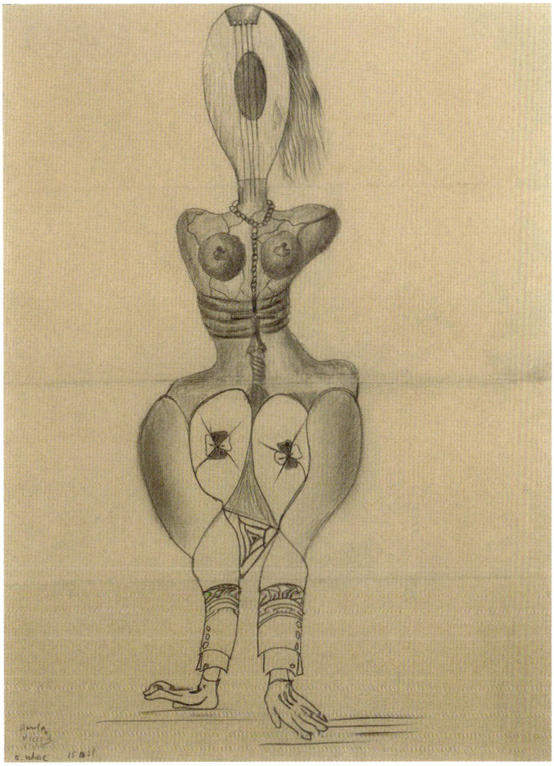

Fig. 5
Victor Brauner, Jacques Hérold, Violette Hérold, Yves Tanguy, and Raoul Ubac
Untitled "Cadavre exquis" ("Exquisite Corpse"), 1938
Graphite and collage on paper, 10 3/8 x 8 1/16"

The drawings, Breton asserted, were endowed "to the highest degree with the power of *dérive*," the subjection of the self and its representations to the vagaries of pure circumstance, as against predetermination.[27] Yet where exactly is chance in this game? The rules that govern the exquisite corpse clearly structure and dominate the associative range of iconography registered in the course of play. The game effects a reassuring rhythm, predictable and consistent; an assertion of stability that would seem to be incompatible with the aleatory dynamism associated with free-play (and the improvisations of automatism), and which reveals an alliance with convention that would run counter to the discourse of liberation informing Surrealist practices.

This incongruously autocratic aspect of the exquisite corpse is a function of games in general. While all play-forms claim chance as a definitive component, games form a singular category within play for the specific way that they treat chance—that is, they subject it to rules, directives that guarantee the game's consistency in repetition. These rules are constitutive of the game: it is not merely that games enclose aleatory phenomena within strict parameters, but that the game itself would not exist without those limitations; they "create the very possibility of playing."[28] Chance depends on the rules simply to show itself—it is pronounced against the regulations by its extreme difference from them.

The demand in the game for a measure of unpredictability explains why, in spite of the rigor of its regulations, the dominant impression of any exquisite corpse is figurative chaos: paper is marked in the exquisite corpse as script or scribble, as a variety of recognizable figures, amorphous masses, allusions to spatial depth, repetitions of geometric pattern, and so on, and the game distributes them in a seemingly endless array of permutations.[29] Thus the exquisite corpse could claim to be liberating from within its regulations (in the manner of all realizable—as opposed to purely utopian or imaginary—liberations), and, as the play directly engages the graphic trace, is particularly well positioned to reconfigure the possibilities available to representation at large.

The new Surrealist codes drafted and enacted through the exquisite corpse game allowed for the manifestation of a combinatorial and indeterminate freedom that had been denied to the more purely conceived automatic drawing and writing. Abandoning the unverifiable discourse of automatism, the Surrealists developed a system that employed the indexical, the anomalous, and the ineffable as signs of the displacements and doublings of unconscious processes, signs available to be manipulated into structures, inserted into practices, and materially deployed against represented codes of ratiocination.[30] Automatism could thus be seen to have been reified into a machinelike game, with effects that

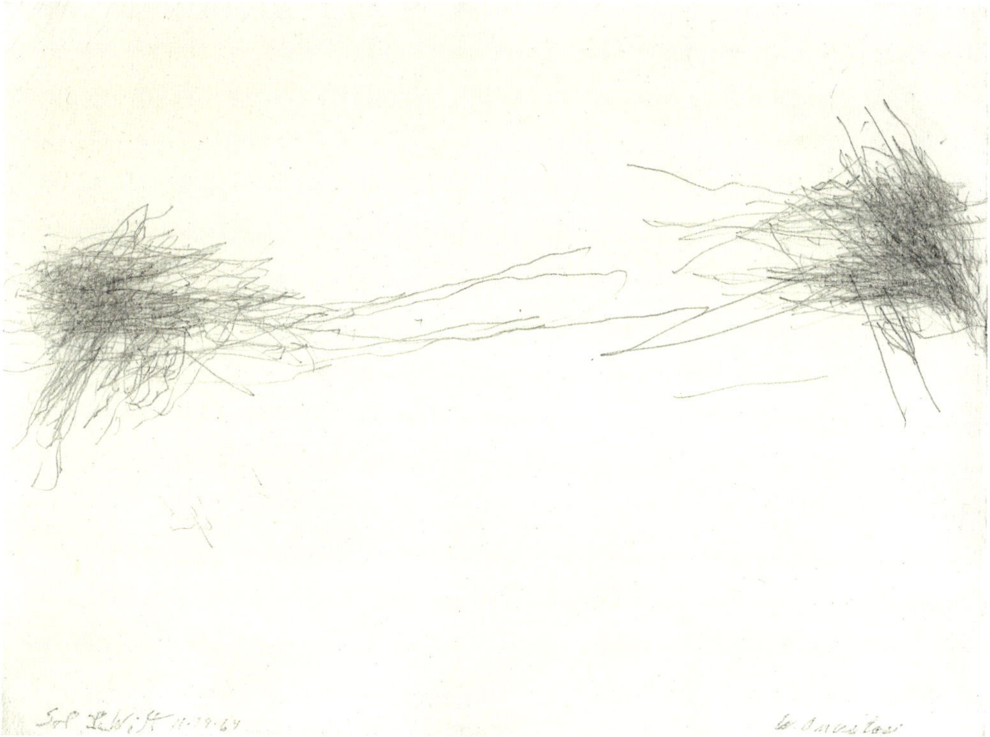

could circulate with all of the reliability of a mechanical device to ensure the repeatability of chance.

It is this last aspect of Surrealist games—the repeated staging of textual production—that would ultimately become the legacy of Surrealist chance strategies. While Robert Motherwell as early as the 1940s understood automatic drawing as utterly "original," the founding "creative principle" (and therefore an instance of unmediated chance, as Bürger would have it),[31] arguably William Anastasi's mechanically determined subway drawings of the 1960s, with their stark replacement of the expressive artistic subject with a subject mediated by technology, would more productively restate the Surrealist critical mandate in a postwar context [Fig. 6; Cat., p. 120]. Similarly, while in the late 1950s the Situationist International reclaimed the practices of *dérive* and *détournement* for the reshaping of urban experience toward a "geographical unconscious," it was the contemporary Fluxus group, with their deadpan games and event scores, that most consistently reproduced the radical open-endedness of reception-based meaning in the arts that had been the *effective* outcome (acknowledging secondary revision) of

Fig. 6
William Anastasi
Untitled (Sol LeWitt 11 19 69), 1969
Pencil on paper drawing, 7 1/2 x 11 1/2"

automatic processes. Of these, Öyvind Fählstrom's politically inflected works, as sites for processes drawing on both regulation and subjective choice, directly recall the game of exquisite corpse in their insistence on the viewer's active participation in determining the outcome—Bürger's "stated goal"—of the artwork [Fig. 7; Cat., p. 152].

Perhaps it was the game of exquisite corpse that Peter Bürger had in mind when he calculated the efficacy of avant-garde deployments of chance. The game's rigid regulations, reliable as an assembly line, effectively mirror the conditions of modern mass production, in a nearly literal expression of Bürger's critical practice, "mediated chance." The difference, of course, lies in the degree of heteroglossia evoked in the final composite image as an effect of its collective construction. Ultimately the game depends entirely on the subjective variety of its players for its chance element, yet, ironically, it is precisely through the displacement of a single authorial voice in favor of a final outcome that cannot be fully attributed to any one of its makers that the alienation of the image is experienced most emphatically.

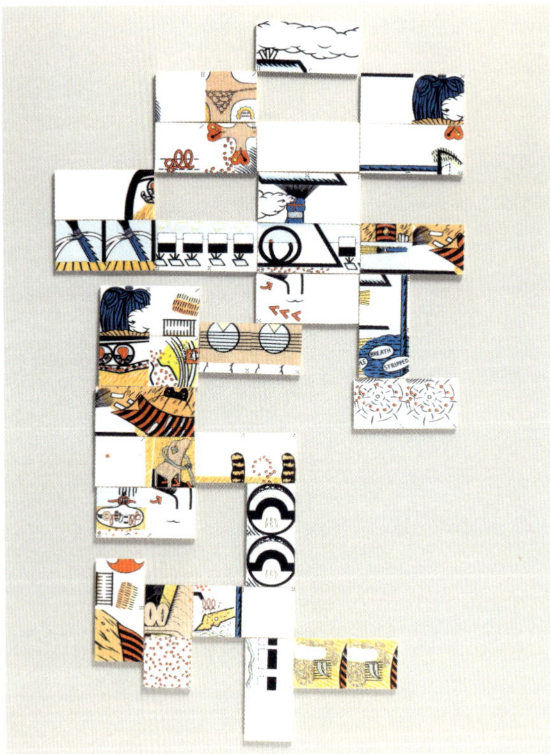

Fig. 7
Öyvind Fahlström
Sitting ... Dominoes, 1966
Color silkscreen on vinyl, magnets, metal, and Plexiglas, 40 3/8 x 28 1/4 x 11/16"

This lays a decisively negative gloss on the play process—a sense that one is *being played* rather than playing the game—and is echoed by a radical disorientation at the level of the reception of the image, rising from a perceived disaggregation that reaches back to the first efforts of automatism and the collaborative model provided by *Magnetic Fields*, where Soupault and Breton depended on one another to deepen the quality of juxtaposition—the "extreme degree of immediate absurdity"—in the text. In the case of *Magnetic Fields*, difference is articulated not so much at the level of the production of the text—in, for example, the marked dissimilarity between the contributions of the two writers—but rather, as Breton emphasized, through estrangement at the level of the reception of the work: an alienation that derives not so much from an encounter with the foreign utterances of other authors, but from the unrecognizability of one's own contribution. "To you who write," he stresses, "these elements are, on the surface, as strange to you as they are to anyone else and naturally you are wary of them."[32] For Breton, the chance encounter, the "spark" of "two distinct realities," occurs when image or text are able, "by removing our systems of reference, to disorient us within our own memories...."[33] That is, in the ideal Surrealist encounter, the subject is confronted with a recontextualization of his or her writing or drawing so radical as to render it alien. "Upon opening my eyes," Breton wrote, describing the first sight of his own automatic drawings, "I would get the very strong impression of something 'never seen.'"[34] Likewise, when he would reread his transcriptions of dream images, they would "surprise" him, and he claimed that they "left me with the impression of their being so gratuitous that the control I had then exercised upon myself seemed to me illusory...."[35] In this light, the perceived likenesses within the works—those smoothly linked parts that at first would seem to be at odds with the tenets of juxtaposition—turn out to be yet another point from which the principle of contradiction is inscribed. The Surrealist desire to collapse the boundaries between subject and object, as it is played out in automatist-based games and techniques, opens unexpectedly onto the revelation that this collapse can only ever be an illusion, as the Surrealist subject is itself presented in the finished image or text as an exoteric object.

This wholesale rejection of volition for chance was ultimately received as a threat by Jean-Paul Sartre: "We have to look on them with the eyes of a stranger," he wrote in 1947. "Automatic writing is above all the destruction of subjectivity."[36] Yet, by the 1970s, Roland Barthes would counter that automatism could never claim the full abnegation of originality that Sartre decried, as even unconscious utterances are constituted in language. "If we were to imagine," Barthes claimed, "that the Good Fairy Automatism were to touch the speaking or writing subject with her wand, the toads and vipers that would spring from his mouth would just be stereotypes."[37] If the conflict summarized by Sartre's and Barthes's statements measures the distance between humanist and poststructuralist criticism, it also raises the structural paradoxes of the automatist paradigm itself: the tensions between associative scrawl and secondary revision in automatic drawing, frottage, and decalcomania; the irony of a normalizing "cure" deployed to elicit unconventional results; the politics of a primitivist model that attempts to replace a willful, conventional subject by an inchoate, alien "other" and, above all, the problem of the psychoanalytic rejection of chance in favor of parapraxes motivated by unconscious desire. If the negotiation of this terrain very quickly drove Surrealist art past the naive model of transcribing "pure thought" to mechanical systems developed to guarantee ludic outcomes, then the aim of the Surrealists must be seen as the desire to demonstrate the ultimate *inability* to achieve the goal of a return to organic, prelinguistic unity—the inability to tap the inchoate unconscious. What Surrealist chance practices repeatedly demonstrate is the inevitability of mediation in all experience, including artistic processes, even as they insist on "making strange" as a resistance to a means–ends continuity. Risking accusations of frivolity, the Surrealists steered automatism toward the development of a modern critical ludic, consistently destabilizing the mechanistic structures of apprehension, ceaselessly reasserting the revolutionary potential of visual language.

NOTES

1. Peter Bürger, *Theory of the Avant-Garde*, trans. Michael Shaw (Minneapolis: University of Minnesota Press, 1984), 65.

2. André Breton, *Conversations: The Autobiography of Surrealism* (1969), trans. Mark Polizzotti (New York: Paragon House, 1993), 106.

3. André Breton, *Mad Love* (1937), trans. Mary Ann Caws (Lincoln: University of Nebraska Press, 1987).

4. Bürger, *Theory of the Avant-Garde*, 65.

5. The fundamental text for this concept of automatism is Pierre Janet, *L'Automatisme psychologique* (1889) (Paris: Éditions Odile Jacob, 1998), but Janet only named the "reality function" as such in 1903. See Pierre Janet, "La Perte de la function du reel," in *Les Obsessions et la psychasthenie*, vol. 1 (Paris: Alcan, 1903), 431–39. For general accounts of automatic phenomena, see Henri F. Ellenberger, *The Discovery of the Unconscious: The History and Evolution of Dynamic Psychiatry* (New York: Basic Books, 1970), 331–417, 835–37; and Wilma Koutstaal, "Skirting the Abyss: A History of Experimental Explorations of Automatic Writing in Psychology," *Journal of the History of the Behavioral Sciences* 28 (January 1992): 5–27. Janet himself recounts a history of automatism that reaches back to cures derived from "magnetism," which provides yet another link, through the title *Magnetic Fields*, to Breton's version of the process. See Pierre Janet, *Principles of Psychotherapy*, trans. H. M. and E. R. Guthrie (New York: Macmillan Company, 1924), 3–91.

6. Philippe Soupault, in his preface to *Magnetic Fields*, as cited in Elizabeth Roudinesco, *Jacques Lacan & Co.: A History of Psychoanalysis in France, 1925–1985*, trans. Jeffrey Mehlman (Chicago: University of Chicago Press, 1990), 12 (originally published as *Les Champs magnétiques* [Paris: Au Sans-Pareil, 1920]), emphasis mine. For an overview of Surrealist automatic writing and the role of trance sessions in its development, see André Breton, Paul Eluard, and Philippe Soupault, *The Automatic Message* (1933), trans. David Gascoyne, Anthony Melville, and J. Graham (London: Atlas Press, 1997): 39–54.

7. Bürger, *Theory of the Avant-Garde*, 66.

8. Ibid., 67.

9. Ibid.

10. In a note to the first manifesto, Breton refers the reader to number 36 of the French review *Les Feuilles libres* for several examples of automatic drawings. André Breton, "Manifesto of Surrealism" (1924), in *Manifestoes of Surrealism*, trans. Richard Seaver and Helen Lane (Ann Arbor: University of Michigan Press, 1972), 21.

11. André Masson, *Écrits*, 37, cited in David Lomas, *The Haunted Self: Surrealism, Psychoanalysis, Subjectivity* (New Haven, CT: Yale University Press, 2000), 33.

12. Max Ernst, *Beyond Painting* (1936), trans. Dorothea Tanning (New York: Wittenborn, Schultz, 1948), 14. The drawing out of ready-made images in Ernst's work is demonstrated as commensurate with Freudian secondary revision in Rosalind E. Krauss, *The Optical Unconscious* (Cambridge, MA: MIT Press, 1993), 53–72. The term "*détournement*," or appropriation and distortion of existing images in order to destabilize the structures of perception they affirm,

is a term now associated with the Situationist International, but which was originally used as early as 1923 by Louis Aragon to describe the effects of Ernst's early collages. See Louis Aragon, "Max Ernst, peintre des illusions," in his *Les Collages* (Paris: Hermann, 1965), 26.

13. Leonardo da Vinci, as cited in Ernst, *Beyond Painting*, 10.

14. Ernst, *Beyond Painting*, 8.

15. Krauss, *Optical Unconscious*, 53.

16. André Breton, "Max Ernst" (1921), in *The Lost Steps*, trans. Mark Polizzotti (Lincoln: University of Nebraska Press, 1996), 60.

17. Ibid.

18. See Benjamin Péret, "D'une décalcomanie sans objet préconçu (décalcomanie du désir)," *Minotaure* 8 (June 1935): 18–25.

19. André Breton, "Pour ouvrir a volonté sa fenêtre sur les plus beaux paysages du monde et d'ailleurs," *Minotaure* 8 (June 1935): 18.

20. Salvador Dalí, "Communication: Visage paranoiaque," *Le Surréalisme au service de la révolution* 3 (December 1931): 40.

21. Salvador Dalí, *Conquest of the Irrational*, trans. David Gascoyne (New York: Julien Levy Gallery, 1935), n.p.

22. Ibid.

23. André Breton, "Words without Wrinkles" (1922), in *The Lost Steps*, 100.

24. Dalí, *Conquest of the Irrational*. See also Raymond Roussel, *How I Wrote Certain of My Books and Other Writings* (1932), ed. Trevor Winkfield, trans. John Ashbery, Kenneth Koch, Harry Mathews, and Trevor Winkfield (Boston: Exact Change, 1995).

25. The maxim is from Comte de Lautréamont's *Chants de Maldorer* and is cited by Andre Masson in his essay, "D'où viens-tu, cadavre exquis? Un des jeux (serieux) des surréalistes," in *Le Cadavre exquis, son exaltation*, ed. Arturo Schwarz (Milan: Galleria Schwarz, 1975), 28.

26. The rules have been tersely related in the *Dictionnaire abrégé du surréalisme* (Paris: Galerie des Beaux Arts, 1938), 6; Tristan Tzara's more specific "recipes" for the game are in *Le Cadavre exquis*, 18, 24. Philippe Audoin makes the comment about viability and judgment in "Surréalistes," his entry on Surrealist games in *Le Dictionnaire des jeux*, ed. René Alleau (Paris: Tchou, 1966), 484.

27. André Breton, "Le Cadavre exquis, son exaltation," in *Le Cadavre exquis*, 12.

28. John R. Searle, *Speech Acts: An Essay in the Philosophy of Language* (Cambridge: Cambridge University Press, 1969), 33.

29. In this the game resembles Deleuze and Guattari's "desiring machine" (Gilles Deleuze and Félix Guattari, *Anti-Oedipus: Capitalism and Schizophrenia*, trans. Robert Hurley, Mark Seem, and Helen R. Lane [New York: Viking Press, 1977]). David Shapiro has referred to exquisite corpse drawings as such in his essay "Art as Collaboration: Toward a Theory of Pluralist Aesthetics, 1950–1980," in *Artistic Collaboration in the Twentieth Century*, ed. Cynthia Jaffee McCabe (Washington, DC: Smithsonian Institution Press, 1984), 52. Similarly, Jean-Jacques Lebel's approach to the exquisite corpse is entirely Deleuzean; see Jean-Jacques Lebel, "La Erupción de la vida," in his *Juegos Surréalistas: 100 Cadáveres exquisitos* (Madrid: Fundacion Coleccion Thyssen-Bornemisza, 1996), 17–41.

30. For an account of the shift away from automatism and toward sign systems, see Laurent Jenny, "The Adventures of Automatism," *October* 51 (1989): 105–14.

31. See Robert Motherwell's letter to Edward Henning (18 October 1978), reprinted in *The Collected Writings of Robert Motherwell*, ed. Stephanie Terenzio (Oxford: Oxford University Press, 1992), 230. Like André Masson, Motherwell characterized automatic drawings as "doodles," and, like Louis Aragon, linked their unpremeditated outcomes to collage principles of juxtaposition.

32. Breton, "Manifesto of Surrealism," 24.

33. Breton, "Max Ernst," 60.

34. Breton, "Manifesto of Surrealism," 21.

35. Ibid., 22.

36. Jean-Paul Sartre, "Situation de l'ecrivain en 1947," in *Qu'est-ce que la littérature?* (Paris: Gallimard, 1948), 215–16.

37. Roland Barthes, "The Surrealists Overlooked the Body," in his *The Grain of the Voice: Interviews 1962–1980*, trans. Linda Coverdale (Berkeley: University of California Press, 1981), 244. He further explained: "The idea of automatic writing implies an idealist view of man as divided into a speaking subject and a profound inner subject. As for the text, it can only be a braid, woven in an extremely twisted and devious fashion between the symbolic and the image-repertoire. One cannot write without the image-repertoire."

PRECARIOUS PRACTICES

CHANCE AND CHANGE IN NOUVEA

RÉALISME AND FLUXUS

PRECARIOUS PRACTICES
PRECARIOUS PRACTICES
CHANCE AND CHANGE IN NOUVEA
PRECARIOUS PRACTICES
RÉALISME AND FLUXUS
PRECARIOUS PRACTICES
CHANCE AND CHANGE IN NOUVEA
PRECARIOUS PRACTICES
RÉALISME AND FLUXUS
PRECARIOUS PRACTICES
CHANCE AND CHANGE IN NOUVEA
PRECARIOUS PRACTICES
RÉALISME AND FLUXUS
PRECARIOUS PRACTICES
CHANCE AND CHANGE IN NOUVEA
PRECARIOUS PRACTICES
RÉALISME AND FLUXUS
PRECARIOUS PRACTICES
CHANCE AND CHANGE IN NOUVEA
PRECARIOUS PRACTICES
RÉALISME AND FLUXUS
PRECARIOUS PRACTICES
CHANCE AND CHANGE IN NOUVEA
PRECARIOUS PRACTICES
RÉALISME AND FLUXUS
PRECARIOUS PRACTICES
CHANCE AND CHANGE IN NOUVEA
PRECARIOUS PRACTICES

Precarious Practices: Chance and Change in Nouveau Réalisme and Fluxus

Meredith Malone

The late 1950s and early 1960s witnessed an enthusiastic embrace of chance-based compositional strategies. To different degrees and with varying outcomes, artists in the United States and in Europe experimented with diverse forms of nondeterminism. Inscribing elements of chance and randomness into their artworks provided a welcome release from the tyranny of the self, signifying a pronounced aversion to both the private ego as the source of art making and the mystification of the artist's role as something that transcends daily life. The stance of quasi-heroic individualism, epitomized by the image the art world had fabricated of some of the more famous artists of Abstract Expressionism in the United States and *art informel* in Western Europe, ceased to seem credible in a context where every new, ostensibly inimitable, painterly gesture was enthusiastically co-opted by a rapidly expanding art market.

Members of Nouveau Réalisme and Fluxus, two international groups of artists that developed roughly parallel to one another during this postwar moment, demonstrated a particularly pronounced interest in the aesthetics of chance. While their projects evince a marked diversity of artistic practices (from object-based assemblage, to participatory environmental installations, to protoconceptual practices merging language, music, and performance), a comparison of the strategic implementation of a range of chance-based procedures on the part of these two groups highlights a shared aspiration to radically rethink the paradigms of artistic production and (artistic) subjectivity in the face of the dominance of late-modernist abstraction and the rise of an affluent consumerist society. Chance appealed to artists such as Daniel Spoerri, Jean Tinguely, George Brecht, and Allan Kaprow because it advanced a more contingent and temporal model of art, one that was not linked to any transcendent or metaphysical ideals but to the concrete realm of the everyday.

Nouveau Réaliste and Fluxus attempts to rearticulate the boundaries between art and life stemmed both from longstanding avant-garde impulses to challenge the autonomy of art and the bourgeois notion of the artist as genius, as well as from actual transformations in postwar daily life. The significant shift in artistic practice at this time was bolstered by a growing historical awareness of Dada's early liberating practices in general (the embrace of non-art materials through assemblage and collage aesthetics, experiments with performance, and the use of chance as a compositional method) and Marcel Duchamp's antiexpressive strategies of nonsubjective, chance-based composition in particular.[1] Yet these artists navigated the avant-garde impulse to challenge and test the boundaries between aesthetic production and the everyday under dramatically different social structures than their historical predecessors.

In postwar Western Europe and the United States, a managerial ethos of efficiency and productivity spurred and sustained unprecedented modernization and consumerism, generating a climate of both hopeful anticipation and intense anxiety concerning the social realities of a burgeoning consumer society. Artists working in the United States made art in the midst of the corporatization of American culture, the expansion of mass media, and a growing market for contemporary art. The situation in Western Europe, and especially in France, was even more extreme. As opposed to the continued modernization of American society that occurred throughout the twentieth century, the state-led modernization drive in France was unusually swift. The rise of consumer culture, shifting conceptions of public and private space, new definitions of work and leisure, and the wars of decolonization irrevocably altered the foundations and daily routines of modern life.[2]

The heightened engagement with the everyday by artists in this moment has conventionally been seen as marking the beginnings of an overt negation of artistic autonomy in favor of a more ironic, and a seemingly casual, immersion in the realities of the modern world.[3] The recourse to chance-based procedures and the associated release of an element of authorial control on the part of Nouveau Réaliste and Fluxus artists would appear to support such a claim. Yet, as art historian Alex Potts convincingly argues, positing a straightforward trajectory from autonomy to heteronomy, from a quasi-heroic stance of opposition to a relaxed attitude of acknowledgment, is deceptive in that it misconstrues the larger stakes involved in the rethinking of artistic subjectivity that took place at this time.[4] The fascination with the everyday and the apparent assumption of a stance of indifference might instead, Potts suggests, be read not so much as an endeavor to transgress or negate autonomy, but as an attempt to achieve a more compelling form of autonomy—a sense of purpose emancipated from the confining imperatives of high art and the self-regarding norms then associated with the image of the modern artist as a heroic individual.

The turn to chance as a compositional principle by Nouveau Réaliste and Fluxus artists, I propose, is indicative of this pervasive attempt to address the fundamental instability of artistic subjectivity in the postwar period. Rather than an overt gesture of repudiation or negation, however, the embrace of chance processes on the part of these artists was always more strategic in aim. Chance provided a necessary means through which unorthodox aesthetic approaches, as well as alternative subject positions, could be readily explored and tested within the context of emerging systems of control and their false offer of stability in a world forever in flux. The dominant preoccupation was to seek a more viable way for the artist producing art, and for the viewer engaging with it, to arrive at a provisional integrity of practice amid the endless permutations and contradictions of capitalism. Such integrity, however, was itself manifestly contingent and precarious, further inciting the production of experimental works of art that aimed to acknowledge and incorporate the changeability of experience by critically probing boundaries between aesthetic production and everyday life, fixed object and temporal event, stasis and change.

Nouveau Réalisme: New Perceptions of the Real

Founded in 1960 in Paris, the Nouveaux Réalistes were a group of artists loosely united by shared opposition to what they perceived to be gestural abstraction's remove from the modern world and by a desire to express what Pierre Restany, the group's chief organizer and theorist, described as "new perceptions of the real" without recourse to painterly or illusive means.[5] Instead of approaching the work of art through personal introspection, members turned their gazes outward and directly appropriated commodity objects, debris, and other scraps of modern industrial culture, initiating a trajectory out of the autonomous realm of painting and into the expansive arena of urban life. In opposition to the nostalgic use of the *objet trouvé* in Surrealism, the Nouveau Réaliste method was closer to that of the readymade, selecting quotidian objects to rescue from oblivion, thereby revaluing the throwaway commodity by creating works in which everyday life as planned obsolescence is brought under the control of the artist. The appropriated items were subsequently transformed through performative chance-based processes, such as ripping, gluing, shooting, amassing, and eradicating.

For Restany, Nouveau Réaliste practice coalesced around a central project: the "positive" appropriation and display of "the real," "perceived in itself and not through the prism of conceptual or imaginative transcription."[6] Mimicking modern day myths of scientific objectivity and technocratic rationalism, he understood the objects chosen, be they fragments of torn posters, bits of junk, used cars, or plastic toys, as immediately revealing something of the greater totality of postwar French society.[7] For many of the leading Nouveaux Réalistes, the introduction of an element of contingency into the work of art was central to the elaboration of this new methodology for directly perceiving and presenting the new reality of contemporary urban life, yet its aim and application were never as straightforward or as positivist as Restany claimed.[8] A closer examination of individual practices reveals a much more dynamic oscillation between an open embrace of a new-found "real" and an implicit wariness concerning the place of the subject in an ever-more controlled society. The theorization of the dialectical relationship between chance and determinism as played out in various Nouveau Réaliste projects, I propose, fundamentally shaped their particular form of "realism," a skeptical version evincing both optimism and pessimism, endorsement and critique, about the categories and classifications with which individuals shape and understand their existence.

For Arman and Daniel Spoerri, two artists who practiced what might accurately be described as pseudosociological methods of art production, the mobilization of chance provided a compelling means for negotiating the changes in contemporary experience wrought by accelerated cycles of production, consumption, and decay. The release of an element of authorial agency through chance signified a desired degree of objectivity on the part of both artists. With his *poubelles*, or trash cans, Arman literally presents the viewer with garbage—debris, obsolete industrial products, and other urban waste—left to rot in his now signature vitrines [Cat., p. 94]. Ostensibly allowing only the force of gravity to determine their arrangement, his trash cans look like core samples taken from contemporary garbage dumps, and demonstrate what he saw as the plight of the postwar period, "the flooding of our world with junk and rejected odd objects."[9] When discussing his practice of amassing found objects and trash in the form of his *poubelles*, Arman often employed the distanced language of a social scientist collecting data, yet his self-proclaimed role as "witness" to society was always counterbalanced by that of a consuming subject.[10] As suggested by Jaimey Hamilton, Arman sought to understand and convey cultural processes precisely by being involved in them, paradoxically assuming multiple subject positions at once: detached observer, consumer of mass-produced items, and prolific producer of industrial-age art objects.[11] His accumulation and subsequent aestheticization of trash performatively mimic the cycle of objects in postwar culture, with his *poubelles* highlighting the end of an object's intended commercial life. By extracting and preserving a moment in this cyclical process, his assemblages effectively elevate the found object back to the status of the autonomous art object, yet concurrently extend the instant indefinitely through a process of gradual decay, thereby defying the notion of a work of art as fixed and finite.

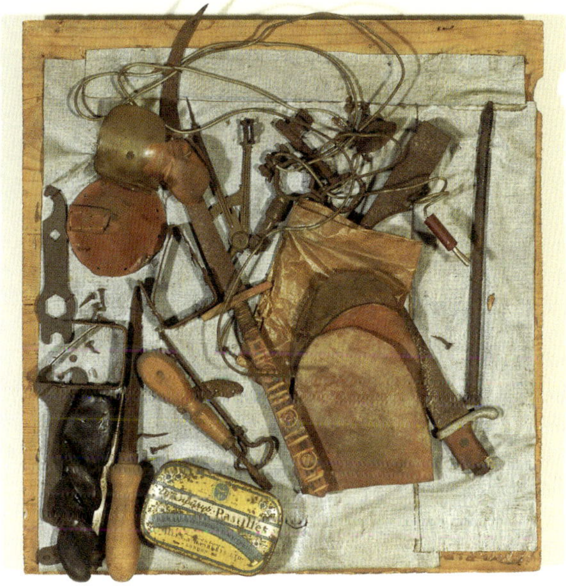

Fig. 1
Daniel Spoerri
Le Tiroir de ma mère, 1960
Objects on wood,
15 7/16 x 15 x 5 1/8"

Daniel Spoerri claimed a similarly remote authorial position, describing himself as a mere "attendant to the accidental," thus denouncing individual creative accomplishment and claims to originality in favor of an aesthetic of factual reporting.[12] To create his *tableaux-pièges*, also known as trap or snare pictures, he systematically glued down random arrangements of quotidian objects or the remains of a meal to the very support on which they rested. The only alteration, the artist claimed, occurred in the shift of plane from horizontal to vertical, as the work hangs on the wall—a sort of readymade still life, arranged

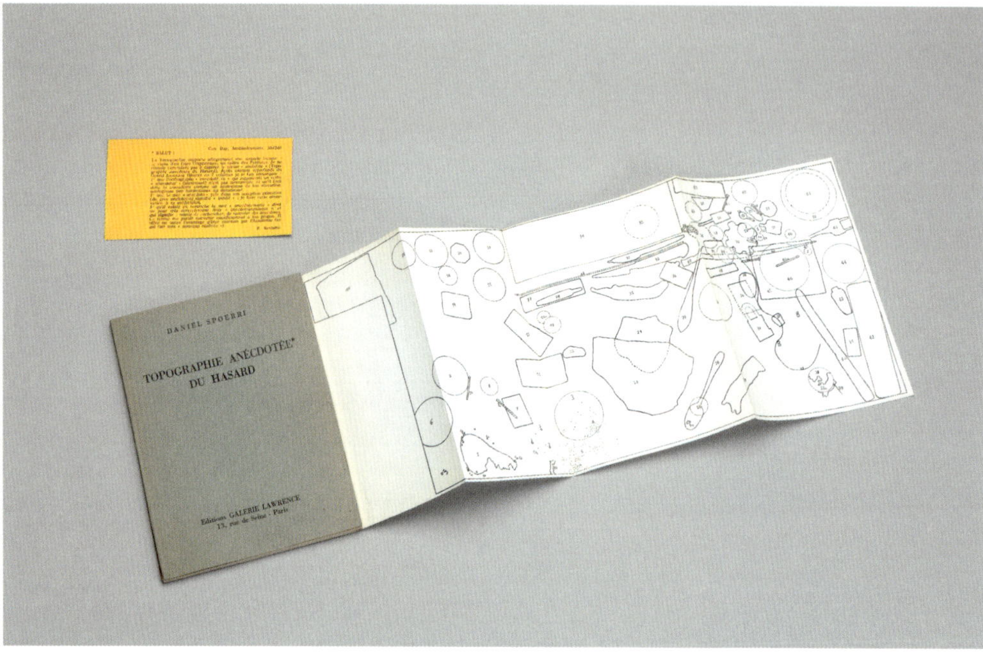

Fig. 2
Daniel Spoerri
Topographie anécdotée du hasard (*An Anecdoted Topography of Chance*), published 1962
Artist's book, 7 1/4 x 5 5/16"

by chance. Describing his snares as "optical lessons" or "provocations," Spoerri espoused a desire to confront the comfortable regularity of the viewers' perceptions of reality, directing attention to the overlooked objects that populate the spaces of their everyday lives. In *Le Tiroir de ma mère* (1960), for example, we see the contents of his mother's drawer, including a bottle opener, knives, a compass, and a large key [Fig.1; Cat., p. 86]. While the sheer banality of these objects infuses them with a sense of universal meaning, the fact that the items are taken from his mother's drawer transforms the piece into a type of portrait of this absent woman, one instilled with an intimate and private sensibility. The dialetic of the particular and the universal is at the heart of Spoerri's meticulous project, which evinces a constant relay between the impersonal character of mass-produced objects and the very specific associations they attain once possessed.

Spoerri's practice of trapping accidental situations allowed him to straddle the realms of art and life, sustaining a productive tension between authorial control and circumstance, fixation and change. Like Arman, he reveled in the contradiction inherent in the act of removing objects from their temporal existence. "I like the contrast provoked by fixating objects," he stated, "to extract objects from the flow of constant changes and from their perennial possibilities of movement; and this despite my love for change and movement."[13] The *tableau-piège* perpetually reveals this conflict. It can be understood as both an event and an object—it freezes a random moment in time, yet, once hung on the wall, it becomes divorced from the particular instant from which it was drawn. By defying the natural flow of daily life and undermining the laws of gravity, the snare pictures facilitate a sense of estrangement at the level of reception, resulting in a decentering effect designed to counter any stable sense of self. By downplaying his subjective bias through the seemingly casual appropriation of accidental situations, Spoerri aimed to lessen the aesthetic distance for the viewer, guiding the heretofore complacent spectator to new levels of self-awareness.

That being said, Spoerri's meticulous if not obsessive drive to trap and preserve accidental situations and quotidian items also manifests a pronounced desire to assert control over an increasingly unwieldy system of objects. His artist's book *An Anecdoted Topography of Chance* offers a twist on the snare picture while extending his bid to conceptualize the processes whereby people relate to and consume objects as well as the behavioral practices that result there from [Fig. 2; Cat., p. 144]. The book tells the story of various objects found on a table in the artist's hotel room in Paris, on October 17, 1961, at 3:47 pm. As he explained on the first page, Spoerri set out "to see what the objects on a section of this table (which I could have made into a snare picture) might suggest to me, what they might spontaneously awaken in me in describing them."[14] Comparing his practice to that of a detective solving a crime through the investigation of a series of objects or an archeologist at Pompeii unpacking the history of a civilization through preserved remains, he attempted to lay out the unforeseen directions of a life through a series of encounters related to the objects present in his room at a specific, yet arbitrary, date and time. In addition to the pages of text, Spoerri attached a map to the end of the book denoting the exact position and shape of each object on the table. These items were then assigned numeric identifiers, and readers were invited to play the game of matching up the numbers and shapes on the map to their textual descriptions.

The *Topography* is thus based on a fundamental absence: it records something that once existed but is now gone, present only through memory. In this respect, it departs considerably from the visually seductive and physically present objects in a snare picture. We might best understand these two projects as mirror images, reflecting and inverting one another. Like his snare pictures, an elemental opposition between structured experimentation and the arbitrariness of chance inform the look and feel of the book. On the one hand, the parameters of the project are specific and strictly followed, enabling the artist to exploit the creative possibilities of constraint. On the other hand, Spoerri generates his anecdotes through a very unsystematic method, following the subjective mechanisms of memory, recording whatever came into his mind as he looked at a given object. Object 26, for example, a small aluminum spoon, is described as:

> A real bargain, bought at the drugstore on Rue Lacépède opposite the Hotel Beau Séjour, where Madame Marabelle claims that someone is tapping her gas and threatens to write the city gas company about it. She has also sent countless complaints to the transport authorities because the buses stand at the bus stop in front of her house with their engines running, and pollute the air. On the spoon, remains of egg yolk.[15]

At one point he compares his *Topography* to a "human garbage can" in that nothing restrained him from accepting what could be accumulated in it. Spoerri was moved to create his book, in part, after seeing one of Arman's *poubelles* and being inspired to consider how he could "retrace the history of each scrap" within his own garbage.[16] Whereas Arman chose to display undifferentiated mounds of accumulated garbage, Spoerri was less interested in the sheer volume of items. Rather, by recounting the story of these random objects as they moved through society and intersected with his daily life, he created a constant relay between the universal character of mass-produced commodities and the very particular meanings they take on once acquired. Thus, while the book exists as a detailed document of personal events and random associations, it also represents a sort of sociological record of artistic relationships and the increasingly prominent role played by commercial products in shaping identity and subjectivity in the early 1960s.

Spoerri and Arman were certainly not alone in examining the cycles of production and consumption in this postwar period. Their activities should be seen as part of a larger effort by sociologists and theorists to study the increasing systematization of objects under capitalism and the resultant effects on everyday life.[17] In the aftermath of World War II and the subsequent shifts toward massive commercialization and Americanization in Europe's city centers, a range of intellectuals, historians, and sociologists, including Henri Lefebvre, Roland Barthes, and Jean Baudrillard, took up the analysis of everyday life, focusing their attention on the regularities, repetitions, and naturalization of consumption that sustained the late-capitalist system. Their aim was not just to analyze but to demystify these naturalized systems, confronting the way they function while unveiling the social, economic, and historical conditions they disguise.[18] Spoerri and Arman's rigorous attention to common items and quotidian phenomena unquestionably resonates with contemporary anxieties concerning how one might negotiate a life within a spectacularized society. While their works, unlike the sociologists', tend to downplay national agendas and other historical or political specifics, their assemblages of random petrified objects nevertheless capture the general concept of the late-capitalist system, characterized by an incredible flow of capital and things in which everything becomes paradoxically static.

As Spoerri and Arman were amassing, fixing, and examining random bits of urban detritus in the form of their trash cans and snares, Jacques Villeglé, one of a group of artists collectively known as the *affichistes*, was engaging in the appropriative practice of *décollage,* literally the ungluing of paper.[19] Wandering the streets of Paris, he would seek out and furtively peel off from public walls already lacerated posters—torn by anonymous passersby, aggressively defaced by vandals, or worn by the weather—as a means of collecting random linguistic and graphic arrangements, what the artist regarded as a kind of raw visual poetry.[20] On one level, Villeglé's practice enacts a pseudosociological project comparable to that of Arman and Spoerri. His *affiches lacerées* exist as both historical documents that record and preserve an otherwise ephemeral street culture and, as Benjamin Buchloh argues, as visual manifestations of political revolt enacted not by the artist but by "anonymous lacerators" enraged by the increased domination of public space by advertising's commodified language.[21] On a more formal level, Villeglé's process evinces an aggressive attack on postwar abstraction. Instead of emphasizing the originality or skill of an individual author, his performative process—a direct response to both Duchamp and the legacy of Surrealist automatism with its emphasis on random selection and chance encounters—signals an interest in artistic creation as a matter of recognizing and choosing existing objects in opposition to the existentialist rhetoric underwriting abstract painting at the time. The relatively anonymous and collaborative practice of *décollage* provided

Villeglé with a trove of ready-made imagery that liberated him from the need to invent new forms from scratch, thus allowing for a reduction of his own subjective expression and personal taste. A work such as *Rue de Crimée, 28 novembre 1969* [Fig. 3; Cat., p. 90], abounding with layers of paper fragments and vivid coloration, directly evokes the gestural brushstrokes and all-over field of *art informel*, revealing Villeglé's project as one deeply engaged in reinscribing abstraction as an idiom with new relevance in light of the glut of visual information produced by an ever-more pervasive media culture.

Niki de Saint Phalle employed a similarly unorthodox mixture of chance and destruction as a means of working through the legacy of postwar abstraction. The creation of her *tirs*, or shooting paintings, involved a two-part process [Cat., p. 88]. First, found objects, including plastic toys and a range of various perishable or discarded materials, were filled with sacks of colored pigment and covered in white plaster to produce a singular assemblage. Next, a rifle was fired at the assemblage, causing the bags of paint to burst, releasing uncontrollable streams of paint down the surface of the work. The rifle—wielded by the artist or, at other times, by spectators in her many public performances staged throughout the early 1960s—assumed the decisive role, thereby severing the connection between the creative hand and the painterly mark. The burst of the gun and the unpredictable explosion of paint across the surface of the piece were always primary, with the remaining assemblage existing as a secondary trace of a fleeting action. "There is always a letdown for me after the shooting is over," Saint Phalle stated. "The result doesn't really interest me except as a document or a photograph. The only thing which really interests me is the spectacle, the event itself."[22] For Saint Phalle, there was a moment of liberation in the act of shooting. By inviting others to take part, by literally putting the gun in their hands, she encouraged the participant to experience the sense of elation that comes with performing such a forceful and damaging action. Saint Phalle's *séances de tir*, as she called them, mimic a world in chaos, internalizing and confounding distinctions between destruction as an expression of aggression and as a positive tool for creative renewal. "Oil painting is finished," she stated in a 1961 interview with David Brinkley. "It is finished now because we are concerned with other things. We are concerned with death, with objects, with the end of things. We want to find a renewal. We want to find beauty in a new way."[23] References to the Cold War and nuclear proliferation abound in her early assemblages, evoking two distinct sides of chance as experienced in the late 1950s and early 1960s: the life-affirming side—its ability to defy total rational control and the status quo—and the apocalyptic side of potential nuclear accident and mass devastation.

Like Saint Phalle's work, Jean Tinguely's production of erratic, self-destructing junk assemblages, such as his *Study for an End of the World, No. 2*, which spectacularly exploded in the desert outside of Las Vegas in 1962, reveals his fascination with the dialectical relationship between destruction and creation. More than a mere publicity stunt, the staging of such violent events reveals the absurdity and danger of technological progress in the postwar period, raising serious questions about the conditions of contemporary experience. Tinguely's contemporaneous production of automated machines for making drawings, his *Metamatics*, reveals another facet of his engagement with elements of contingency and disorder as a wry critique of modern ideals of technological efficiency and rational control. Constructed from used objects found in the junkyards of Paris and animated by secondhand electronic motors, the *Metamatics* were widely recognized by critics as a clever questioning of the skill involved in abstract painting, particularly the presumably inimitable and spontaneous gestures of practitioners of American action painting and European lyrical abstraction.[24] Each machine consisted of a motorized arm capable of holding a pen or marker, and spectators were encouraged to "do-it-yourself" by choosing between the colors, their variety, and the speed of a given machine [Fig. 4; Cat., p. 114].[25] The artist frequently described his sculptures as "anti-machine machines" because they never did the same thing twice, characterizing their random and uncontrollable movements as "the functional use of chance."[26] Through his humorous combination of mechanization and chance, Tinguely subjected art to what Helen Molesworth describes as "a perverse Taylorization of the artistic process."[27] Along the same lines, critic Art Buchwald wryly pointed out that the production of a painting using one of Tinguely's machines could

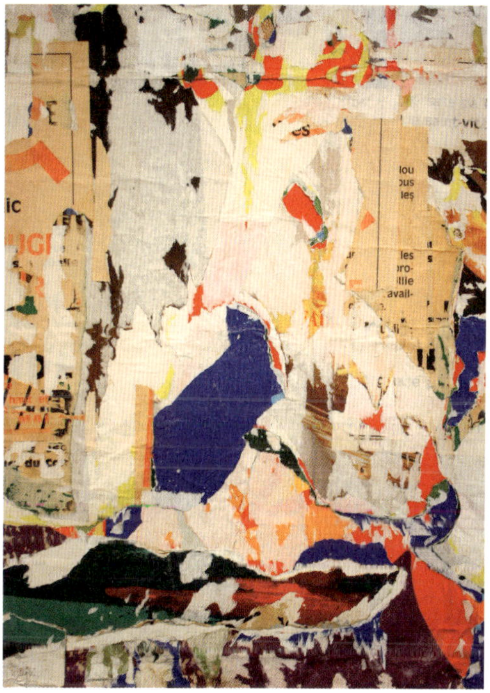

Fig. 3
Jacques Villeglé
Rue de Crimée, 28 novembre 1969, 1969
Décollage on canvas, 39 1/4 x 28 3/4"

be made with marked rapidity, requiring less than ten minutes of a participant's time.[28]

Tinguely, like many of his fellow Nouveaux Réalistes, was fundamentally concerned with creating art capable of registering the changeable and fragmented, yet paradoxically standardized and homogenized, nature of the modern experience. In his 1959 manifesto "For Statics," for example, he insisted that change is an essential condition of existence, the one aspect of reality that is constant: "Today we can no longer believe in permanent laws, defined religions, durable architecture, or eternal kingdoms. Immutability does not exist. All is movement...; stop evoking movement and gesture. You are movement and gesture."[29] While his presentation of his *Metamatics* appears, upon first glance, as a benevolent call for spectator participation—anyone could come in off the street, whether artistically inclined or not, and create their own drawings—implicit in this gesture was a sarcastic acknowledgment that such sanguine aspirations could only be imagined and articulated through the language of a technologically driven postwar consumer society.[30] After each new drawing was produced, it was promptly stamped on the back as a means of authentication. The stamp read: "Painting executed in collaboration with Tinguely's méta-matic N. _____." Lines for the name of the "artist," date, and place of collaboration were left blank for the visitor to fill in. Each painting, although nominally unique, was thus always recognized as part of a series originating from the artist's *Metamatics*.

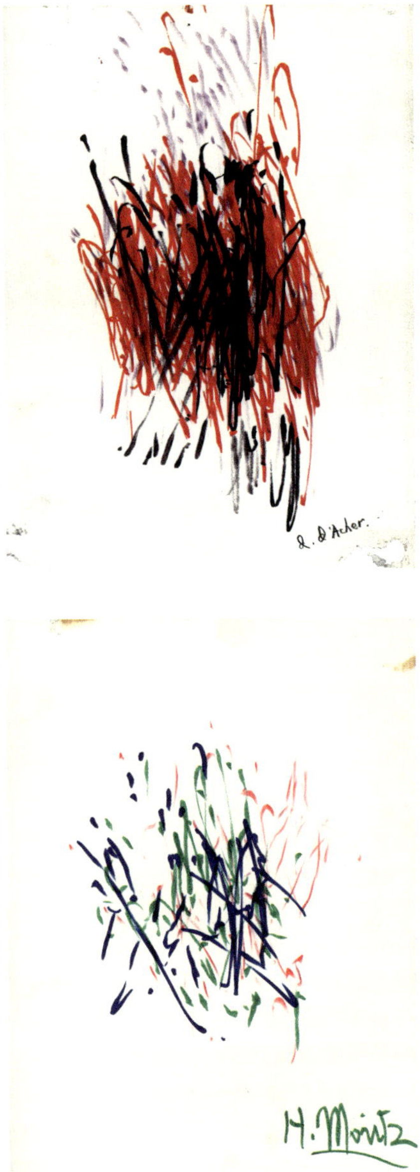

Fig. 4
Jean Tinguely
Two *Metamatic* drawings from *Metamatic No. 9*, 1959
Ink on paper, 12 3/4 x 9 3/4" each

Tinguely reveled in the paradox of industrial automation; while human energy is saved from carrying out repetitive tasks, the individual is deprived of the possibility of contributing something truly personal to the final product. Although he offered his participants the appearance of choice in the form of a variety of ways to personalize a given work, the style was always predetermined by the unpredictable movements of his unstable machines. His *Metamatics* critically demonstrate how the ostensibly liberatory elements of chance and choice can all too easily become tools of commodification and programmed individualism within the strictures of capitalist society.

In each of the approaches examined here, the implementation of chance-based procedures signified a release of subjective agency on the part of the artist, yet the Nouveaux Réalistes' process-driven strategies were never intended to entirely eliminate authorial intervention. Ironically, it was precisely through the regular repetition of each distinct action—ripping, gluing, accumulating, amassing, shooting, or mechanizing—that the members arrived at their signature styles. As unabashed producers, their performative and temporal acts almost always resulted in singular artworks that reinstate the autonomy of the individual art object. The recourse to chance was thus deliberately employed as a halfway gesture, allowing these artists to explore new aesthetic terrains and subject positions while still operating within the conventions of the art market, an attitude that plainly sets them apart from the more radically utopian aspirations of their contemporaries in Fluxus.

Fluxus: Chance Operations and Indeterminate Procedures

Fluxus, an informal international artist group active in both the United States and Germany, was formed around the same time as Nouveau Réalisme. While members of both groups grounded their art in a concrete, quotidian reality, Fluxus was characterized by its more conceptually based practices driven by a desire to achieve a closer integration of art and everyday life and to collapse defined boundaries between language, music, performance, and the visual arts.[31] Chance was from the very beginning associated with the group's pervasive concern with process, fluidity, and experience. It was regularly incorporated into works as means of establishing an active engagement with the ever-changing flux of life, and it served as a critical strategy for transforming the symbolic organization of subject-object relationships, if not the actual conditions of social exchange, within a functionalist society shaped by corporate cultures of control.[32]

Situated squarely within the avant-garde tradition of anti-art—characterized by its overt negation of the art market, rejection of the notion of a great individual creator, and refusal of the art object as a reified commodity—Fluxus attempted to fundamentally decenter the artist's position of mastery and privilege. Its members believed that the simple and habitual objects and activities of everyday life should be regarded as artistic events. Unlike Jean Tinguely's playful call for spectator participation in his "do-it-yourself" exhibition, Fluxus ardently declared that "anything can be art and that anybody can do it."[33] In opposition to the rhetoric employed by Pierre Restany to theoretically frame the diverse work of the Nouveaux Réalistes as an enthusiastic and overtly positive embrace of postwar modernization, the language of George Maciunas, the founder and impresario of Fluxus, took a more militantly revolutionary tone.[34] In his 1962 manifesto pronounced during a concert inaugurating a series of Fluxus performances in Germany, Maciunas called for a radical anti-individualism in art. He advocated the rejection of predetermined or fixed forms, favoring instead open compositions that allow nature "either in the form of an independent performer or indeterminate-chance compositional methods" to complete the work without the guidance of the artist-composer.[35] The primary contribution of the artist would consist in "creating a *concept* or a *method* by which form can be created independently of him," thus signifying an important theoretical shift from the notion of the artist as primary arbiter of meaning to a more conceptually open-ended practice based on reception.[36]

Maciunas lays out here two of the central strategies of Fluxus practice: the use of chance-based procedures at the level of composition, and the introduction of indeterminacy through spectator participation in the creation or performance of a work. While these two methods complement one another and are frequently employed in tandem, they should not be conflated, as they demonstrate different degrees of artistic control or release over an artwork from conception to realization.[37] Whereas chance, in this context, implies the maintenance of a productive tension between a priori systems necessarily set up by an author and the unforeseen results subsequently generated, indeterminacy entails a more extreme gesture toward the effacement of the determining role of the author in favor of the subjective choices and experiences of the performer.

An Anthology (1963) [Cat., p. 136], the first of many compendia offered by Fluxus, is full of such chance-based and indeterminate devices spanning a wide range of media, including poetry, music, and dance.[38] Several contributions, including those by George Brecht, Jackson Mac Low, La Monte Young, and Dick Higgins, took up the form of the event score—instruction-like texts that engage performers in one or more actions based on everyday situations. In Higgins's *Telephone Music (Concretion No. 6)*, for instance, the performer throws a die to determine how he or she will respond to a ringing phone. If the number thrown is a two, the performer is instructed to disconnect the phone. If the number is a six, he or she answers the phone and listens without saying anything until the other party hangs up. While the order of events to be carried out by the performer is left to chance, the actual execution provides little room for variation, as the range of actions are predetermined by the artist. This is similar to experimental composer John Cage's highly programmatic scoring practices, such as in *Music of Changes* (1951), a piece inspired by the divinatory techniques presented in the Chinese *I Ching*, or *Book of Changes*, and created by flipping coins to decide tempos, the number of simultaneous layers, dynamic levels, pitches, and sound categories [Cat., p. 130].

Cage pioneered the use of such laborious chance operations in composition in an effort to open music to a wider world of unforeseen and unintended sounds as well as a larger ethics of nonhierarchical appreciation, advocating for an acceptance of "that continuity that happens" rather than imposing "particular continuity that excludes all others."[39] While the score for *Music of Changes* was arrived at through chance-based procedures in which the results were impossible to predict, the enactment of the resultant musical notation allowed for no deviation on the part of the performer. By the late 1950s, Cage himself criticized the rigidity of such scores and their imposition of tremendous constraints on the performer: "The function of the performer in the case of *Music of Changes* is that of a contractor who, following an architect's blueprint, constructs a building."[40] In a 1958 lecture, he drew a clear distinction between his earlier use of chance procedures on the level of *composition* and his shift toward an emphasis on indeterminate elements in the *performance* of musical works. With a piece such as *Fontana Mix* (1958), which consists of a complex, quasi-topographical system of graphic notation, Cage offers the performer the tools, however complex and opaque, to create any number of scores that can be variously applied to instrumental, vocal, and theatrical purposes [Cat., p. 130].

While Cage never truly severed the relationship between notational sign and performative realization (he repeatedly condemned undisciplined performances of his music), the practitioners of Fluxus event scores, as evidenced in Higgins's *Telephone Music*, took this type of experimentation with indeterminacy one step further by removing musical notation altogether, drastically reducing the score to minimal verbal instructions, the realization of which is left open to a number of complex or simple, public or private, individual or collective interpretations. Mac Low's page of randomly overlapping typewritten letters and symbols in *An Anthology* and the accompanying instructions that detail how the page "may be used in any way as a score for solo or group readings, musical or dramatic performances, looking, smelling, anything else & / or nothing at all," is a case in point. Young's *Composition 1960 #13 to Richard Huelsenbeck* is even more unstructured, merely stating that "the performer should prepare any composition and then perform it as well as he can." The generativity of such a score, a flexible template that can be used to produce unlimited realizations of any shape and duration, comes from its radical contingency. Although such an open work appears to teeter precariously on the edge of absolute arbitrariness and a concomitant lack of meaning, what a piece like Young's purports is an altered perceptual and spectatorial position, as the boundary between author and interpreter is significantly blurred.

If the overt suppression of authorial agency was liberating for an artist such as Young, there were others who could not completely accept it. As suggested by Julia Robinson, the divide between Fluxus and Allan Kaprow's related Happenings, for instance, is built on this very distinction.[41] Kaprow chose to create purposely scripted, time-based events that involved a multiplicity of variables and required active audience participation, but which ultimately had to be orchestrated by the artist himself. *18 Happenings in 6 Parts*, performed at the Reuben Gallery in New York in October 1959, embodies the highly structured character of his Happenings. Upon arriving, spectators were given instruction cards directing them to seats in one of three rooms. The performance was divided into six parts, with each part containing three happenings that were to occur simultaneously. At the end of every two parts, a bell rang, and the audience moved to the next room according to their cards.[42] Elements of chance were incorporated into the temporal structure of *18 Happenings* so as to build noncontrol into the work, effectively guaranteeing variation in the order of the scripted events, but Kaprow always remained as overseer, with the audience just one component in the larger composition. While attempting to activate viewers, to physically engage them in the creation of the work, he also realized that the release of too much control could lead to disaster, as lack of cooperation on the part of the spectator would result in the failure of the piece.[43] Kaprow was ultimately less interested in engaging with chance operations as such than with the production of endlessly changeable aesthetic experiences capable of reflecting the impermanence of a post-World War II environment shaped by planned obsolescence and mass consumerism. His insistence on the "ambiguous, fluid existence" of the art form in opposition to traditional values of permanence and skill was, he thought, the key to destroying old principles and discovering a new field of aesthetic possibility, one as "open and fluid as the shapes of our everyday experience."[44]

George Brecht, now known chiefly as a key member of Fluxus, was a friend of Kaprow's in the 1950s and similarly grappled with the efficacy of chance as a constructive principle for creating new art practices. Fueled by a keen understanding of the application of the forces of chance in twentieth-century art, science, and physics and by a markedly empirical mentality, Brecht's engagement with chance and accident ultimately moved in a decidedly different direction from Kaprow's more theatrical aesthetic.[45] Both artists embraced chance procedures as a compelling means of addressing the problem of individual experience in the context of an increasingly commodified subjectivity. Yet from the start, Brecht's work reveals a more emphatic desire to efface authorial control through the production of radically open forms, the ultimate goal being not to create art, but to instigate, on the part of the spectator, a heightened attention to and perception of the phenomena of daily life.

While working as a research chemist in the early 1950s, Brecht embarked on a concerted examination of chance as a method for creating experimental works of art. Using Jackson Pollock's model of aleatory composition as his point of departure, he focused not on the metaphysical interpretations built up around the painter's drip technique, but rather on more pragmatic concerns such as Pollock's relinquishing of authorial control, his foregrounding of process over product, and his blurring of the line between body and canvas. Brecht's series of *Chance Paintings* (1957) [Cat., p. 134], made by pouring water and ink on bed sheets and then crumbling the sheets into balls so that the ink would dry in unforeseeable patterns, represents one such investigation.[46] By focusing solely on the arbitrary flow of natural processes, he effectively deconstructed the highly individualized practice of 1950s action painting, voiding any exploration of the unconscious mind or expressive content in favor of depersonalized, technical concerns such as process and medium.

In 1957 and 1958, Brecht, along with Kaprow, attended John Cage's experimental composition class at the New School for Social Research in New York. The decisive influence of Cage led to a fundamental shift in both Brecht's and Kaprow's work—a shift that signified a broader movement in the aesthetics of chance away from Pollock's model and its link to a late-Surrealist automatism with its emphasis on a liberating unconscious, and toward a more rigorously programmed form of chance operations.[47] The class was effectively a workshop that centered on the

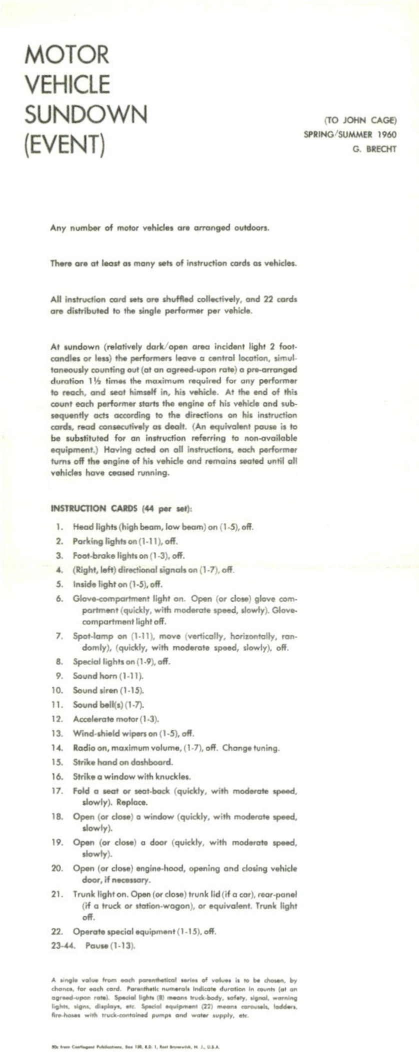
MOTOR VEHICLE SUNDOWN (EVENT)

(TO JOHN CAGE)
SPRING/SUMMER 1960
G. BRECHT

Any number of motor vehicles are arranged outdoors.

There are at least as many sets of instruction cards as vehicles.

All instruction card sets are shuffled collectively, and 22 cards are distributed to the single performer per vehicle.

At sundown (relatively dark/open area incident light 2 foot-candles or less) the performers leave a central location, simultaneously counting out (at an agreed-upon rate) a pre-arranged duration 1½ times the maximum required for any performer to reach, and seat himself in, his vehicle. At the end of this count each performer starts the engine of his vehicle and subsequently acts according to the directions on his instruction cards, read consecutively as dealt. (An equivalent pause is to be substituted for an instruction referring to non-available equipment.) Having acted on all instructions, each performer turns off the engine of his vehicle and remains seated until all vehicles have ceased running.

INSTRUCTION CARDS (44 per set):

1. Head lights (high beam, low beam) on (1-5), off.
2. Parking lights on (1-11), off.
3. Foot-brake lights on (1-3), off.
4. (Right, left) directional signals on (1-7), off.
5. Inside light on (1-5), off.
6. Glove-compartment light on. Open (or close) glove compartment (quickly, with moderate speed, slowly). Glove-compartment light off.
7. Spot-lamp on (1-11), move (vertically, horizontally, randomly), (quickly, with moderate speed, slowly), off.
8. Special lights on (1-9), off.
9. Sound horn (1-11).
10. Sound siren (1-15).
11. Sound bell(s) (1-7).
12. Accelerate motor (1-3).
13. Wind-shield wipers on (1-5), off.
14. Radio on, maximum volume, (1-7), off. Change tuning.
15. Strike hand on dashboard.
16. Strike a window with knuckles.
17. Fold a seat or seat-back (quickly, with moderate speed, slowly). Replace.
18. Open (or close) a window (quickly, with moderate speed, slowly).
19. Open (or close) a door (quickly, with moderate speed, slowly).
20. Open (or close) engine-hood, opening and closing vehicle door, if necessary.
21. Trunk light on. Open (or close) trunk lid (if a car), rear-panel (if a truck or station-wagon), or equivalent. Trunk light off.
22. Operate special equipment (1-15), off.

23-44. Pause (1-13).

A single value from each parenthetical series of values is to be chosen, by chance, for each card. Parenthetic numerals indicate duration in counts (at an agreed-upon rate). Special lights (8) means truck-body, safety, signal, warning lights, signs, displays, etc. Special equipment (22) means carousels, ladders, fire-hoses with truck-contained pumps and water supply, etc.

Fig. 5
George Brecht
Motor Vehicle Sundown (Event), 1960
Printed sheet, folded

composer's adherence to nonintention on the part of the artist and his notion of the score as an open field capable of incorporating a wide range of found sounds, actions, and durations.[48] Cage's fundamental belief that the function of art is to imitate nature "in her manner of operation" and that chance is "at the point of potentiality" was also informed by the Zen Buddhist teachings of Daisetz Suzuki, the main promoter of Zen in the West at that time.[49] The nondualistic philosophy of Zen complemented and advanced Brecht's and other Fluxus members' interest in opening the work of art to forces outside of the artist's subjective decisions and offered a new ideological basis for the use of chance.[50] The philosophical emphasis on detachment, spontaneity, and the elimination of hierarchies provided an ostensibly functional counter-model to a dominant administrative culture.

It was while attending Cage's class that Brecht began to move away from his earlier systematic experiments with painting, adapting Cage's techniques of musical composition to produce his conceptually hybrid event scores, a form that could be realized as language, object, and performance. Brecht's first events were akin to Kaprow's Happenings in that they were performed by participants following a complex score that prescribed a series of actions distributed in time through a series of chance operations. For example, the score for *Motor Vehicle Sundown (Event)*, a piece initially inspired by Brecht's routine experience of waiting in a car for his wife with the motor running, called for the distribution of instruction cards directing the action of performers both in and on any number of motor vehicles assembled outdoors [Fig. 5]. Once the performers turned on their engines, they were instructed to act out the directions on the cards—which included turning on and off headlights, sounding horns, opening windows, and operating the windshield wipers—in the order they were dealt, arriving at what Henry Martin has aptly described as a "delicately ordered chaos" in which groups of sounds and activities "become significant by virtue of their being constantly repeated in constantly changing sequences."[51] The piece's complex arrangement and chance juxtaposition of sounds and acts exist "as a temporal extension of collage aesthetics" and directly recall Dadaist performances of simultaneity.[52]

Brecht soon gravitated away from the model of programmatic chaos provided by Cage and practiced by Kaprow in favor of more discrete or monostructural language-based events. Comprised of short, simple words, his event scores produced in the early 1960s tend to involve either minimal task-based instructions or focused observations of single everyday occurrences.[53] In a work such as *Two Vehicle Events* from 1961, for instance, which consists of only two words, "start" and "stop" (each proceeded by a bullet point), the limited directives result in an incredible amount of freedom of choice and subjective interpretation on the part of the reader / performer. Through its extreme generality, this score generates an open work whose ultimate form and duration can never be known until performed, fusing process and reception in endlessly unfixed variation. In hyper-banal scores such as this one, intended to cut into the flow of everyday life by creating a specific mode of attention, chance is essentially no longer at play: the pronounced lack of direction in Brecht's wholly indeterminate pieces now shifts the formation of the work off of the artist and onto the performer, who must assume the authoritative role of decision maker.[54] It is precisely this crucial change that marked what Brecht would come to articulate, in an addendum to his manifesto-type essay *Chance-Imagery*, as "the resolution of the distinction between choice and chance" in his practice—between works driven almost exclusively by performer preferences and programmed, necessarily author-centered, chance procedures.[55]

Maciunas heralded Brecht's indeterminate scores as a model for Fluxus production, emblematic of the group's desire to create nonpersonal works that would eventually lead to such a time when fine art can be totally eradicated and man can "experience the world, the concrete world surrounding him ... in the same way he experiences art."[56] Whether or not he shared Maciunas's extremist agenda to eliminate the role of the artist completely, Brecht's practice, like the majority of his fellow Fluxus artists', reveals a fundamental desire to achieve, in the face of the rapid standardization of experience attributable to the homogenizing tactics of commodity culture, a more viable relationship between the self and the changing world of everyday phenomena.

***

Considered together, these diverse practices and agendas, ranging from the openly utopian outlook offered by Fluxus to the more ambivalent position of the Nouveaux Réalistes, draw critical attention to the ambiguities then facing postwar society at large: immediate experience versus commercial mediation; technological liberation versus social repression; collective benevolence versus individual egoism. Acknowledging the way in which subjects are absorbed within postwar spectacle culture, these artists commonly turned to chance-based practices as means of cleaving what Benjamin Buchloh has described as "sudden ruptures within that system's mesmerizing totality and numbing continuity."[57] Arman and Spoerri asserted a point of tension in the conceptualization of experience by preserving or freezing the flow of commercial objects and urban refuse in their tracks. Kaprow's Happenings and Brecht's event scores similarly pointed to the changing realm of everyday experience through object and event-production that aimed to supplant individual creation with discourse and active social participation. Unlike their postmodern successors who conceived "reality" as inherently mediated by language, technology, and socioeconomic structures, these artists still held a belief, however tenuous, that access to some form of valid experience was still possible. The introduction of performativity and temporality through aleatory procedures and indeterminate strategies allowed for a critical exploration of the experience of the subject as contingent and changing. By upholding this rather precarious position, they propelled alternative models for artistic production while simultaneously advancing a more complex and multifaceted notion of subjectivity that radically expanded the parameters for the relationship between artist, artwork, and viewer—developments that would fundamentally change the direction and shape of artistic production for decades to follow.

NOTES

1. For an overview of the revived interest in Dada strategies by this postwar generation, see Susan Hapgood, *Neo-Dada: Redefining Art, 1958–1962* (New York: American Federation of Arts, 1994).

2. For a reading of the impact on the arts of the rise of American corporate culture of control at mid-century, see Jackson Lears, "Out of Control: Art and Accident in a Managerial Age," in *Off Limits: Rutgers University and the Avant-Garde, 1957–1963*, ed. Joan M. Marter (New Brunswick, NJ: Rutgers University Press, 1999), 48–64. For a discussion of socioeconomic shifts and the culture of control as it arose in the postwar French context, see Kristin Ross, *Fast Cars, Clean Bodies: Decolonization and the Reordering of French Culture* (Cambridge, MA: MIT Press, 1995).

3. See Alex Potts, "Autonomy in Post-war Art, Quasi-heroic and Casual," *Oxford Art Journal* 27, no. 1 (2004): 46–47. Peter Bürger's seminal text, *Theory of the Avant-Garde* (1974), set the frame for debate about the duality between the historical avant-garde's imperative for autonomy from the reified realities of the modern world and the impulse to sublate art and life. Important critiques of Bürger's rubric include Benjamin H. D. Buchloh, *Neo-Avantgarde and Culture Industry: Essays on European and American Art from 1955 to 1975* (Cambridge, MA: MIT Press, 2000); Hal Foster, "Who's Afraid of the Neo-Avant-Garde?" in his *The Return of the Real: The Avant-Garde at the End of the Century* (Cambridge, MA: MIT Press, 1996), 1–32; Dietrich Scheunemann, ed., *Avant-Garde / Neo-Avant-Garde* (Amsterdam: Rodopi, 2005); and David Hopkins, ed., *Neo-Avant-Garde* (Amsterdam: Rodopi, 2006).

4. Potts, "Autonomy in Post-war Art," 46.

5. "Nouveau Réalisme = nouvelles approches perceptives du réel" (translation mine). This declaration by Pierre Restany was made the day Nouveau Réalisme was officially founded, on October 27, 1960, in Yves Klein's apartment. Those in attendance included Klein, Jean Tinguely, Arman, François Dufrêne, Raymond Hains, Martial Raysse, Daniel Spoerri, and Jacques Villeglé. Christo, Niki de Saint Phalle, Gérard Deschamps, and César soon joined, bringing the group to thirteen members.

6. Pierre Restany, "The Nouveaux Réalistes Declaration of Intention" (1960), in *Theories and Documents of Contemporary Art*, ed. Kristine Stiles and Peter Selz (Berkeley: University of California Press, 1996), 306.

7. Jill Carrick offers a valuable critique of Restany's theorization of the group and his dream of a neutral language of unmediated presentation. See Jill Carrick, "Le Nouveau Réalisme: Fetishism and Consumer Spectacle in Post-War France" (Phd diss., Bryn Mawr, 1998), 66–71.

8. According to Restany, Nouveau Réalisme represented "the incarnation of the optimistic metaphor of European consumer society." See Pierre Restany, "Nouveau Réalisme: The Richness of the World of Objects," in *Nouveaux Réalistes* (New York: Zabriskie Gallery, 1988), 5. Statements such as this have led numerous critics, both in the 1960s and today, to denigrate Nouveau Réalisme as a naïve pastiche of capitalist spectacle.

9. Arman, as quoted in Henry Martin, *Arman; Or, Four and Twenty Blackbirds Baked in a Pie; Or, Why Settle for Less When You Can Settle for More* (New York: Harry N. Abrams, 1973), 9. In a related series, the *Portraits-Robots*, Arman made "portraits" of friends and fellow artists out of their trash. Rather than anonymous garbage, the collections of personal trash become stand-ins for their "sitters."

10. Ibid.

11. See Jaimey Hamilton, "Arman's System of Objects," *Art Journal* 67, no. 1 (Spring 2008): 55–56.

12. See Daniel Spoerri, "Trap Pictures" (1961), reprinted in *Zero* (Cambridge, MA: MIT Press, 1973), 217.

13. Ibid.

14. Daniel Spoerri, *An Anecdoted Topography of Chance* (London: Atlas Press, 1995), 23. First published in February 1962 in lieu of a catalog for an exhibition of the artist's *tableaux-pièges* at the Gallery Lawrence in Paris, the book has gone through numerous editions and substantial augmentation in the form of anecdotes offered by various friends and collaborators. Each edition presents an increasingly complicated system of footnotes, with additional narratives branching off from Spoerri's earliest descriptions to create various levels of thoughts and random observations.

15. Ibid., 83.

16. Ibid., 131.

17. Jill Carrick has convincingly argued for a contextual connection between the classificatory impulses in sociology in 1960s France and the practice of the Nouveaux Réalistes. See Carrick, "Le Nouveau Réalisme," 75–79

18. For more on (de)mystification in this postwar period, see Michael Kelly, "Demystification: A Dialogue between Barthes and Lefebvre," in *The French Fifties: Yale French Studies*, ed. Susan Weiner (New Haven, CT: Yale University Press, 2000), 79–97.

19. The other *affichistes* included Raymond Hains, François Dûfrene, and Mimmo Rotella.

20. Villeglé's work has been the subject of several recent studies, including François Bon, Nicolas Bourriaud, and Kaira Marie Cabañas, *Jacques Villeglé* (Paris: Flammarion, 2007); and *Jacques Villeglé: La comédie urbaine* (Paris: Centre Pompidou, 2008).

21. Buchloh's rigorously political reading of Villeglé's work has led the scholarship on these works since the early 1990s. See Benjamin H. D. Buchloh, "Villeglé: From Fragment to Detail," in his *Neo-Avantgarde and Culture Industry*, 443–60. See also Tom McDonough, "Authorial Intervention," *Artforum* (March 2009): 216–23, for a revised interpretation of Villeglé's posters that stresses how little of the artist's output actually corresponds to the dominant reading of his work.

22. Niki de Saint Phalle, letter to Harry Mathews, 1961, Harry Mathews Archives, Rare Books and Manuscripts, Van Pelt Library, University of Pennsylvania, Philadelphia, Pennsylvania.

23. Saint Phalle, televised interview with David Brinkley, 1961 (NBC). A tape of this program is housed at the Niki Charitable Art Foundation, Santee, California.

24. Calvin Tomkins wittily observed that the results of Tinguely's machines "as often as not are not only distinctly pleasing but uncomfortably close to certain contemporary paintings produced by the unaided human hand." See Calvin Tomkins, *The Bride and the Bachelors: Five Masters of the Avant-Garde* (Middlesex, England: Penguin Books, 1976), 163. One of Tinguely's most famous exhibitions of his *Metamatics* took place at the Iris Clert Gallery in Paris in July 1959. Recounting the exhibition, Clert noted the participation of several prominent abstract painters, stating: "The machine was resolutely *tachiste*. Funny thing though. Artist Hans Hartung tried it and his canvas resembled a Hartung." Iris Clert, as quoted in Waverly Root, "The Fine Art of Press Agentry," *Washington Post*, June 2, 1963, E5.

25. The announcement card passed out at the opening read: "Come to create for yourself with ardor, furor, sweetness or elegance your painting in collaboration with Tinguely's sculptures that paint at the Iris Clert gallery."

26. Jean Tinguely, as quoted in William R. Byron, "Wacky Artist of Destruction," *Saturday Evening Post*, April 21, 1962, 76.

27. Helen Molesworth, "Jean Tinguely," in *Work Ethic*, ed. Helen Molesworth (Baltimore: Baltimore Museum of Art; University Park: Pennsylvania State University Press, 2003), 204.

28. Art Buchwald, "The Latest in Abstract Art," *New York Herald Tribune*, Paris edition, June 3, 1959.

29. Jean Tinguely, "Für Statik"(1959), translated and reproduced in *Zero*, 119.

30. Benjamin Buchloh makes a similar observation in regard to Andy Warhol's *Dance Diagram* (1961) and series of *Do It Yourself* paintings (1962). See Benjamin H. D. Buchloh, "Andy Warhol's One-Dimensional Art," in *Neo-Avantgarde and Culture Industry*, 482–84. Warhol and Tinguely both parody the methods and legacy of earlier Abstract Expressionist painters while ironically evoking the participatory rituals of popular entertainment.

31. Fluxus debuted in a series of European festivals that took place in 1962 and 1963.

32. See Jackson Lears, "Out of Control."

33. George Maciunas, "Fluxus Art-Amusement" (1965), reproduced in *Fluxus Etc: The Gilbert and Lila Silverman Collection*, ed. Jon Hendricks (Bloomfield Hills, MI: Cranbrook Academy of Art Museum, 1981), 9.

34. Maciunas explicitly associated the Fluxus project with that of the LEF (Left Front of the Arts) group of Soviet productivists, attempting to collectivize artistic production and deprofessionalize the artist. Many of the Fluxus artists contested the leftist language used by Maciunas to speak on their behalf. For more on Maciunas's disputed role as impresario and his leftist agenda, see Julia Robinson, "Maciunas as Producer: Performative Design in the Art of the 1960s," *Grey Room* 33 (Fall 2008): 56–83. Daniel Spoerri, who participated in select Fluxus performances and publications in the early 1960s in Europe, considered Fluxus an extremely tentative development and rejected Maciunas's dictatorial role. According to Spoerri, "New Realism was a movement: people did work together and exhibit together, and have a gallery. But Fluxus was always only Maciunas, who decided who was in and who was not." Daniel Spoerri, interview with Susan Hapgood, Paris, April 26, 1992, in *Neo-Dada*, 132.

35. George Maciunas, "Neo-Dada in Music, Theater, Poetry, Art," in *In the Spirit of Fluxus*, ed. Elizabeth Armstrong and Janet Jenkins (Minneapolis: Walker Art Center, 1993), 157.

36. Ibid.

37. For more on this distinction, see Anna Dezeuze, "Origins of the Fluxus Score: From Indeterminacy to the 'Do-It-Yourself' Artwork," *Performance Research* 7, no. 3 (September 2002): 82–85. Dezeuze's more recent exploration of performer choice as an alternative to chance is also critical to the evolving discourse on this topic. In particular, she illuminates the emergence of spectator participation in the late 1950s and early 1960s through Neoconcrete works and early Fluxus event scores. Anna Dezeuze, "'Open Work,' 'Do-it-yourself Artwork' and Bricolage," in *The 'Do-it-Yourself Artwork': Participation from Fluxus to Relational Aesthetics*, ed. Anna Dezeuze (Manchester: Manchester University Press, forthcoming). I am grateful to her for sharing a draft of this essay with me.

38. *An Anthology* was initially assembled in 1960 by composer La Monte Young for a planned issue of *Beatitude East*, an extension of a West Coast experimental musical periodical, *Beatitude West*. It was designed and published by George Maciunas in 1963. The contents served as the central material that Maciunas brought to Europe to be performed during the first Fluxus festivals in 1962.

39. John Cage, "Lecture on Something," in his *Silence* (Middletown, CT: Wesleyan University Press, 1961), 132.

40. John Cage, "Composition as Process: Indeterminacy" (1958), in *Silence*, 36. For more on this shift in Cage's practice as well as his seminal influence on Fluxus and the neo-avant-garde more broadly, see Liz Kotz, *Words to Be Looked At: Language in 1960s Art* (Cambridge, MA: MIT Press, 2007), esp. chapters 1 and 2. See also Branden W. Joseph, "Robert Morris and John Cage: Reconstructing a Dialogue," *October* 81 (Summer 1997): 59–69.

41. See Julia Robinson, "The Sculpture of Indeterminacy: Alison Knowles's Beans and Variations," *Art Journal* 63, no. 4 (Winter 2004): 98–99.

42. For descriptions of *18 Happenings* and a reproduction of Kaprow's script, see *Happenings: An Illustrated Anthology*, ed. Michael Kirby (New York: E.P. Dutton, 1965), 53–83.

43. See Allan Kaprow, *Assemblage, Environments & Happenings* (New York: Harry N. Abrams, 1966), 174 and 181. See also William Kazen, "Framed Space: Allan Kaprow and the Spread of Painting," *Grey Room* 13 (Fall 2003): 96–98.

44. Allan Kaprow, "Notes on the Creation of a Total Art," in his *Essays on the Blurring of Art and Life*, ed. Jeff Kelley (Berkeley: University of California Press, 1993), 12.

45. In his 1957 essay *Chance-Imagery*, Brecht framed chance as an underlying principle of our worldview, an aspect "of the way in which we structure our universe" and thus of direct relevance to trends in contemporary artistic practice. See George Brecht, *Chance-Imagery* (New York: Great Bear Pamphlet / Something Else Press, 1966), 2. Two essential monographs on Brecht's work are Henry Martin, *An Introduction to George Brecht's "Book of the Tumbler on Fire"* (Milan: Multhipla Edizioni, 1978); and Julia Robinson, *George Brecht Events: A Heterospective*, ed. Alfred M. Fisher (Cologne: Walther König, 2005).

46. Brecht's other experiments included the use of random numbers to plot coordinates on a canvas and "rolling marbles dipped in ink over plywood, so that irregularities in the surface appeared in the resultant form." George Brecht, interview with Michael Nyman (1976), reproduced in Martin, *An Introduction to George Brecht's "Book of the Tumbler on Fire"*, 114.

47. Brecht spells out Pollock's influence on his early chance-based experiments in *Chance-Imagery*. At the same moment, Kaprow authored his own essay evincing his deep understanding of the primacy of action in Pollock's process of creation. See Allan Kaprow, "The Legacy of Jackson Pollock," *ARTnews* 57, no. 6 (October 1958): 24–26, 55–57. Douglas Kahn offers an insightful analysis of Kaprow's and Brecht's negotiation of the simultaneous influences of Pollock and Cage in his *Noise, Water, Meat: A History of Sound in the Arts* (Cambridge, MA: MIT Press, 1999), 270–88.

48. In the period before the formation of Fluxus, c. 1958–1962, Brecht, Kaprow, Dick Higgins, Jackson Mac Low, and others attended Cage's seminal class. Soon thereafter they all branched off in different directions. For more on the impact of Cage's class, see Bruce J. Altshuler, "The Cage Class," in *Flux Attitudes*, ed. Cornelia Lauf and Susan Hapgood (Buffalo, NY: Hallwalls Contemporary Arts Center, 1992), 17–23; and Joseph Jacobs, "Crashing New York à la John Cage," in *Off Limits*, 65–99.

49. John Cage, "Where are we going? And what are we doing?," in *Silence*, 194. Recent scholarship devoted to Cage has provided new insights into his theories and practices as well as his relationship to Eastern philosophy. Alexandra Munroe notes, for example, that "Cage cared less about the actual practice and history of Zen than his creative application of it, both for his compositions and the work of artists he admired." Alexandra Munroe, "Buddhism and the Neo-Avant-Garde: Cage Zen, Beat Zen, and Zen," in *The Third Mind: American Artists Contemplate Asia, 1860–1989*, ed. Alexandra Munroe (New York: Solomon R. Guggenheim Museum, 2009), 207–8.

50. As revealed in his *Chance-Imagery* essay, Brecht's interest in Zen predated his meeting Cage. See also Alfred M. Fischer's examination of Brecht's evolving interest in Zen philosophy, "No Words Will Ever...," in Robinson, *George Brecht Events*, 182–202; and Anna Dezeuze, "'Neo-dada,' 'Junk Aesthetic' and Spectator Participation," in *Neo-Avant-Garde*, 62–65.

51. Martin, *An Introduction to George Brecht's "Book of the Tumbler on Fire"*, 8.

52. Kotz, *Words to Be Looked At*, 73.

53. Many of Brecht's event scores were assembled and distributed as small printed cards in *Water Yam* (1963), the first in a series of Fluxus editions planned by George Maciunas intended to offer collected artist works in a cheap, easily distributed manner.

54. See Kahn, *Noise, Water, Meat*, 285.

55. Brecht, *Chance-Imagery*, 15.

56. Maciunas, "Neo-Dada in Music, Theater, Poetry, Art," 157.

57. Benjamin H. D. Buchloh, "Robert Watts: Inanimate Objects—Inanimate Subjects," in Buchloh and Judith F. Rodenbeck, *Experiments in the Everyday: Allan Kaprow and Robert Watts, Events, Objects, Documents* (New York: Columbia University, Miriam and Ira D. Wallach Art Gallery, 1999), 22.

CATALOG

Entries by Bradley Bailey (BB), Karen K. Butler (KB), Emily Hage (EH), Meredith Malone (MM)

COLLAGE, ASSEMBLAGE, AND THE FOUND OBJECT

The strategies of collage and assemblage were incredibly generative throughout the twentieth century for numerous avant-garde artists concerned with testing and dismantling sanctioned categories of art such as painting and sculpture.

TRISTAN TZARA
RICHARD HUELSENBECK
MARCEL JANCO
MARCEL DUCHAMP
RAOUL HAUSMANN
JEAN (HANS) ARP
ELLSWORTH KELLY
JEAN DUBUFFET
DANIEL SPOERRI
NIKI DE SAINT PHALLE
MIMMO ROTELLA
JACQUES VILLEGLÉ
DIETER ROTH
ARMAN

These methods offered inventive means for constructing an image from preexisting materials and found objects while simultaneously destabilizing existing views of the world through fragmentation and juxtaposition. The deliberate deployment of chance and accident in the creation of a work furthered the radical act of introducing non-art materials into the realm of art. The extent to which chance procedures were employed, and to what ends, varied considerably from artist to artist. Some turned to chance as a nihilistic gesture, superseding all purposeful organization and rational control. Others selected found objects through chance processes but carefully arranged, applied, or manipulated their findings according to strict standards of composition.

Many of the artists associated with Dada, for instance, viewed any coherence or order with contempt. They embraced chance as an irreverent means of shocking a complacent bourgeoisie and overthrowing the artistic status quo. Artworks such as Jean Arp's series of collages "arranged according to the laws of chance" (1916–17), in which the artist dropped pieces of paper onto a support and, as the story goes, glued them down "in the order that they had chosen themselves,"[1] and Marcel Duchamp's unaltered readymades, such as *Hat Rack* (1917), represent critical hallmarks of chance-based practices that informed a wide range of subsequent artistic explorations aimed at escaping the notion of the artist as a primary arbiter of meaning. In negating traditional elements that served as baseline criteria for judging a work of art, such as the direct trace of the artist's hand or the reliance upon a learned set of skills, the Dadaists prompted a productive dialectic between deskilling and reskilling by way of unorthodox tools and materials, provoking a fundamental rethinking of artistic subjectivity and originality.

The embrace of chance as an anti-art strategy by the Dadaists was followed in the mid-1920s by the Surrealists' championing of the magical frisson created when two unrelated, found objects are brought strangely together as art, epitomized in the metaphor of French writer Isidore Ducasse (the "Comte de Lautréamont") of the chance encounter of a sewing machine and an umbrella on a dissecting table. André Breton, the principal founder of Surrealism, would often cite this phrase to articulate the Surrealist belief that beauty, or the marvelous, could be found in chance encounters in the street, what he paradoxically termed "objective chance." Breton described chance as objective insofar as it represented for him not a fully random coincidence but an encounter with an object that is both "fortuitous" and "foreordained."[2] Such serendipitous intersections were thought to cause moments of "sublime illumination" that were experienced as positive dislocations in which internal impulses and external signs were confused and the individual was left feeling simultaneously like and unlike himself.[3] This radical decentering was infused with sociopolitical implications, as it was thought to provide a means of overcoming habitual actions and assumptions to find the marvelous within the everyday. Unlike the nihilistic stance taken by Dada artists, the Surrealists' use of found objects aimed at nothing less than the total transformation of the way people perceived reality, with the goal of freeing humankind from the constraints of logic and reason that had led to the domination and destruction of World War I.

In the post-World War II period, the strategies of collage, assemblage, and the found object appeared for many artists as compelling means of critically negotiating the expansion of mass culture in the industrialized urban environment. These production techniques were especially appealing to a generation emerging in the late 1950s and early 1960s, offering a means of reconnecting art with the stuff and actions of everyday life. This shift in practice was, in part, a reaction to the metaphysical ideals subscribed to by proponents of gestural abstraction and the formal purity then associated with institutionalized modernism. Daniel Spoerri's fixing of chance encounters with daily objects in the form of his *tableaux-pièges*, Jacques Villeglé's and Mimmo Rotella's appropriated lacerated posters, and Dieter Roth's experiments with the natural process of decomposition reveal the diversity of approaches undertaken as artists worked to redefine artistic paradigms while grappling with the changes in contemporary experience wrought by a burgeoning consumer society characterized by accelerated cycles of consumption, disposal, and decay. The emphasis on the act of finding and juxtaposing everyday items, combined with an intense desire to interrogate the artwork's status as an unchanging object through the incorporation of contingent and temporal elements, would prove essential in pushing the trajectory of artistic production toward Process art and performance-based events in the decades to follow.

NOTES

1. Jean (Hans) Arp, as quoted in Richard Huelsenbeck, "Arp and the Dada Movement," in *Arp*, ed. James Thrall Soby (New York: Museum of Modern Art, 1958), 18.
2. André Breton, *Mad Love* (1937), trans. Mary Ann Caws (Lincoln: University of Nebraska Press, 1987), 19. The clearest illustration of objective chance can be found in the beginning of *Mad Love*, as Breton tells of his trip to a Parisian flea market with Alberto Giacometti, where he found a wooden spoon with a little shoe carved out of its handle, recalling a phrase running through Breton's head some months earlier: "the Cinderella ash-tray." Breton, *Mad Love*, 32–33.
3. See Ross Hamilton, *Accident: A Philosophical and Literary History* (Chicago: University of Chicago Press, 2007), 276.

Tristan Tzara (French, b. Romania, 1896–1963)
Richard Huelsenbeck (German, 1894–1972)
Marcel Janco (Israeli, b. Romania, 1895–1984)

"L'Amiral cherche une maison à louer," 1916

Simultaneous poem published in *Cabaret Voltaire*, no. 1 (1916)

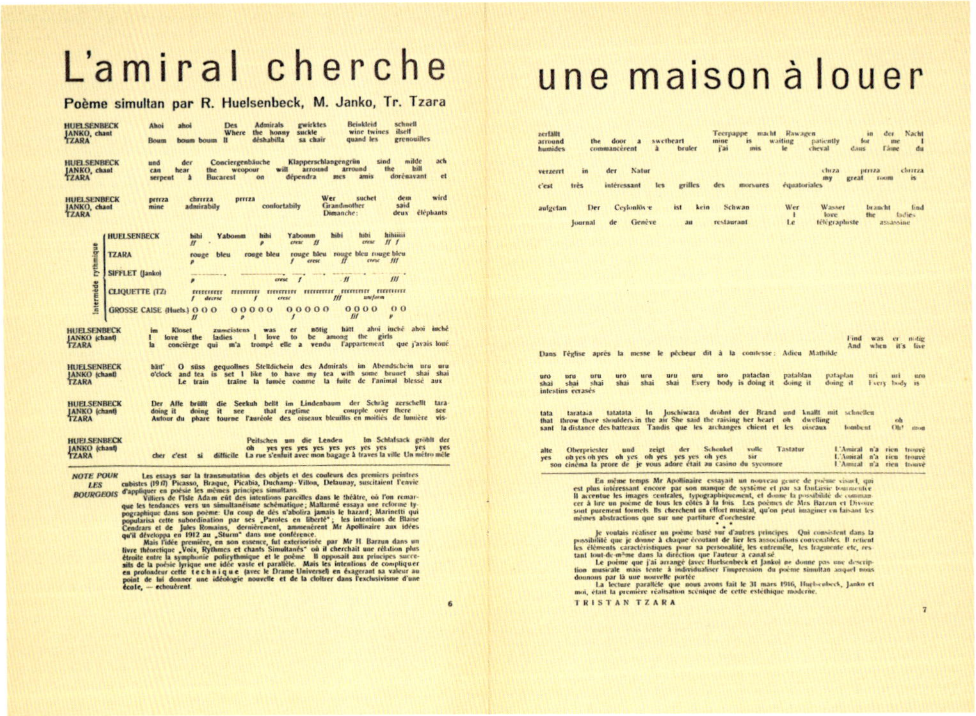

L'amiral cherche une maison à louer

Poème simultan par R. Huelsenbeck, M. Janko, Tr. Tzara

HUELSENBECK Ahoi ahoi Des Admirals gwirktes Beinkleid schnell
JANKO, chant Where the honny suckle wine twines ilself
TZARA Boum boum boum Il déshabilla sa chair quand les grenouilles

HUELSENBECK und der Conciergenbäuche Klapperschlangengrün sind milde ach
JANKO, chant can hear the weopour will arround arround the hill
TZARA serpent à Bucarest on dépendra mes amis dorénavant et

HUELSENBECK prrrza chrrrza prrrza Wer suchet dem wird
JANKO, chant mine admirabily confortabily Grandmother said
TZARA Dimanche: deux éléphants

Intermède rythmique

HUELSENBECK hihi Yabomm hihi Yabomm hihi hihi hihiiiii
ff p cresc ff cresc ff f

TZARA rouge bleu rouge bleu rouge bleu rouge bleu rouge bleu
p f cresc ff cresc fff

SIFFLET (Janko)
p cresc f ff fff

CLIQUETTE (TZ) rrrrrrrrrr rrrrrrrrrr rrrrrrrrrr rrrrrrrrrr rrrrrrrrrr rrrrrrrrrr
f decresc f cresc fff uniform

GROSSE CAISE (Huels.) O O O O O O O O O O O O O O O O O O O O
ff p f fff p

HUELSENBECK im Kloset zumeistens was er nötig hätt ahoi iuché ahoi iuché
JANKO (chant) I love the ladies I love to be among the girls
TZARA la concièrge qui m'a trompé elle a vendu l'appartement que j'avais loué

HUELSENBECK hätt' O süss gequollnes Stelldichein des Admirals im Abendschein uru uru
JANKO (chant) o'clock and tea is set I like to have my tea with some brunet shai shai
TZARA Le train traîne la fumée comme la fuite de l'animal blessé aux

HUELSENBECK Der Affe brüllt die Seekuh bellt im Lindenbaum der Schräg zerschellt tara
JANKO (chant) doing it doing it see that ragtime coupple over there see
TZARA Autour du phare tourne l'auréole des oiseaux bleuillis en moitiés de lumière vis-

HUELSENBECK Peitschen um die Lenden Im Schlafsack gröhlt der
JANKO (chant) oh yes yes yes yes yes yes yes yes yes yes
TZARA cher c'est si difficile La rue s'enfuit avec mon bagage à traves la ville Un métro mêle

NOTE POUR LES BOURGEOIS Les essays sur la transmutation des objets et des couleurs des premiers peintres cubistes (1907) Picasso, Braque, Picabia, Duchamp-Villon, Delaunay, suscitaient l'envie d'appliquer en poésie les mêmes principes simultans.

Villiers de l'Isle Adam eût des intentions pareilles dans le théâtre, où l'on remarque les tendances vers un simultanéisme schématique; Mallarmé essaya une reforme typographique dans son poème: Un coup de dés n'abolira jamais le hazard; Marinetti qui popularisa cette subordination par ses „Paroles en liberté"; les intentions de Blaise Cendrars et de Jules Romains, dernièrement, ammenèrent Mr Apollinaire aux idées qu'il développa en 1912 au „Sturm" dans une conférence.

Mais l'idée première, en son essence, fut exteriorisée par Mr H. Barzun dans un livre théoretique „Voix, Rythmes et chants Simultanés" où il cherchait une rélation plus étroite entre la symphonie polirythmique et le poème. Il opposait aux principes succesifs de la poésie lyrique une idée vaste et parallèle. Mais les intentions de compliquer en profondeur cette t e c h n i q u e (avec le Drame Universel) en éxagerant sa valeur au point de lui donner une idéologie nouvelle et de la cloitrer dans l'exclusivisme d'une école, — echouèrent.

6

zerfällt Teerpappe macht Rawagen in der Nacht
arround the door a swetheart mine is waiting patiently for me I
humides commancèrent à bruler j'ai mis le cheval dans l'âme du

verzerrt in der Natur chrza prrrza chrrrza
my great room is
c'est très intéressant les grilles des morsures équatoriales

aufgetan Der Ceylonlöwe ist kein Schwan Wer Wasser braucht find
I love the ladies
Journal de Genève au restaurant Le télégraphiste assassine

Find was er nötig
And when it's five
Dans l'église après la messe le pêcheur dit à la comtesse: Adieu Mathilde

uro uru uru uro uru uru uru uro pataclan patablan pataplan uri uri uro
shai shai shai shai shai shai Every body is doing it doing it doing it Every body is
intestins ecrasés

tata tarataia tatatata In Joschiwara dröhnt der Brand und knallt mit schnellen
that throw there shoulders in the air She said the raising her heart oh dwelling oh
sant la distance des batteaux Tandis que les archanges chient et les oiseaux tombent Oh! mon

alte Oberpriester und zeigt der Schenkel volle Tastatur L'Amiral n'a rien trouvé
yes oh yes oh yes oh yes oh yes yes yes oh yes sir L'Amiral n'a rien trouvé
son cinéma la prore de je vous adore était au casino du sycomore L'Amiral n'a rien trouvé

En même temps Mr Apollinaire essayait un nouveau genre de poème visuel, qui est plus intéressant encore par son manque de système et par sa fantaisie tourmentée. Il accentue les images centrales, typographiquement, et donne la possibilité de commancer à lire un poème de tous les côtés à la fois. Les poèmes de Mrs Barzun et Divoire sont purement formels. Ils cherchent un éffort musical, qu'on peut imaginer en faisant les mêmes abstractions que sur une partiture d'orchestre.

* * *

Je voulais réaliser un poème basé sur d'autres principes. Qui consistent dans la possibilité que je donne à chaque écoutant de lier les associations convenables. Il retient les éléments caractéristiques pour sa personalité, les entremêle, les fragmente etc, restant tout-de-même dans la direction que l'auteur a canalisé.

Le poème que j'ai arrangé (avec Huelsenbeck et Janko) ne donne pas une description musicale mais tente à individualiser l'impression du poème simultan auquel nous donnons par là une nouvelle portée.

La lecture parallèle que nous avons fait le 31 mars 1916, Huelsenbeck, Janko et moi, était la première réalisation scénique de cette estéthique moderne.

T R I S T A N T Z A R A

7

On March 30, 1916, Tristan Tzara, Richard Huelsenbeck, and Marcel Janco performed Tzara's simultaneous poem, "L'Amiral cherche une maison à louer" (The Admiral Is Looking for a House to Rent) at the Cabaret Voltaire in Zurich. They spoke in three languages—German, French, and English—with a brief "rhythmic interlude" in which they played musical instruments and made vocal sounds. The words of the poem are nonsensical and for the most part they do not seem to relate to the title in any obvious way. Janco's line, for example, consisted in part of: "see that ragtime coupple over there see that throw there shoulders in the air She said the raising her heart oh dwelling oh oh."[1] The multiplicity of languages contributes to the incoherence of the piece, punctuated at the end when the three voices announce in unison: "L'amiral n'a rien trouvé" (The admiral has found nothing). In his diary entry for March 30, 1916, Dadaist Hugo Ball described the performance of the piece and defined the simultaneous poem as "a contrapuntal recitative in which three or more voices speak, sing, whistle, etc., at the same time in such a way that the elegiac, humorous, or bizarre content of the piece is brought out by these combinations."[2] An affront to the strident nationalism of the time, Tzara's trilingual poem resisted the logic and reason that many Dadaists blamed for the atrocities of World War I and used the arbitrary juxtaposition of multiple voices to thwart any predetermined outcome or coherent meaning. In this last regard, "L'Amiral cherche une maison à louer" is much like Tzara's instructions from 1920 regarding how to write a Dada poem, which call for the poet to randomly cut out words from a newspaper and arrange them as they are pulled out of a hat.

Although Tzara seems to have composed "L'Amiral cherche une maison à louer" so that certain words would be uttered at the same time, by having three voices speak at once he invited unpredictable variations in the actual performance, which changed significantly depending on the cadence, intonation, volume, and pitch of each participant's voice, as well as on the noises and interruptions from the audience, which at the cramped and smoky Cabaret Voltaire was usually a rowdy, intoxicated crowd.[3]

Given the cacophonous and raucous nature of the live presentation of the poem, its appearance later that same year in the journal *Cabaret Voltaire* is startlingly conventional. Tzara chose to print this poem in a manner that resembles a musical score, with each part carefully arranged over two pages in uniform typography, even with dynamic markings.[4] The striking contrast between the printed and the performed versions of Tzara's composition suggests that while Tzara and his fellow Dadaists were eager to share this piece with a broad, international readership, it was only through live performance that the mutability and uncertainty at the heart of the poem became manifest.[5] The poem thus manifests the Dadaists' emphasis on art as a collaborative and ephemeral enterprise that resists notions of originality, uniqueness, and collectability.

EH

NOTES

1. This excerpt is from the poem as it was first published in the art journal *Cabaret Voltaire*, in 1916.

2. Hugo Ball, *Flight Out of Time: A Dada Diary*, ed. John Elderfield, trans. Ann Raimes (Berkeley: University of California Press, 1996), 57.

3. See T. J. Demos, "Zurich Dada: The Aesthetics of Exile," in *The Dada Seminars*, ed. Leah Dickerman and Matthew S. Witkovsky (Washington, DC: National Gallery of Art, 2005), 13.

4. The poem, notes Tzara in his "Note pour le bourgeois" included at the bottom of the page, builds upon the radical experiments with text and image in the work of Stéphane Mallarmé, Filippo T. Marinetti, and Guillaume Apollinaire, among others.

5. See Demos, "Zurich Dada." The Dadaists' emphasis on performance is reflected in Hugo Ball's statement in his diary entry for March 2, 1916: "Reciting aloud has become the touchstone of the quality of a poem for me." Ball, *Flight Out of Time*, 54.

Marcel Duchamp (French, 1887–1968)

Hat Rack, 1964 (4th version of 1917 original)

Wood, 8/8, 9 7/16 x 17 5/16 x 13"

When, in 1913, Marcel Duchamp affixed an upside-down bicycle wheel to the seat of a stool in his Rue Sainte-Hippolyte studio in Paris, he produced an object of such random and bizarre revelation that it became the seed of what is generally considered to be his most significant contribution to the history of art: the readymade. Defined essentially as a commercially manufactured object (generally mass produced), chosen rather than created by the artist, the readymade is transformed into a work of art through the intervention of the artist and the change of context the object undergoes when it is exhibited. This process fundamentally transformed the understanding of art in the twentieth century. Indeed, not only did the readymade introduce conceptualism (in which the idea is paramount to the object) into art, but it laid the foundation for appropriation art, a postmodern concept in which innovation is measured not through a further self-critical distillation of media into their leanest, purest forms, but rather through one's ability to manipulate, juxtapose, and reference that which has already been produced in order to reveal the underlying social and cultural substructures that inform both artistic process and content.

If the chance operations employed by Duchamp in the creation of his *Three Standard Stoppages* (1913–1914) or detailed in his extensive notes in *The Green Box* (1934) [Cat., p. 126] were, in his words, "the way to escape from the traditional methods of expression long associated with art," then the introduction of the readymade can be considered an all-out assault on the past.[1] While the distinction of the true or "unrectified" readymade is that only the context of the object has been modified, not the object itself, Duchamp often displayed these objects in markedly unfamiliar ways that impeded their functionality. The readymade *Hat Rack* of 1917, for example, was suspended in mid-air from a string hanging down from the ceiling in Duchamp's New York City studio at 33 West 67th Street, with the intention, as he explained, "to escape from conformity, which demands that works of art be hung on the wall or presented on easels."[2]

Duchamp's indifference toward the original or utilitarian function of these objects was mirrored in his selection process. According to him, readymades such as *Hat Rack* should be acquired "as if you had no aesthetic emotion. The choice of readymades is always based on visual indifference and, at the same time, on the total absence of good or bad taste."[3] This notion of "visual indifference" is critical to the understanding of the readymade, as it implies a sort of qualified chance procedure, one that Duchamp elucidated in his note "Specifications for Readymades" in *The Green Box*. He described the process for selecting readymades as a "kind of rendezvous" between the artist and object that will happen at a precise moment specified by the artist.[4] The "meeting" Duchamp described in the process of selecting readymades has the *appearance* of randomness or "indifference," but is actually a rigorous selection process based on aesthetic and linguistic factors. This brand of chance, described as a "kind of subjective determinism" and practiced by Duchamp in a number of projects, came out of the artist's peculiar understanding of chance as being far from random. "My chance is not the same as yours," Duchamp argued. "What is lucky for one person may be unlucky for somebody else. I was interested in expressing this concept physically."[5] Such contradiction, coming from

Duchamp, should be far from surprising, as he once famously pronounced: "I have forced myself to contradict myself in order to avoid conforming to my own taste."[6]

BB

NOTES

1. Marcel Duchamp, in Katharine Kuh, "Marcel Duchamp," in her *The Artist's Voice: Talks with Seventeen Artists* (New York: Harper & Row, 1962), 81.

2. Marcel Duchamp, *The Complete Works of Marcel Duchamp*, third edition, ed. Arturo Schwarz (New York: Delano Greenridge, 1997), 656. Duchamp had a particular penchant for racks and hanging objects during the period when the readymades were produced (between 1914 and 1917), which included, in addition to the *Hat Rack*, the *Bottlerack* (1914) and *Trébuchet*, or *Trap* (1917), a coat rack that he obstinately nailed to the floor after tripping over it several times.

3. Marcel Duchamp, "A Window onto Something Else," in *Dialogues with Marcel Duchamp*, ed. Pierre Cabanne, trans. Ron Padgett (New York: Da Capo Press, 1987), 48.

4. Marcel Duchamp, "Conditions of a Language," translated and reprinted in *The Writings of Marcel Duchamp*, ed. Michel Sanouillet and Elmer Peterson (New York: Da Capo Press, 1989), 32.

5. Ibid., 127.

6. Duchamp, as quoted in Harriet and Sidney Janis, "Marcel Duchamp, Anti-Artist," in *Marcel Duchamp in Perspective*, ed. Joseph Masheck (Englewood Cliffs, NJ: Prentice-Hall, 1975), 31.

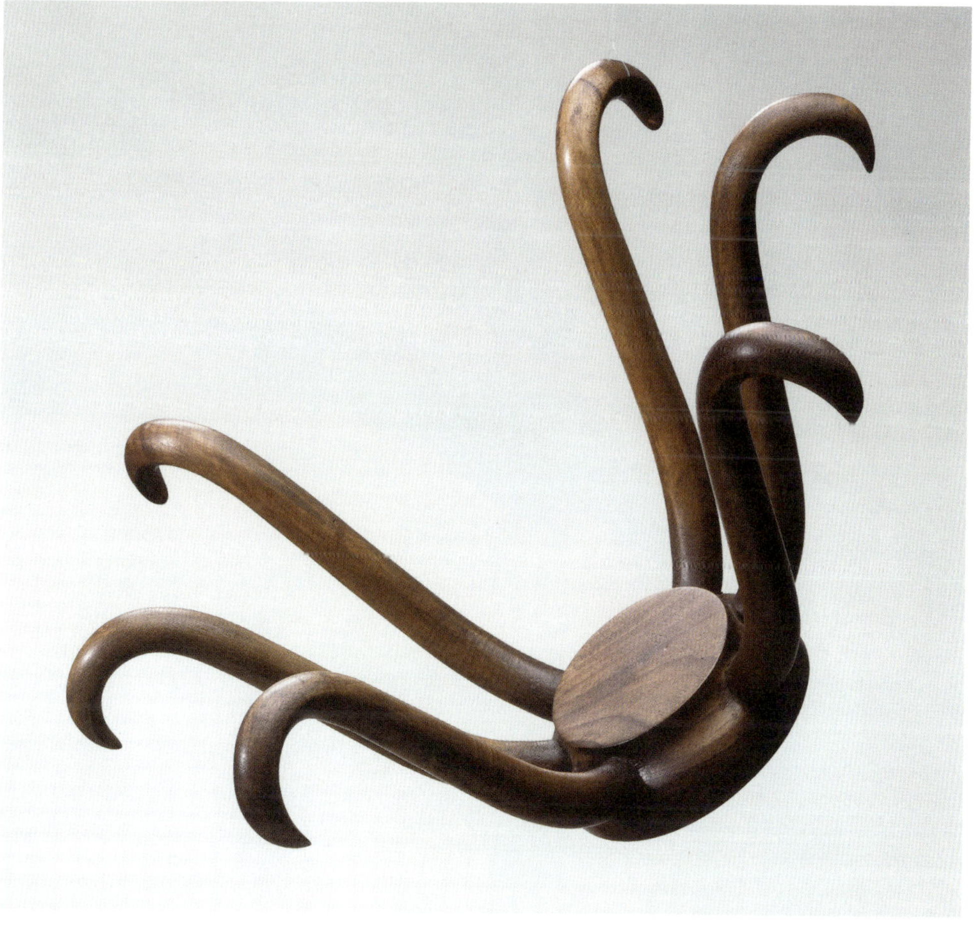

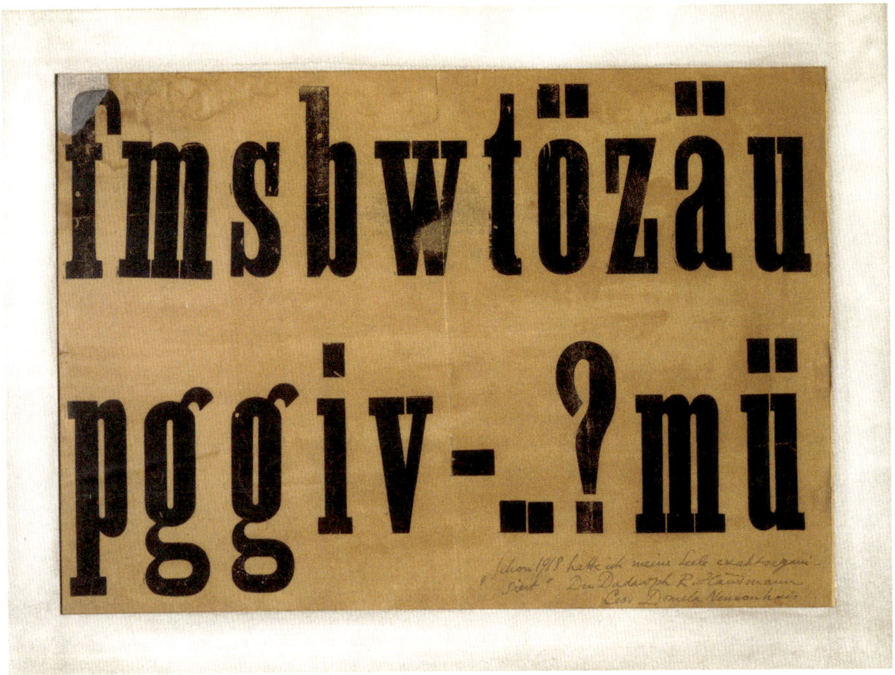

Raoul Hausmann (Austrian, 1886–1971)

Fmsbwtözäu, 1918
Photomechanical reproduction with typography on brown paper, 12 13/16 x 19"

Fmsbwtözäu is one of four phonetic poster poems that Berlin Dadaist Raoul Hausmann created in 1918.[1] These poems, composed of nonsensically combined letters printed large, were intended solely for auditory and visual effect. In the context of trauma and heightened nationalism following World War I, Hausmann, like his fellow Dadaists, attacked conventional language as debased and discredited, focusing instead on the abstract, arbitrary, and acoustic qualities of words.[2] He set out to destabilize language by breaking it down into letters and recombining them in nonliteral ways, thus drawing attention to the arbitrary nature of words, both printed and spoken. Like the other poster poems, *Fmsbwtözäu* is a string of letters and punctuation marks that do not seem to have any logical relationship with one another. The deliberate typographic layout of the poster-sized letters and symbols neatly arranged in two straight lines further highlights the absurdity of their combination and the aleatory means by which they were said to be assembled.

According to Hausmann, he asked his printer, Robert Barth, to select large letters "as they came out of their box—just according to his own mood and chance."[3] This dimension of the unexpected is augmented by Hausmann's chosen medium of block printing and the mechanical means by which it is executed, as the overall appearance of each poster necessarily varied according to how well the ink transferred from the woodblock letters to the paper.

Hausmann retrospectively described his poster poems as "automatic writing with question marks, exclamation points and even a pointer!"[4] His language—specifically his reference to the later Surrealist technique of automatic writing—casts doubt, however, on the veracity of his remarks about the degree to which he actually employed chance. Hausmann himself later admitted that he exerted some artistic agency in the arrangement of the letters in order to achieve the desired acoustic effect. He explained that after seeing the arrangement of the printer's selected letters, "for reasons of sonority, I subsequently eliminated *m ü* from the first and I replaced it with *qu i i é* (sic) from the second phonetic poem."[5]

Hausmann also harnessed the creative potential of chance in his performances of his poster poems. Isolating the letter as a single unit, he maintained that the letter, and thus his poems, must be understood both acoustically and visually:

> I thought the poem is the rhythm of the sounds. Why words? From the rhythmic flow of consonants and diphthongs and the countermovement of their vowel complements results the poem, which should be oriented optically and phonetically at once.[6]

Audio versions of the poem reveal the degree to which the performance of the poem was largely indeterminate. As Hausmann would recite the printed letters, like the appearance of the type, his voice demanded attention but was straightforward, lacking emotion. However, at the same time, in the recording included in the exhibition, he seems to have spontaneously augmented the poem, adding sounds and expressive bursts, suggesting that he would have welcomed improvisations from future "readers" as well as the random noises of the audience at Café Austria where he most likely first performed his poster poems.[7]

EH

NOTES

1. Two of the original four poster poems, which were printed between April and October of 1918, still exist: *Fmsbwtözäu* and *OFFEAHBDC*. Two copies of one of the other two, ***NVMWNAUR***, are visible in a photograph of Johannes Baader's assemblage, *Plasto-Dio-Dada-Drama* (1920). See Timothy O. Benson, *Raoul Hausmann and Berlin Dada* (Ann Arbor, MI: UMI Research Press, 1987), 94. Of the fourth poster poem, little is known, including the whereabouts of any existing copies.

2. In addition to the Dadaists, other artists in the early twentieth century who were experimenting with language in these ways included the German Expressionists and the Italian Futurists.

3. Raoul Hausmann, "Zur Geschichte des Lautgedichtes," in his *Am Anfang war Dada* (Steinbach, Giessen: Anabas-Verlag G. Kämpf, 1972), 43, as translated by and quoted in Rudolf E. Kuenzli, "The Semiotics of Dada Poetry," in *Dada Spectrum: The Dialectics of Revolt*, ed. Stephen C. Foster and Rudolf E. Kuenzli (Madison, WI: Coda Press Inc.; Iowa City: University of Iowa, 1979), 62.

4. Ibid. The exclamation point and pointer Hausmann mentions are in the poem *OFFEAHBDC*.

5. Raoul Hausmann, *Courrier Dada* (Paris: Éditions Le Terrain Vague, 1958), 63, translation mine. The latter set of letters to which he refers are, in fact, "*q j y E*." The poster poem in the *Chance Aesthetics* exhibition is a signed photomechanical reproduction on brown paper that dates from 1918.

6. Hausmann, *Courrier Dada*, as quoted in Christopher Phillips, "In the Chaotic Cave of the Mouth," in *Raoul Hausmann*, (Saint-Étienne, France: Musée d'art moderne de Saint-Étienne, 1994), 298. In 1922, Hausmann built upon the relationship between sound and image by developing the optophone, a device for transforming sound signals into light signals and vice versa. For more on this and Hausmann's optophonic poems, see Jacques Donguy, "Machine Head: Raoul Hausmann and the Optophone," *Leonardo* 34, no. 3 (2001): 217–20; and Marcella Lista, "Raoul Hausmann's Optophone: 'Universal Language' and the Intermedia," in *The Dada Seminars*, ed. Leah Dickerman and Matthew S. Witkovsky (Washington, DC: National Gallery of Art, 2005), 83-101.

7. Hausmann most likely delivered these poems at a Dada evening at Café Austria in Berlin on June 6, 1918. He also performed them at the "Anti-Dada-Merz" tour undertaken by Hausmann, Hannah Höch, and Kurt and Helma Schwitters in Prague in 1921. As Dorothea Dietrich has pointed out, the tour was one of the "constellations" that emerged in reaction to the politicized definition of Dada advanced by individuals such as Richard Huelsenbeck and George Grosz. (Merz was the name that Schwitters assigned to his art.) See Dorothea Dietrich, "Hanover," in *Dada*, ed. Leah Dickerman (Washington, DC: National Gallery of Art, 2005), esp. 158, 167-68, and 170-71. See also Benson, *Hausmann and Berlin Dada*, 94.

Jean (Hans) Arp (French, b. Germany [Alsace], 1886–1966)

Objets placés selon les lois du hasard III: Configuration symétrique (Objects Arranged according to the Laws of Chance III: Symmetrical Configuration), 1931

Oil on wood, 10 1/8 x 11 3/8 x 2 3/8"

As a founding member of Dada, Alsatian artist Jean Arp adopted Cubist collage to Dadaist ends, transforming it from a medium of semiotic analysis into one of chance composition. His series of collages "arranged according to the laws of chance" begun around 1916, have come to be recognized as iconic works in the history of chance aesthetics. To make these works, the artist purportedly tore pieces of paper of different colors, dropped them onto a surface, and glued them down where they fell. The fact that the pieces appear to have formed a rough grid calls into question the composition as a work of pure chance, however; as argued by T. J. Demos, Arp likely "invoked the former only to attack it with the latter."[1]

Rejecting the logic and rationality that Arp and his fellow Dadaists linked to the violence and corruption of World War I (later, in 1948, Arp declared: "The chaos of our era is the result of that overestimating of reason"[2]), Arp sought in his art what he called "a denial of human egotism," associating individual authorship with authoritarianism. He also attempted to sublimate his own subjectivity through collaboration, primarily with Swiss artist Sophie Taeuber, seeking "an anonymous and collective art." Linked to Arp's suspicion of authorship were his rejection of anthropocentrism and his creation of abstract forms, which he associated with a return to a more primal state. As he asserted of the Dadaists: "We rejected all mimesis and description, giving free rein to the Elementary and the Spontaneous."

Although there is some uncertainty about when this series of collages was titled, and even by whom, titles were important to Arp. In 1948, he explained the title of his series as follows:

> Since the arrangement of planes and their proportions and colors seemed to hinge solely on chance, I declared that these works were arranged "according to the laws of chance," as in the order of nature, chance being for me simply a part of an inexplicable reason, of an inaccessible order.

Arp's statement points out the significance of the organic as a model in his work. It also highlights his understanding of chance as not completely haphazard, but having a certain inherent structure. Despite the importance of the accidental in the creation of these collages, the title most likely came about years after the work was made, after the Surrealists had begun to champion the role of the unpredictable in Arp's art. In 1930, Surrealist writer Louis Aragon allied Arp's collage technique with the Surrealists' attempts to resist direct, authorial composition and subjectivity.[3] Arp's language in his own retrospective explanation of the series title suggests that he, too, reframed his collage technique in terms developed by the Surrealists:

> "The law of chance," which comprises all other laws and surpasses our understanding (like the primal cause from which all life arises), can be experienced only in a total surrender to the unconscious.[4]

In 1930, under the same core title, Arp began a new series of wooden reliefs, which he referred to as "constellations." In *Objects Arranged according to the Laws of Chance III: Symmetrical Configuration*, the first part of the title directly links this work to his earlier collages, while the contradictory nature of the subtitle, "Symmetrical Configuration," underscores the element of control that he exerted over the composition. Throughout this series of wooden reliefs, Arp created different configurations using an identical support and the same set of oval shapes, or "navels," which he considered emblematic of all biological life and open to interpretation. He arranged these ovals so that the shapes seem to jostle together, as if in a state of constant movement and recombination. These reliefs, like his earlier collages and other work, reflect Arp's lifelong interest in a mutable order free from the strictures of an artificial logic.

EH

NOTES

1. T. J. Demos, "Zurich Dada: The Aesthetics of Exile," in *The Dada Seminars*, ed. Leah Dickerman and Matthew S. Witkovsky (Washington, DC: National Gallery of Art, 2005), 22.

2. Jean (Hans) Arp, "Dadaland" (1948), in *Arp on Arp: Poems, Essays, Memories, by Jean Arp*, ed. Marcel Jean, trans. Joachim Neugroschel (New York: Viking Press, 1972), 232. Unless otherwise noted, the following quotations are taken from the same source and page number.

3. As cited in and discussed by Anne Umland, "Jean [Hans] Arp," in *Dada in the Collection of the Museum of Modern Art*, ed. Anne Umland and Adrian Sudhalter with Scott Gerson (New York: Museum of Modern Art, 2008), 47.

4. Jean (Hans) Arp, "And So the Circle Closed" (1948), in *Arp on Arp*, 246.

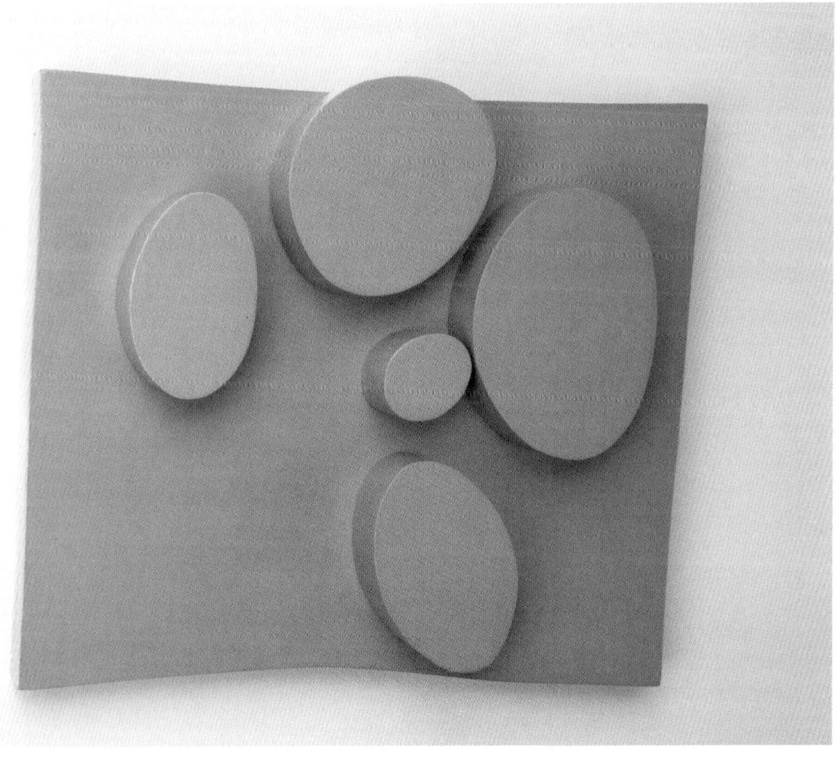

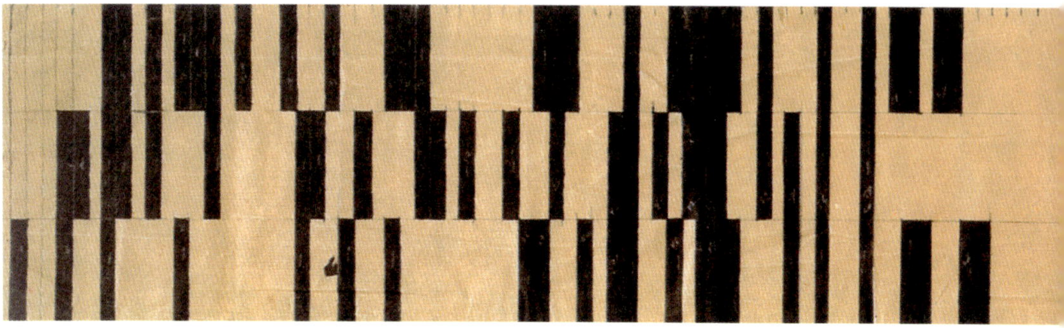

Ellsworth Kelly (American, b. 1923)

Glass Roof Pattern, Charenton, 1950
Pencil and ink on paper, 8 1/4 x 59 1/4"

Ellsworth Kelly's artistic production from his years in France (1948–1954) was shaped largely by his fascination with chance as a compositional strategy. At this time, Kelly set out to develop a distinctive body of work by exploring the creative possibilities of removing his own subjectivity from his work. He later described this period in his career:

> Everywhere I looked, everything I saw became something to be made, and it had to be exactly as it was, with nothing added. It was a new freedom: there was no longer the need to compose. The subject was there already made, and I could take from everything. It all belonged to me: a glass roof of a factory with its broken and patched panels..., paper fragments in the street. It was all the same: anything goes.[1]

Glass Roof Pattern, Charenton is a drawing in which Kelly transcribed the patterned grid of windows on a factory roof. Like other works from his time in Paris, this found composition can be said to rely on what has been called "a kind of objective chance."[2] Kelly claimed to have happened upon the roof, which he perceived as an already made image that he could set down on paper with little intervention.[3] This drawing demonstrates, however, that in fact Kelly did not forfeit artistic control entirely. His choice of subject matter, for one thing, was not accidental. Actively seeking out shapes and compositions, he was drawn to the random pattern created within the regular framework of the roof by the panels that had been damaged during World War II, some of them still shattered, others patched.

The drawing is not free from Kelly's artistic agency, either, although he set out to straightforwardly record exactly what he saw. "Instead of making a picture that was an interpretation of a thing seen, or a picture of invented content," he later noted, "I found an object and 'presented' it as itself alone."[4] In an effort to avoid composing, he counted all the panes of glass and numbered each of them on butcher's paper. On the one hand, these meticulous markings support Kelly's assertion that he was

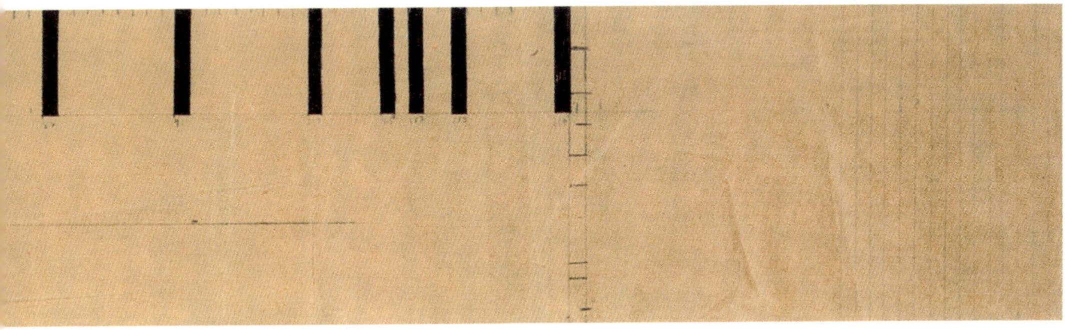

merely recording what he observed. On the other hand, they remind us that the artist chose the scale of the work and the paper size, and carefully calculated the translation of what he saw onto paper.

Further removing *Glass Roof Pattern, Charenton* from merely documenting what Kelly saw is the simplified pattern that he devised. He omitted extraneous details from the drawing, so that the roof became a series of black rectangles. His chosen angle—it is unclear whether we see the roof from below or above—renders the original form even more unrecognizable, an effect compounded by the drawing's vertical placement on the wall. The painting he created based on this drawing, entitled *Rouleau bleu* (*Blue Roll*) (1951), is even further removed from the subject matter that initially inspired it, appearing as a completely abstract composition made up of white rectangles on a long stretch of blue awning.[5]

EH

NOTES

1. Ellsworth Kelly, "Notes from 1969," in *Theories and Documents of Contemporary Art: A Sourcebook of Artists' Writings*, ed. Kristine Stiles and Peter Selz (Berkeley: University of California Press, 1996), 92.

2. Yve-Alain Bois, "Ellsworth Kelly in France: Anti-Composition in Its Many Guises," in *Ellsworth Kelly: The Years in France, 1948–1954*, ed. Yve-Alain Bois, Jack Cowart, and Alfred Pacquement (Washington, DC: National Gallery of Art, 1992), 23. Ellsworth Kelly was encouraged to use chance by his encounters with the work of Jean Arp and the Surrealists, whose interest in found objects correlated with his interest in found compositions.

3. Yve-Alain Bois describes this kind of transcription as a "transfer" analogous to the "index" in semiotic terms. Yve-Alain Bois, "Kelly's Trouvailles: Findings in France," in his *Ellsworth Kelly: The Early Drawings, 1948–1955* (Cambridge, MA: Harvard University Art Museums; Winterthur, Switzerland: Kunstmuseum Winterthur, 1999), 14.

4. Kelly, "Notes from 1969," 92.

5. In this painting, Kelly reproduced the pattern in the drawing almost exactly, although he turned the entire piece 180 degrees. The original drawing measures 8 1/4 x 59 1/4"; the painting is 17 1/2 x 117".

Ellsworth Kelly (American, b. 1923)

Children's Leftovers Arranged by Chance, 1950
Collage on paper, 15 3/4 x 10 1/4"

[right]

Brushstrokes Cut into Forty-Nine Squares and Arranged by Chance, 1951
Cut-and-pasted paper and ink, 13 3/4 x 14"

[below]

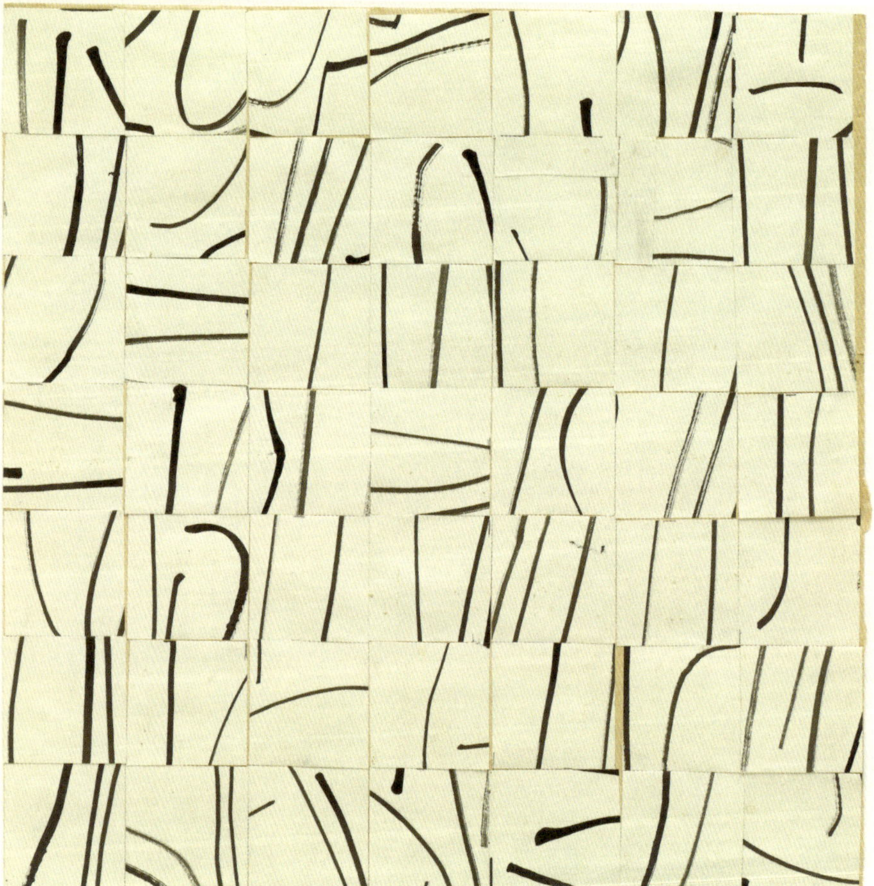

In 1950, Ellsworth Kelly met Jean Arp in Paris.[1] Arp's earlier Dada collages "arranged according to the laws of chance," in their effort to counter rational composition and tap the creative potential of the illogical, became an inspirational model for the young artist [Cat., p. 78].[2] Kelly experimented with a similar approach, and *Children's Leftovers Arranged by Chance* exemplifies one of the many techniques he employed as a means of manipulating the tension between chance and control. Created while Kelly was teaching children at the American School in Paris, this collage is made up of scraps of paper that his students had left in his classroom. At first glance, the pieces seem to bear a random relationship with one another, particularly as they transgress the boundaries of a strictly rectangular composition. At the same time, however, as in Arp's compositions, the visual rhymes between shapes and colors strongly suggest that their selection and placement was not entirely accidental.

In a desire to highlight the aleatory process by which he composed his work, Kelly began to apply random techniques within a strictly ordered system.[3] Of particular interest was the order of the grid, as exemplified in works such as *Brushstrokes Cut into Forty-Nine Squares and Arranged by Chance*. To create this collage, he first made a drawing comprised of a series of black lines. He then cut it into squares of identical dimensions and reglued the squares next to one another on a piece of paper of the same dimensions as the original drawing, creating a grid in which the lines intersect with one another in an ostensibly haphazard way.[4] The uniformly unaligned arrangement of each piece, however, suggests that here too Kelly asserted some degree of control over the final composition.

EH

NOTES

1. In 1948, after serving in World War II, Kelly, then twenty-five years old, moved to Paris and enrolled at the École des Beaux-Arts with the help of the G.I. Bill. He returned to the United States in 1954.

2. Kelly's interest in collage may also have been further encouraged by Henri Matisse's large cutouts, which were exhibited in the late 1940s and early 1950s in Paris. See Michael Plante, "'Things to Cover Walls': Ellsworth Kelly's Paris Paintings and the Tradition of Mural Decoration," *American Art* 9, no. 1 (Spring 1995): 41.

3. For more on this, see Yve-Alain Bois, "Ellsworth Kelly in France: Anti-Composition in Its Many Guises," in Yve-Alain Bois et al., *Ellsworth Kelly: The Years in France: 1948–1954*, ed. Yve-Alain Bois, Jack Cowart, and Alfred Pacquement (Washington, DC: National Gallery of Art, 1992), 23.

4. See ibid., 25.

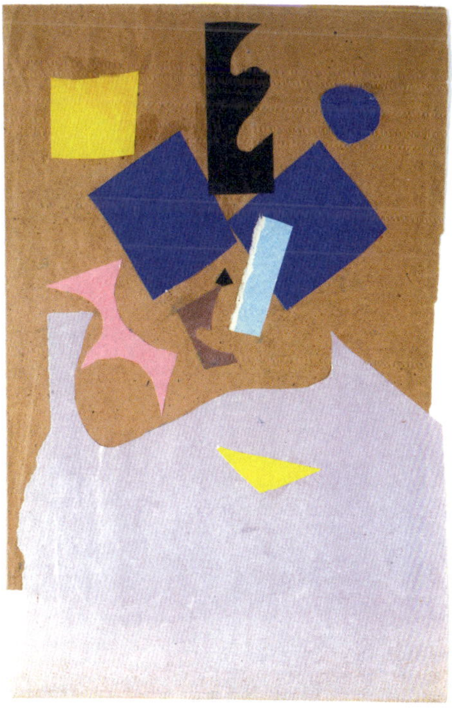

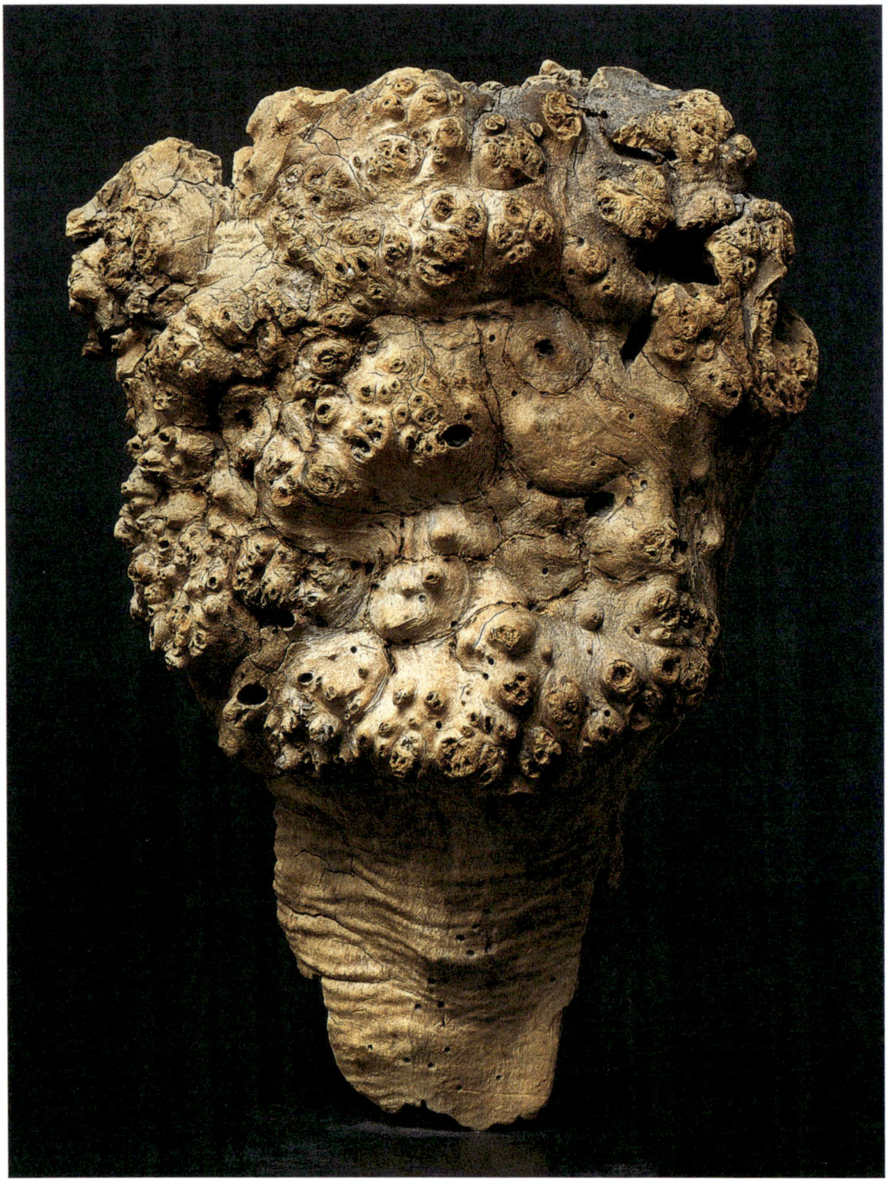

Jean Dubuffet (French, 1901–1985)

Tête barbue (Bearded Head), 1959
Driftwood with barnacles, 11 1/8 x 8 1/2 x 4"

In the immediate aftermath of World War II, as after World War I, many artists waged a critique of the protocols and decorum of Western culture. After deciding to become an artist in 1942, Jean Dubuffet set out to repudiate received notions of taste, value, and beauty, proposing instead an art free of all conventions. The models for his reinvented art were found in the works produced by untrained individuals "untouched by artistic culture," what he termed "*art brut*."[1] Equating Western culture with a dead language, Dubuffet aimed for an art "which would be in immediate connection with daily life, an art which would start from this daily life, and which would be a very direct and very sincere expression of our real life and our real moods."[2] He believed that true art must spring spontaneously and obsessively from the individual, resulting in a direct and singular expression of the self. While Dubuffet, by his own definition, could not be considered a maker of *art brut*, he embraced its conventions of compulsive repetition, bricolage, automatism, and chance throughout his career.

In 1954, Dubuffet combined his interest in assemblage and his desire to employ non-art materials to produce a series of sculptures titled *Petites statues de la vie précaire* (Little Statues of a Precarious Life).[3] Employing various ordinary and ephemeral materials, such as cinders, charcoal, sponges, and, in a second group of related works created in 1959–60, *papier-mâché*, aluminum foil, and driftwood, the artist developed a radical approach to sculpture in which the final work arose from the chance configuration and intrinsic nature of the given material. Made from a found piece of driftwood picked up after storms on the beaches of the Côte d'Azur, *Tête barbue* is essentially an *objet trouvé*. The artist's hand performed a minimal amount of intervention in order to heighten the human semblance already existing in the amorphous but suggestive natural material. By burning a few lines and dotting the wood, a pair of eyes, a nose, and other subtle details emerged. Instead of attempting, like the Surrealists, to use found objects to evoke a transcendent reality, Dubuffet replaced the evocative object with banal materiality. "I'm a glutton for banality," he stated in 1959. "A roadway free of any unevenness or peculiarity, a dirty floor, a bare and dusty terrain, that no one would ever dream of looking at ... are reaches of intoxication and jubilation for me."[4] In his drive to highlight values and materials dismissed by Western culture, what mattered to Dubuffet was unfettered spontaneity and truth to the self—and with that, a spirit of brazen opposition and impertinence.

MM

NOTES

1. Jean Dubuffet, "*Art Brut* in Preference to the Cultural Arts" (1949), trans. Paul Foss and Allen S. Weiss, *Art and Text* 27 (1988): 31–33. In 1945, Dubuffet began the systematic collection of more than five thousand artworks by those regarded as outside mainstream culture. The collection is now housed at the Musée de l'*Art Brut* in Lausanne, Switzerland.

2. Jean Dubuffet, "Anticultural Positions" (1951), reprinted in *Theories and Documents of Contemporary Art: A Sourcebook of Artists' Writings*, ed. Kristine Stiles and Peter Selz (Berkeley: University of California Press, 1996), 192.

3. The first series of statues was created in 1954 and consisted of forty-four sculptures. Dubuffet created a second group of thirty-two related sculptures between October 1959 and November 1960, including *Tête barbue*. For a complete overview of these related series, see Andreas Franzke, *Jean Dubuffet: Petites statues de la vie précaire* (Berlin: Verlag Gachnang & Springer, 1988).

4. Jean Dubuffet, "Célébrations du sol," *Les Lettres Nouvelles* (April 1959), translated and reproduced in Mildred and Marc Glimcher, *Jean Dubuffet: Towards an Alternate Reality* (New York: Abbeville Press, 1987), 167.

Daniel Spoerri (Swiss, b. Romania, 1930)

Le Tiroir de ma mère, 1960

Objects on wood, 15 7/16 x 15 x 5 1/8"
[p. 49]

Meal Variation No. 2 Eaten by Marcel Duchamp, c. 1967

Glass-covered photo-laminated tabletop mounted on wood with metal pedestal and four rubber spacers, 28 3/4 x 25 x 21 1/8"
[below]

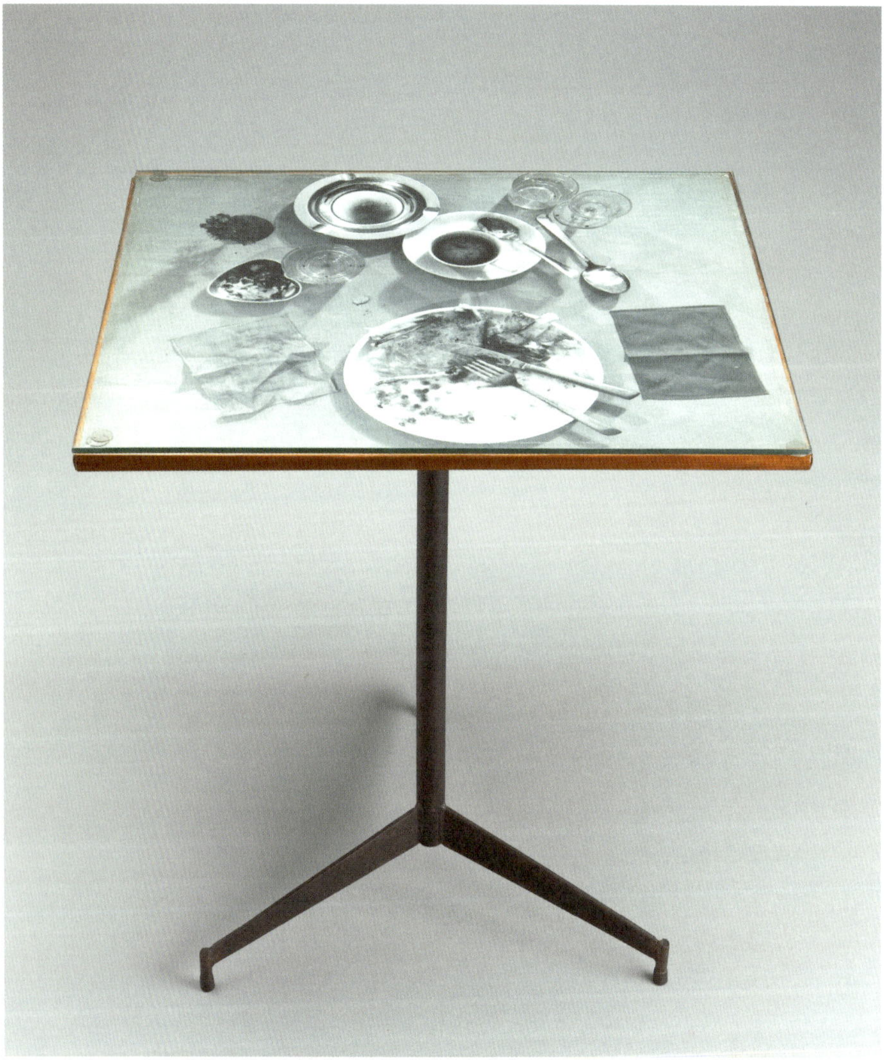

In 1960, Daniel Spoerri began creating his *tableaux-pièges* (trap or snare pictures), sculptural assemblages made by meticulously gluing in place chance arrangements of everyday objects to whatever surface on which they were found. The initial displacement of an ephemeral moment into a permanent work of art, divorced from the ubiquitous flow of daily life, was heightened by its subsequent vertical display as a three-dimensional still life. In *Le Tiroir de ma mère*, for example, Spoerri fixed the random assortment of items found in his mother's drawer, including a bottle opener, some string, and a knife with a wooden handle, to the very drawer in which they resided. Shortly after his invention of the snare picture, Spoerri became a member of the Paris-based Nouveaux Réalistes. Instead of approaching the creation of art through overt personal introspection, as did their contemporaries practicing *art informel* abstraction, the Nouveaux Réalistes directed their gaze outward, toward materials and events encountered in their daily lives. Spoerri's undiscriminating selection of objects and foodstuffs in the form of his snare pictures is an apt illustration of what Pierre Restany, critic and founder of the group, described as a form of art created by objective observations of direct encounters with "the real."[1]

Spoerri often downplayed the notion of his snare pictures as works of art, choosing to present them as provocations intended to "make the viewer uneasy," aggravating spectators in order to provoke a change in their perception of the world by "focusing attention on situations and areas of daily life that are little noticed, if at all."[2] While the singular snare picture abruptly freezes an arbitrary moment in time, Spoerri's gastronomic banquets, beginning with his *Restaurant de la Galerie J* in Paris in 1963, expanded this initial gesture and infused it with the intensity of a sensual, collective experience. After each sitting, the progression of a meal from order to disorder was documented in the form of a snare picture. Although the basic parameters, such as the menu and the table settings, were predetermined by "Chef Daniel," chance still played a dominant role, as the composition of each *tableau-piège* was completely contingent on the gestures and choices of the participants carried out over the course of a given meal.

Fluxus impresario George Maciunas enacted a further reworking of Spoerri's *tableaux-pièges* in 1965.[3] Maciunas photographed several snare pictures produced from Spoerri's 1964 series titled *31 Variations on a Meal* and developed full-size, black-and-white reproductions to be laminated and sold as real tabletops in an edition of *Flux-Furniture*.[4] This step not only added a rather humorous level of mediation, fixing through the medium of photography Spoerri's already petrified chance compositions and returning them to their original horizontal orientation, but also literalized the conceptual link between the *tableau-piège* and the mechanical arbitrariness of the photographic snapshot, which records the transient and transcribes the mundane.

MM

NOTES

1. Pierre Restany's notion of "the real" was characterized as uniquely industrial, urban, and aggressive. He optimistically embraced the technological and social changes facing Paris and its inhabitants in the late 1950s and early 1960s. See Pierre Restany, *Les Nouveaux Réalistes* (Paris: Éditions Planète, 1968).

2. Daniel Spoerri, "Trap Pictures" (1960), reprinted in *Zero* (Cambridge, MA: MIT Press, 1973), 217.

3. Daniel Spoerri participated in select Fluxus performances and publications in the early 1960s in Europe.

4. In March 1964, Spoerri presented *31 Variations on a Meal* in New York at the Alan Stone Gallery. Thirty-one identical tables were altered through the activities of the various invited guests, including Arman, Marcel Duchamp, Dick Higgins, Ray Johnson, Allan Kaprow, Alison Knowles, Roy Lichtenstein, Robert Rosenblum, and Andy Warhol, among others. In addition to the tabletops, Maciunas also produced tablecloths silkscreened on canvas. See Jon Hendricks, *Fluxus Codex* (Detroit: Gilbert and Lila Silverman Fluxus Collection; New York: Harry N. Abrams, 1988), 486–88.

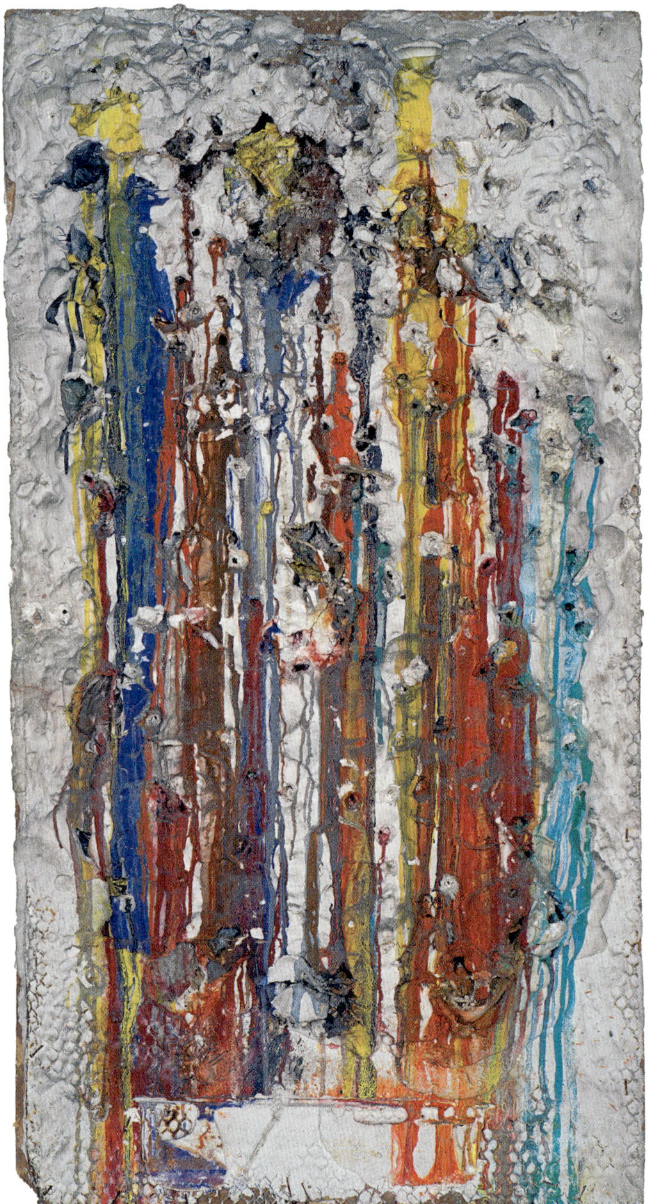

Niki de Saint Phalle (French, 1930–2002)

Grand tir–séance Galerie J, 30 June–12 July 1961
Plaster, paint, wire mesh, string, and plastic, 56 5/16 x 30 5/16"

Violence and chance were the key elements in Niki de Saint Phalle's *tirs*, or shooting paintings. To create these volatile works, she would first cover perishable and found objects—such as eggs, spaghetti, old shoes, plastic toys, and a diversity of junk items—along with several bags filled with paint, in white plaster. Then, taking up a rifle, she would fire at the assemblage, causing the paint sacks to burst, bleeding streaks of vibrant colors onto the white assemblage. The rifle, wielded by the artist or, at other times, by participants, assumed the decisive role in the creation of the work of art, thereby severing the direct connection between the artist's hand and the painterly mark. It was ultimately the skill of the shooter, the trajectory of the bullet, and the force of gravity that determined the final outcome.

Grand tir–séance Galerie J was created on the occasion of Saint Phalle's exhibition *Feu à volonté* (Fire at Will) at the Galerie J in Paris in the summer of 1961. Visitors to the exhibition—who notably included Jasper Johns, Robert Rauschenberg, Frank Stella, Jean Fautrier, and many of Saint Phalle's fellow Nouveaux Réalistes—were invited to take up a rifle and shoot at the prepared assemblages, thus transforming the space of the gallery from one of quiet reverence to impromptu, explosive activity.[1] While prized art objects were produced during this event in the form of the assemblages, it was the fleeting, anarchistic moment when the shot was released that held the greatest importance for the artist. In a 1961 television interview with David Brinkley, she explained: "The shooting is the moment. It is the only thing that lives because everything is dead afterwards. Nothing lives. Cézanne, Rembrandt, everything will be dead in the end. The shooting is that one moment in which the miracle happens."[2] The relationship between beauty and brutality, creation and destruction, is thoroughly entangled in her reliefs, which exist as evocative traces of these participatory events.

Many critics from the early 1960s, as well as subsequent scholars, interpret Saint Phalle's violent acts in predominantly biographical terms: as a rejection of her bourgeois upbringing and in reaction to events suffered during her childhood.[3] Although these interpretations reveal important aspects of her work, they tend to overlook the historical specificity of her shooting sessions for audiences in both Europe and America during what was a moment of intense political upheaval and violent unrest.[4] "My problem," she passionately stated during the Brinkley interview, "is creating, is creating now, is creating beauty, is creating something, is creating something which has to do with you, which has to do with now, which has to do with bombs and everything and the end of the world and BANG!"

MM

NOTES

1. Niki de Saint Phalle began her shooting performances in early 1961 and continued to stage them for three years. Her exhibition at the Galerie J was her first shooting performance inside a gallery. The gallery was required to obtain a shooting gallery license before police would allow the show to go on. See Lois Dickert, "Shooting at Malibu" (Spring 1962), unpublished manuscript in the collection of the Niki Charitable Art Foundation, Santee, California.

2. Niki de Saint Phalle, interview with David Brinkley (NBC, New York, 1961). A tape of this program is housed at the Niki Charitable Art Foundation, Santee, California.

3. Saint Phalle has reinforced such interpretations of her work. In her writings on the *tirs*, she referred to them as therapy for trauma reaching back to her relationship with her father. Additionally, Jill Carrick has recently examined Saint Phalle's work in terms of fetishism and feminine masquerade. See Jill Carrick, "Phallic Victories? Niki de Saint Phalle's *Tirs*," *Art History* 26, no. 5 (November 2003): 700–720.

4. Saint Phalle garnered an extraordinary amount of media attention for her shooting sessions, yet few critics reviewing her exhibition at the Galerie J in 1961 drew direct links between the shooting taking place in the art gallery and the violence, occurring right outside the front door, relating to the Algerian War for Independence, which began in 1954 and escalated in the summer of 1961, including a series of terrorist actions in the city of Paris.

Mimmo Rotella (Italian, 1918–2006)

La Dernière Marilyn, 1966
Décollage on canvas, 53 1/2 x 37 3/4"
[below]

Jacques Villeglé (French, b. 1926)

Rue de Crimée, 28 novembre 1969, 1969
Décollage on canvas, 39 1/4 x 28 3/4"
[p. 55]

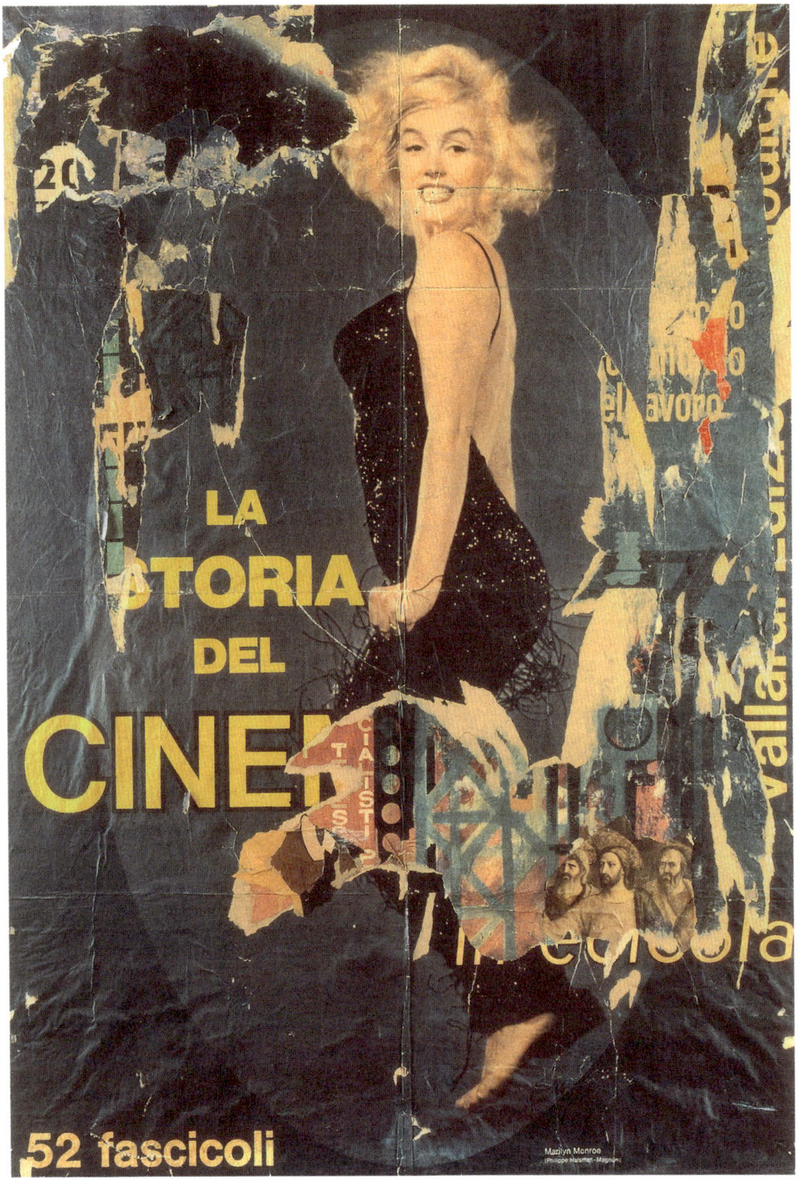

In the late 1940s, French artists Jacques Villeglé and Raymond Hains initiated the practice of *décollage*, literally the ungluing of paper, by ripping large fragments of *affiches lacérées* (lacerated posters) directly from the walls of the city of Paris and eventually presenting the results as a sort of readymade. Shifting their operations from the private space of the studio to the public arena of the street, Villeglé and Hains appropriated these posters as a means of collecting linguistic and graphic configurations produced by random acts of urban vandalism. Instead of highlighting the originality or skill of an individual author, the work of Villeglé and Hains along with their fellow *décollagist* François Dufrêne highlight the destructive gestures of unknown collaborators who vandalized these posters, symbols of the increased domination of public space by advertising's commodified language and its incipient effects on modern everyday life.[1]

Villeglé is one in a long line of Parisian *flâneurs* captivated by the ephemeral and gritty beauty of the urban streets. A work such as *Rue de Crimée, 28 novembre 1969*, with its vibrant repertoire of rips, scratches, slashes, abrasions, and largely illegible textual fragments, epitomizes what the artist regarded as a kind of spontaneous visual poetry.[2] The titles indicate the exact date and location where he happened upon a given poster, highlighting the fundamentally archival character of his appropriative practice.

Independent of any knowledge of his French contemporaries, Italian artist Mimmo Rotella began his first *décollages* in the early 1950s in Rome, a city struggling to rid itself of the memory of fascism.[3] According to Rotella: "To tear posters down from the wall was the sole compensation, the only means of protest against a society that had lost its appetite for change and transformation."[4] His practice of *décollage* is notably different from that of Hains and Villeglé in that he would take down scraps of already torn advertising posters, glue them to canvas, and then cut and tear them again to form complex juxtapositions of color and texture. By the early 1960s, Rotella moved away from his predominately formal concerns, attending to the actual imagery displayed on the posters themselves. His lacerated posters were often populated with brand names and ads for various forms of popular entertainment. Film posters plastered with the seductive figure of American cultural export Marilyn Monroe, produced by the Cinecittà film industry headquartered just outside of Rome, make up some of Rotella's most iconic pieces. A work such as *La Dernière Marilyn* compounds Rotella's rejection of traditional artistic techniques while laying witness to the rapid expansion of the Italian economy and Rome's emergence as an international media capital.

The readymade and unpredictable nature of *décollage* secured for the *affichistes* a new model of artistic agency at a time when the notion of heroic individualism and originality proffered by *art informel* abstraction and American Abstract Expressionism was being reassessed by the postwar avant-garde.[5] Driven by a desire to engage with the changing experience of objects and public space in a newly emerging society of spectacle and consumption, the works of the *affichistes* articulate the profound ambiguities of cultural production in a consumer society.

MM

NOTES

1. This politically inflected interpretation has been most concisely argued by Benjamin H. D. Buchloh, "Villeglé: From Fragment to Detail," in his *Neo-Avantgarde and Culture Industry: Essays on European and American Art from 1955 to 1975* (Cambridge, MA: MIT Press, 2000), 443–60.

2. Further to this, Yve-Alain Bois has eloquently described the effect of the layered and irregularly torn posters as "undifferentiated noise." See Yve-Alain Bois, "Ray Guns," in Yve-Alain Bois and Rosalind E. Krauss, *Formless: A User's Guide* (New York: Zone Books, 1997), 178.

3. In 1960, Raymond Hains, Jacques Villeglé, François Dufrêne, and Mimmo Rotella all became members of Nouveau Réalisme. These four are collectively known as *affichistes*.

4. Mimmo Rotella, "Autopresentazione" (1957), as translated by and quoted in Tomasso Trini, *Rotella* (Milan: Giampaolo Prearo, 1974), xv.

5. See Brandon Taylor, *Urban Walls: A Generation of Collage in Europe & America* (New York: Hudson Hills Press, 2008), 16.

Dieter Roth (Swiss, 1930–1998)

Kleiner Sonnenuntergang (Small Sunset), 1968

Sausage on paper in plastic bag, 16 15/16 x 12 9/16"
[right]

Small Landscape, 1969

Pressing, soft cheese on emery paper, in plastic sleeve, 12 5/8 x 30 15/16"

Big Cloud, 1971

Felt pen and mayonnaise on white paper, 29 1/2 x 39 13/16"
[below]

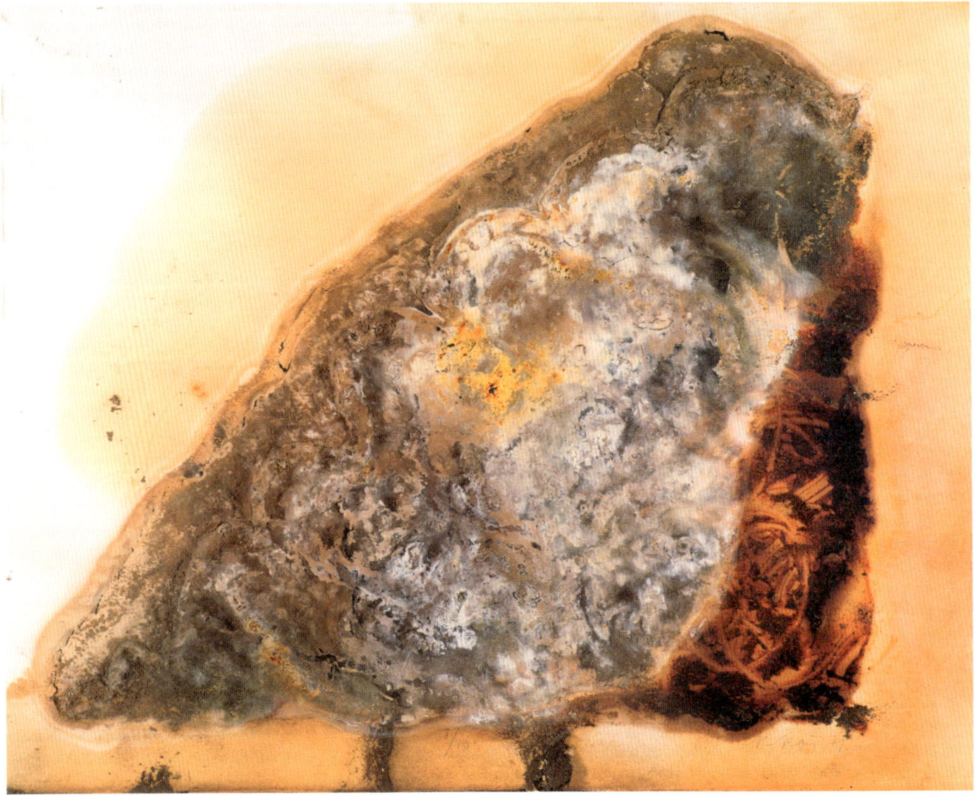

Although initially an adherent to the stringent rules of Concrete art and poetry, by the early 1960s Dieter Roth liberated himself from formal and linguistic conventions and began to use cheap, everyday materials to create objects made from books, newspapers, and various foodstuffs such as cheese, bananas, sausage, mayonnaise, milk, and chocolate. His incorporation of organic materials was a means of displaying the effects of time, letting his works develop through the natural process of decay rather than through the direct interference of the artist's hand. Furthermore, Roth employed decomposition and the chance transformations that came with it as a means of parodying the serious tone and preservationist impulse he perceived in the postwar art world. Roth's works were not to be fully controlled, but to develop according to the environmental conditions under which they were kept—temperature, humidity, and light—continuing to alter over time.[1] One example of this variability is *Small Sunset*, one in a series of multiples he made by placing a slice of sausage between two sheets of paper, enclosing it in plastic, and letting the fat from the sausage slowly soak into the paper to create the composition.[2] Because of the varied conditions in which versions of the work were produced, each *Small Sunset* is essentially unique, arriving at a form of seriality without repetition.

For Roth, an artwork was not so much a product as a process. Rather than striving for permanence, he reveled in the transitory and relished the abject. *Small Landscape* and *Big Cloud* are two similar examples of multiples—made with cheese and mayonnaise, respectively—that parody traditionally romantic themes with decidedly unromantic materials.[3] The works elicit sensations of both attraction and repulsion: visually stunning yet rancid, playful yet putrefying. Created in the aftermath of the student revolts of 1968 and during a volatile period of economic downturn, these multiples reveal a more transgressive side of Roth's work. The use of food and other organic materials was a way for him to defy traditional categories while positing chance and continuous transformation in opposition to the stagnation of institutional art.

MM

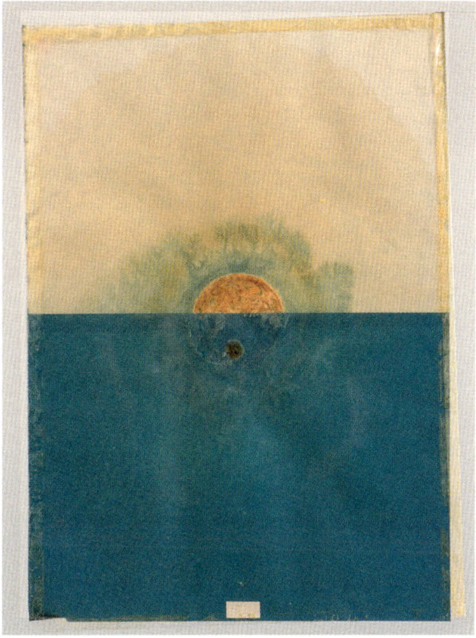

NOTES

1. The question of the proper preservation of Dieter Roth's work is an ongoing one for museums. See Heide Skowranek, "Should We Reproduce the Beauty of Decay? A *Museumsleben* in the Work of Dieter Roth," *Tate Papers* (Autumn 2007), http://www.tate.org.uk/research/tateresearch/tatepapers/07autumn/skowranek.htm (accessed December 21, 2008).

2. Like his contemporaries in Fluxus, Nouveau Réalisme, and Pop art, Dieter Roth was a pioneering figure in the creation of multiples. The format offered the potential for wide-scale distribution beyond art world circles while furthering his challenge to the elite status of the art object.

3. See Tanja Maka, *Eat Art: Joseph Beuys, Dieter Roth, Sonja Alhäuser*, no. 33 (Cambridge, MA: Harvard University Art Museums, 2001), 8.

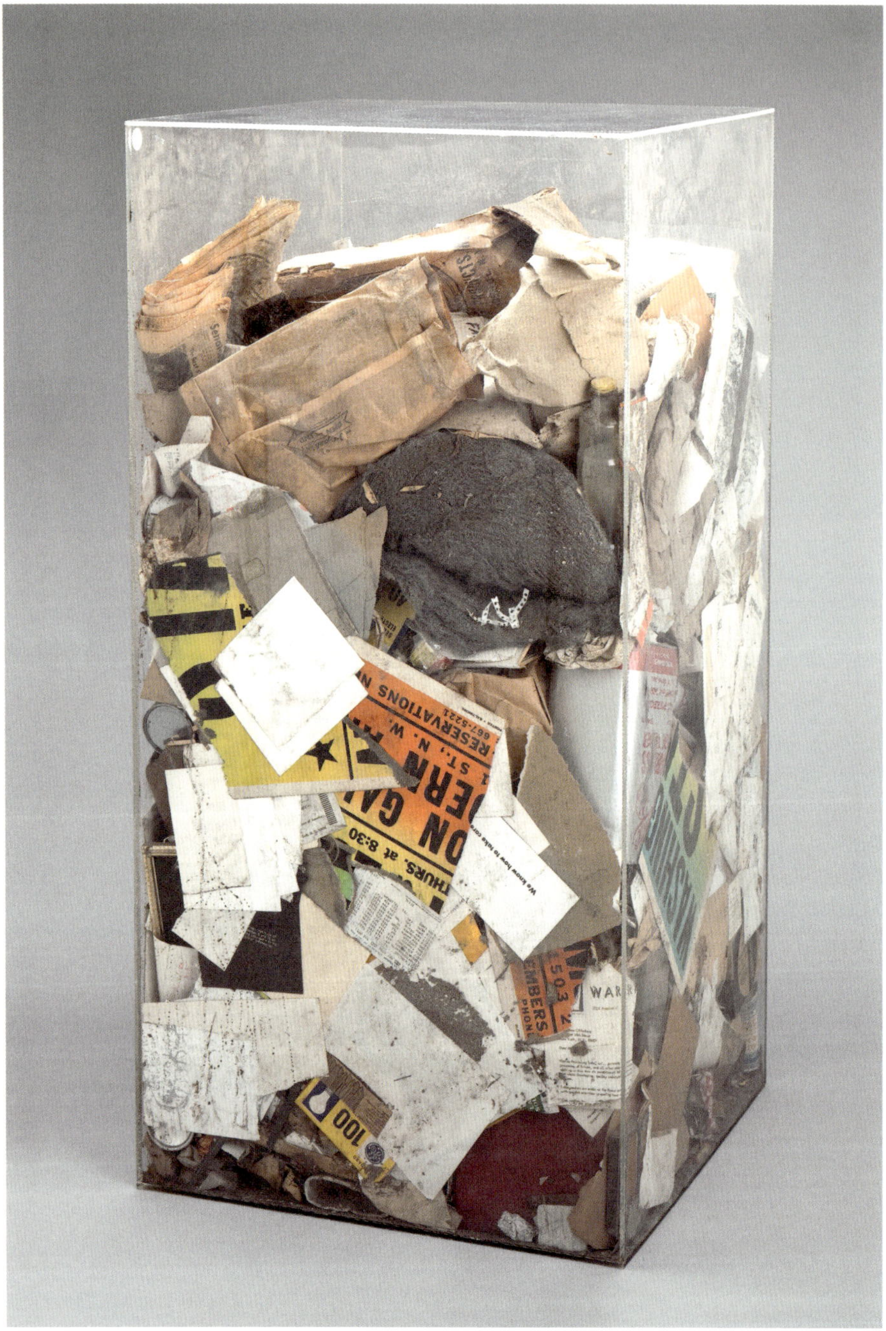

Arman (French, 1928–2005)

Claes Oldenburg's Refuse, 1970–71
Plexiglas box with refuse, 47 1/4 x 23 5/8 x 23 5/8"

To create his first *poubelles*, or trash cans, in the early 1960s, Arman harvested garbage from public dumps and trash bins as potent remnants of the burgeoning consumer society in postwar France, and preserved it in glass (later Plexiglas) vitrines. Taking a cue from Marcel Duchamp, whose readymades advanced the idea that anything could be art by an act of selection, the composition of each *poubelle* was ostensibly left largely to chance; Arman merely stuffed the found refuse into containers, letting the force of gravity determine the ultimate composition.[1] As a member of the Nouveaux Réalistes, a loose group of artists working in Paris in the early 1960s who commonly produced art through the direct appropriation of everyday objects from their urban surroundings, Arman embarked on what he described as a "critical investigation of ... rubbish, refuse, scrap, reworked manufactured goods; in short, useless things."[2] In using a phrase like "critical investigation" to describe his practice, Arman intentionally called upon the language of the archaeologist, anthropologist, and sociologist, all allegedly objective observers of society. However, the fact that he was producing luxury art objects that simultaneously contributed to and mimicked, in the form of his signature vitrines, the strategies of the commodity implicates him as a complicit participant as well. His rather ambiguous position has been a core issue for critics and art historians, who have variously interpreted his practice as that of a detached observer recording industrial forces, a fetishistic consumer of mass-produced items, and an engaged demystifier of capitalism.[3]

Claes Oldenburg's Refuse is part of a related series of works, the *Portraits-Robots*, or robot portraits, in which accumulated trash is no longer anonymous, but rather becomes a stand-in for a particular person. Initially, Arman collected various personal objects from friends and acquaintances, items explicitly connected to the intimate or public personality of the person to whom they belonged, to create his robot portraits. With *Oldenburg's Refuse*, however, he gave up almost all control over the selection of objects. His only intervention was the placement of a three-foot-tall plastic bin in the artist's studio to serve as a receptacle for scraps.[4] Once the box was full, Arman's "work" was finished. Empty cans, old newspapers, bits of cardboard, and junk mail are all haphazardly piled on top of one another and are left to decay over time. Seeing one person's trash encased in such a manner evokes a variety of responses: repugnance, as the substantial heap focuses attention on the stultifying production of waste that exists in an age of mass consumption; voyeuristic fascination, as the trash offers clues into Oldenburg's tastes, interests, and inclinations; and attraction, as the display of trash in a vitrine evinces a certain beauty in its accumulation.

MM

NOTES

1. I use the word "ostensibly" here because it is clear that some of Arman's *poubelles* were more intentionally composed than others.

2. Arman, "The Realism of Accumulations" (1960), reprinted in *Zero* (Cambridge, MA: MIT Press, 1973), 209. In 1960, Arman infamously filled the Iris Clert Gallery in Paris with 250 pounds of garbage and other debris, epitomizing the Nouveaux Réalistes' focus on the urban, industrialized environment.

3. For a discussion of these positions, see Jaimey Hamilton, "Arman's System of Objects," *Art Journal* 67, no. 1 (Spring 2008): 55–67.

4. This process is described by Grégoire Müller, "Arman," *Arts Magazine* (April 1970): 38. Müller explicitly characterizes Arman's accumulative activities in terms of ethnography and sociology.

AUTOMATISM

The release of conscious compositional control through automatic techniques has been variously championed by avant-garde artists in search of more direct, unmediated forms of expressivity—from the Surrealist emphasis on psychic liberation to more phenomenologically oriented practices concerned with the body and the physical materiality of the work of art.

FRANCIS PICABIA
ANDRÉ MASSON
YVES TANGUY
ELLSWORTH KELLY
MAX ERNST
ANDRÉ BRETON
OSCAR DOMINGUEZ
MARCEL JEAN
SALVADOR DALÍ
JACKSON POLLOCK
ROBERT MOTHERWELL
GUY DEBORD
ASGER JORN
JEAN TINGUELY
GEORGE MACIUNAS
KAZUO SHIRAGA
WILLIAM ANASTASI
ROBERT MORRIS

In his first "Manifesto of Surrealism" (1924), André Breton defined Surrealism as "psychic automatism in its pure state ... dictated by thought, in the absence of any control exercised by reason."[1] Appropriated first from physiology and psychiatry, the term "automatism" was applied to various techniques including automatic drawing, frottage (rubbings taken from different surfaces), fumage (passing paper or canvas over a smoking candle), and decalcomania (spreading paint on a given surface and then pressing it onto paper or canvas), among many others. As the cornerstone of Surrealism, automatism was employed with the intention of bypassing the conscious mind, destabilizing perceptions, and opening up new avenues for explorations of unexpected and unpredictable forms. While the rhetoric underscoring these techniques professed the liberatory potential of unmediated spontaneity, a balance was necessarily struck between the ideal of pure psychic automatism and the need for some degree of critical self-awareness, as artists often worked up and revised their involuntary compositions based on what the initial imagery suggested to them.

Surrealist automatic techniques were adopted and adapted by a diverse range of artists into and throughout the post-World War II period. The emergence of *art informel* in Europe, a type of painterly abstraction in which form becomes subservient to the expressive impulses of the artist, was closely aligned with the legacy of Surrealist automatism. The influx of European Surrealists into the United

States in the late 1930s and early 1940s also proved a crucial ingredient in the subsequent rise of American Abstract Expressionism. Jackson Pollock and Robert Motherwell were among numerous American artists who adopted automatic methods in their work, experimenting with the chance effects of gravity and momentum on falling paint. However, a crucial shift in rhetoric occurred as many artists associated with this genre of painting questioned the abdication of aesthetic responsibility through psychological determinism in favor of a practice of direct expressivity that placed emphasis on the painterly gesture as a manifestation of artistic free will.

In the late 1950s and early 1960s, a new generation of artists working within an increasingly consumerist society critically reassessed the liberatory rhetoric associated with automatism and the metaphysical language applied to gestural abstraction. While diverse responses arose in opposition to both legacies, their heightened emphasis on the process of making art was retained and greatly expanded upon. Members of the overtly political group of artists and activists known as the Situationist International (SI), for example, appropriated and redeployed various Surrealist strategies, such as *dérive*, drifting through urban space, and *détournement*, a collage-like technique in which stolen texts and images are reassembled for radically subversive effect. The Swiss sculptor Jean Tinguely took a more humorous and ironic approach, creating automatic drawing machines that moved in unpredictable jerks to produce "gestural" abstractions completely detached from the artist's hand. Tinguely's machines illustrate a pervasive concern among artists at this moment with moving beyond Pollock's powerful and performative model of painting, beyond the confines of the two-dimensional canvas, by actively incorporating elements of time and space into the work of art. As artists shifted emphasis and interest away from the dominant notion of art as a fixed object, they grew increasingly interested in what Robert Morris described as "chance, contingency, indeterminacy—in short, the entire area of process."[2] Emphasis on the contingent was often asserted in an attempt to alter the framework of value placed on art objects while critiquing the oppressive logic of postwar consumerism.

NOTES

1. André Breton, "Manifesto of Surrealism" (1924), reprinted in *Manifestoes of Surrealism*, trans. Richard Seaver and Helen R. Lane (Ann Arbor: University of Michigan Press, 1969), 26.
2. Robert Morris, "Notes on Sculpture, Part 4: Beyond Objects" (1969), reproduced in Robert Morris, *Continuous Project Altered Daily: The Writings of Robert Morris* (Cambridge, MA: MIT Press, 1993), 67.

Francis Picabia (French, 1879–1953)

La Sainte-Vierge (The Blessed Virgin), 1920
Ink blot on paper, published in *391*, no. 12 (March 1920)

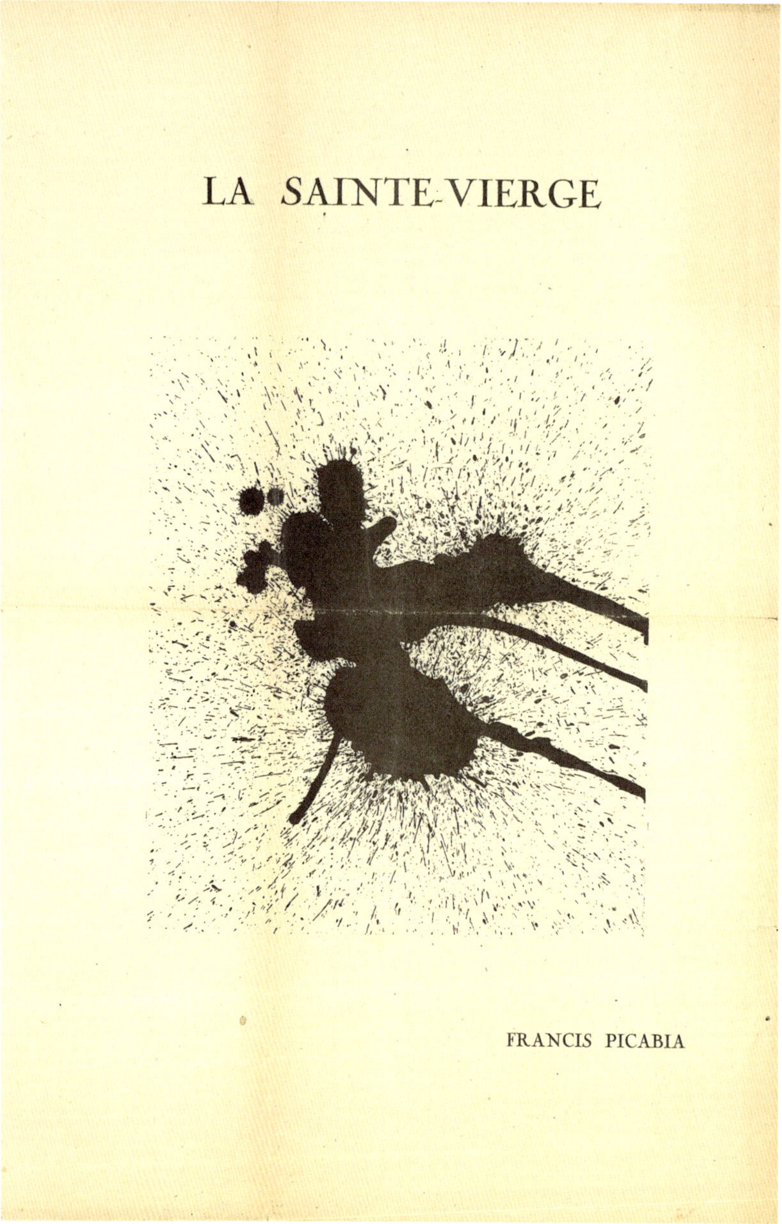

***La Sainte-Vierge* (*The Blessed Virgin*)** by Francis Picabia is an irreverent work that manifests the Dadaists' sustained experimentation with chance procedures.[1] In order to create this image, Picabia splattered black ink onto a piece of paper so that the ink pooled, bled, and sprayed, creating a large amorphous shape surrounded by tiny dots. This ink stain can be interpreted as indexical and autographic: what we see is the direct result of the artist's gesture, an inimitable record of a specific moment impossible to recreate.

Yet despite such interpretations, Picabia repeatedly resisted the autographic mark making typically associated with drawing. In his earlier "mechanomorphic" portraits, for instance, he rendered industrial objects by means of mechanical drawing. With *La Sainte-Vierge*, he literally created a distance between his pen and the paper by flinging the ink onto the paper, allowing the accidental to assert itself.[2]

Further removing this piece from the notion of originality is the fact that Picabia may have decided to create his image in imitation of another, Man Ray's *Art Motes* (1915). Man Ray's abstract black splotch, reproduced in his satirical journal *The Ridgefield Gazook* (March 1915), is itself only a simulation of an ink splotch.[3] The fact that Picabia mechanically reproduced *La Sainte-Vierge* in his own art journal, *391* (March 1920), and distributed copies of it at the Manifestation Dada event at the Maison de l'Oeuvre in Paris in the same month, adds yet another level of mediation.[4] Derivative and duplicated, yet necessarily unique, *La Sainte-Vierge* exemplifies how Picabia performed in the space between the accidental and the deliberate.

EH

NOTES

1. For analyses of the various interpretations that can be assigned to this image, see Elizabeth Legge, "Thirteen Ways of Looking at a Virgin: Picabia's *La Sainte-Vierge*," *Word and Image* 12, no. 2 (April–June 1996): 218–42; David Hopkins, "Questioning Dada's Potency: Picabia's *La Sainte-Vierge* and the Dialogue with Duchamp," *Art History* 15, no. 3 (1992): 317–33; and William A. Camfield, *Francis Picabia: His Art, Life, and Times* (Princeton, NJ: Princeton University Press, 1979), 141–42.

2. The original drawing is believed to no longer exist. A second drawing Picabia made using the same process, *La Sainte-Vierge II* (*The Blessed Virgin II*) (c. 1920), is located at the Bibliothèque Littéraire Jacques Doucet in Paris.

3. Man Ray's *Art Motes* is signed "Kumoff," a pseudonym that exemplifies the sophomoric humor of his entire publication. Only one issue of *The Ridgefield Gazook* was published. For more on the link between Man Ray's and Picabia's works, see Legge, "Thirteen Ways," 220; and George Baker, *The Artwork Caught by the Tail: Francis Picabia and Dada in Paris* (Cambridge, MA: MIT Press, 2007), 35–37.

4. The Manifestation Dada event was a series of Dada performances held on March 27, 1920, to celebrate the twenty-fifth anniversary of Alfred Jarry's play, *Ubu roi* (*King Ubu*).

André Masson
(French, 1896–1987)

Untitled, 1926
Pen and black ink on off-white laid paper, 16 13/16 x 12 1/2"
[p. 31]

Yves Tanguy
(French, 1900–1955)

Untitled, 1927
India ink on paper, 11 9/16 x 7 7/8"
[below]

Ellsworth Kelly
(American, b. 1923)

Automatic Drawing, 1950
Pencil on paper, 12 3/8 x 17 5/8"

[right]

Automatism, according to the Surrealists, entailed giving free reign, whether in writing or in art, to the unconscious, unfettered by logic or willful control. Although poet and founding Surrealist André Breton was chiefly concerned with automatic writing, his concepts of Surrealist aesthetics and automatism were equally influential to visual artists and their related explorations of the creative potential of the imagination. The automatic drawings produced by André Masson and Yves Tanguy, among others, in the 1920s reflect the Surrealists' enthusiasm for this technique.

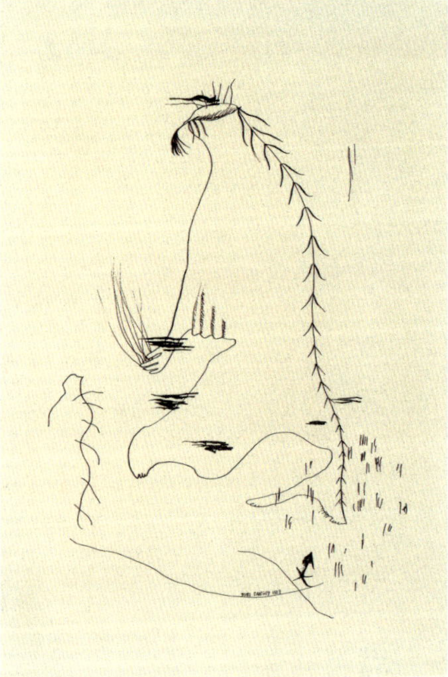

As Masson explained, at that time "a frantic surrender to automatism was the rule with us."[1]

As Masson described the method of automatic drawing, one must clear one's mind and then allow the hand to draw. He characterized himself as being engrossed in his automatic drawing with "such a fever" that he "couldn't see what he was creating."[2] The process he describes is thus a passive one: the artist is surprised by the results of his own hand. "The first graphic apparitions upon the paper are pure gesture, rhythm, incantation," Masson explained, after which "the image (which had been latent) now asserts its rights. Once the image has appeared, it is time to stop."[3] The automatic drawings themselves, however, show evidence of an additional step: upon recognizing shapes in his scribbles, the artist would then augment his drawings. The result is an image that includes recognizable elements with little overall cohesion, thus inviting viewers to make their own associations. The draftsmanship of these drawings, particularly evident in the fluid lines of Masson's drawing, evince the tension between a stream-of-consciousness approach and control.[4]

Although the Surrealists came to acknowledge the impossibility of pure automatism by the late 1920s, their ideas inspired many later artists to experiment with the technique. One such artist is Ellsworth Kelly, who expanded the creative possibilities of employing chance in his efforts to discover a new visual vocabulary in the 1940s and 1950s. While Kelly was attracted to automatism as a strategy that yielded potentially unexpected results, he did not share the Surrealists' interest in the unconscious. Rather, when he set out to draw a particular object,

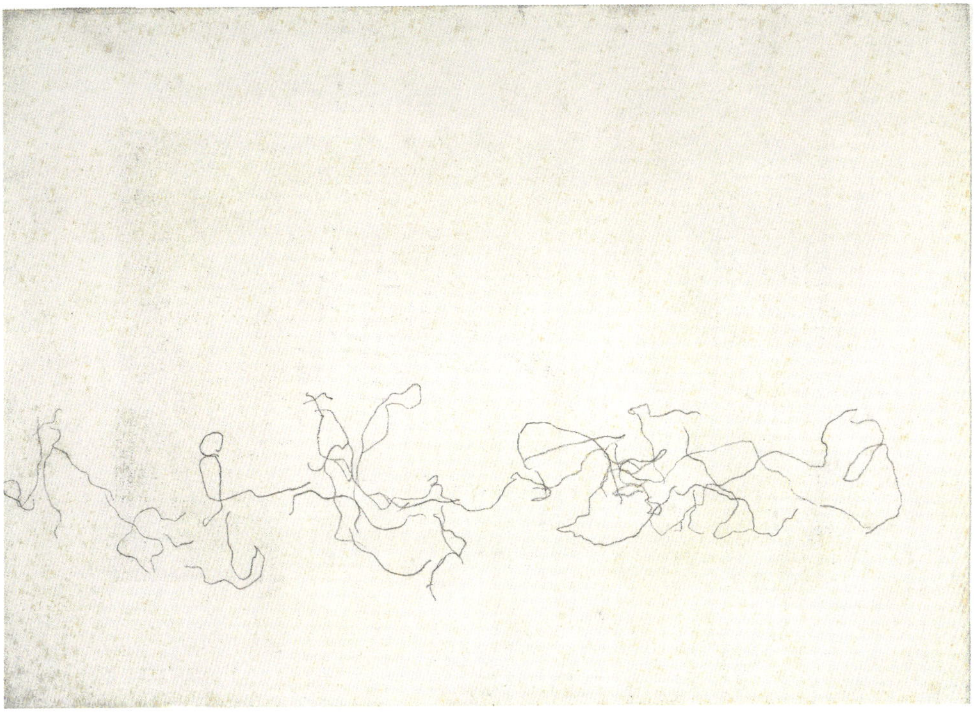

he would limit the amount of control he had by employing two distinct tactics: looking only at the object he was drawing and not at the paper, and drawing blindfolded.

Automatic Drawing, a blind drawing, exemplifies the kind of results Kelly achieved with these strategies. The tension between the deliberate and the whimsical in this piece is paramount. On the one hand, he seems to have proceeded across the paper carefully, lifting his pencil several times as if to sketch yet another part of what was the basis for the drawing. The variations of the lines—from dark to light, thick to thin—also suggest that Kelly was attempting to precisely render something in particular. On the other hand, the lines seem to perform an improvisational dance across the page, with strong verticals giving way to graceful, fading horizontals. Kelly eventually abandoned his experiments with automatism, embarking on a more systematic method for obtaining chance results.

EH

NOTES

1. André Masson, "Painting Is a Wager" (1943), in *Surrealist Painters and Poets: An Anthology*, ed. Mary Ann Caws (Cambridge, MA: MIT Press, 2001), 47.

2. André Masson, interview with Georges Bernier (1955), as quoted and translated by Clark V. Poling, "Automatism and the Fragmented Self," in his *André Masson and the Surrealist Self* (New Haven, CT: Yale University Press, 2008), 52.

3. André Masson, "Propos sur le surréalisme" (1961), as quoted and translated by Roger Cardinal, "André Masson and Automatic Drawing," in *Surrealism: Surrealist Visuality*, ed. Silvano Levy (New York: New York University Press, 1997), 83.

4. As visual manifestations of a defining Surrealist concept, automatic drawings were widely reproduced in Surrealist publications. Masson's drawings appeared in the Surrealists' journal *La Révolution surréaliste*, which was published from 1924 to 1929, for example, and Tanguy's drawings appeared as illustrations for Benjamin Péret's book of poems *Dormir, dormir, dans les pierres* (Paris: Éditions Surréalistes, 1927).

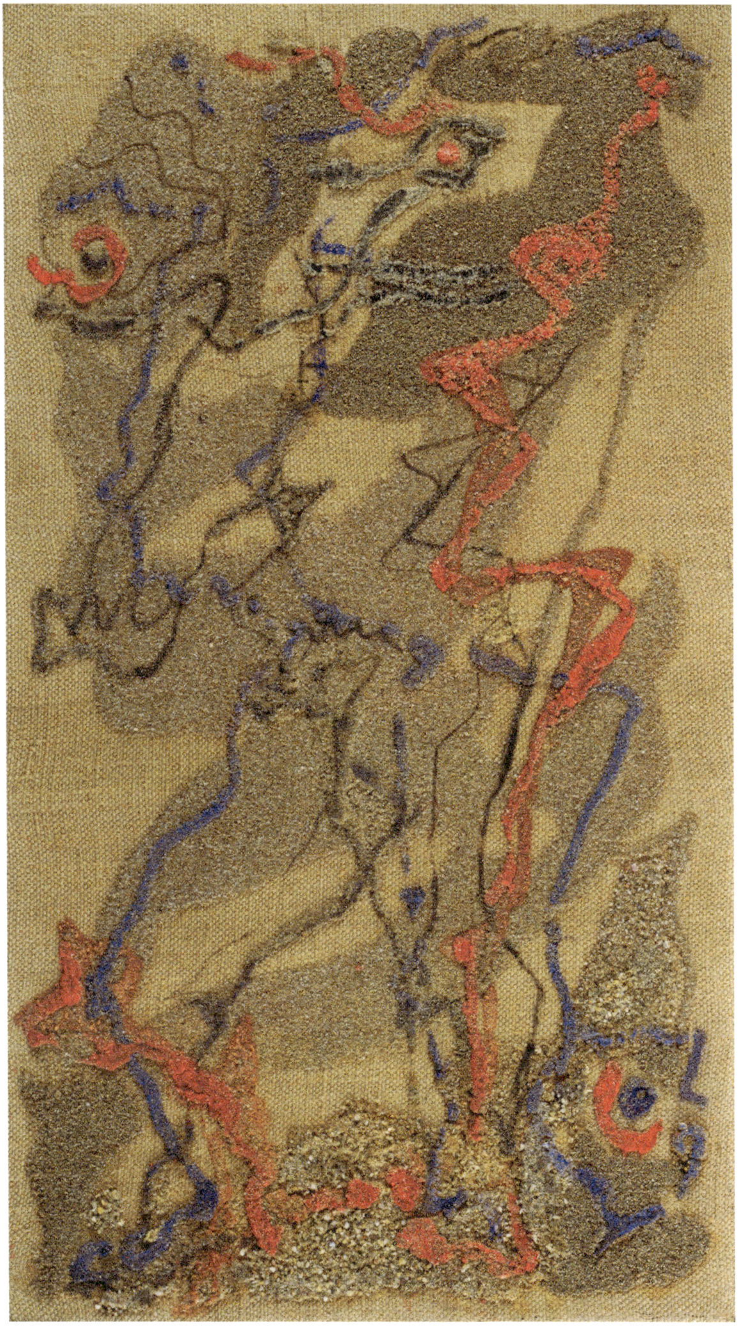

André Masson (French, 1896–1987)

Figure, 1926–27
Oil and sand on canvas, 18 1/8 x 10 1/2"

As one of the founding members of Surrealism, André Masson practiced a variety of automatic techniques as a means of dismantling the bourgeois conventions of illusionist easel painting that for centuries had prioritized rational control and the skilled rendering of reality. Masson's sand paintings, a remarkable interval in Surrealist production, were made in the short period between 1926 and 1927 when Masson was living by the sea at Sanary-sur-mer in the south of France. To make the sand paintings, Masson poured glue on a horizontally placed canvas, letting it randomly puddle, and then quickly sprinkled on layers of sand and liquid paint to devise chance forms that stemmed, he believed, from his unconscious. In *Figure*, the patches of sand, automatist drips of paint, and calligraphic line suggest a humanlike form and two creatures that resemble fish. Skeins of red, blue, and black paint, which Masson probably added toward the end of the creative process, reinforce the vertical orientation of the figure and give shape to the fishlike forms that are only hinted at by the patches of sand. Similar images that seem to document Masson's personal psychic imagery—male and female forms, inchoate animal shapes, and ambiguous symbols such as eyes, wings, and stars—appear in many of his sand paintings. Other sand paintings, such as *The Battle of Fishes* (1926), *Villagers* (1927), and *Two Death's Heads* (1927), evoke bloody, semi-abstract battles, although Masson never defined this vocabulary, leaving it open to interpretation. Violent sexualized imagery appears in Masson's automatic drawings that precede the sand paintings and in the oil paintings that follow them, and probably originated in the Surrealists' understanding of violence, death, and desire as the dominant impulses of the unconscious.

Within Surrealist circles, it was often felt that the pictorial arts were less successful than the written arts, particularly poetry, at registering the flow of psychic material harnessed through automatism. Masson turned to sand painting as a means of bridging the gap between the automatic drawings he had been making since 1924 and his oil paintings, which were not as spontaneous or immediate and hence less successful at accessing the unmediated flow of unconscious thought. Later in life, Masson described the sand painting process in a way that emphasizes this lack of artistic control and the manner in which he considered himself simply an instrument for the transfer of psychic imagery:

> I began by laying flat a piece of canvas or a stretcher covered with unprepared canvas. Onto it I threw pools of glue that I manipulated, and they took on the aspect of Leonardo da Vinci's wall. Then I spread on sand, I shook the picture again so that there were bursts, puddles, sometimes I raked it with a knife. I obtained something that had no sense but which could provoke it.... And all of this was done with the speed of a toss. With the sand, I used different thicknesses, of course. I spread on the glue in successive layers, which ended by making a sort of wall, a very uneven wall, and then, at a certain point, these layers suggested forms, almost always irrational. With a little oil paint, I added some lines, but as quickly as possible, and then, already a little calmer, some touches of color.[1]

Although his production of sand paintings was not sustained, Masson would periodically return to this experimental technique throughout his career as a means of revisiting the automatist method that had been so generative during the heyday of his Surrealist years.

KB

NOTES

1. André Masson, in Jean-Paul Clébert, *Mythologie d'André Masson* (Geneva: Pierre Cailler, 1971), 34 (translation mine).

Max Ernst (German, 1891–1976)

Histoire naturelle, 1926
Portfolio of photogravures, 19 5/8 x 12 3/4"
Published by Jeanne Bucher, Paris
[below; p. 33]

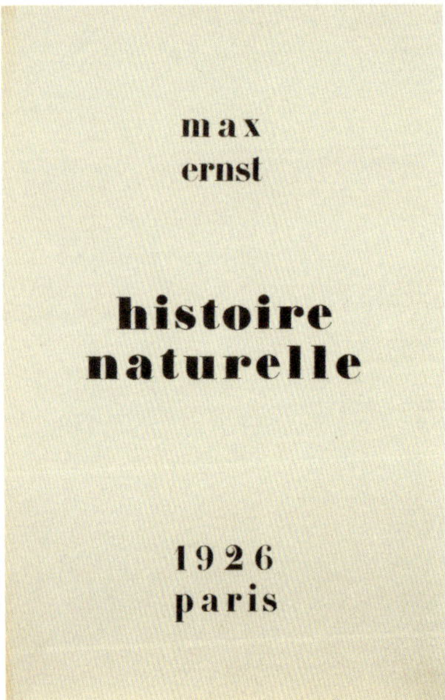
max
ernst

histoire
naturelle

1926
paris

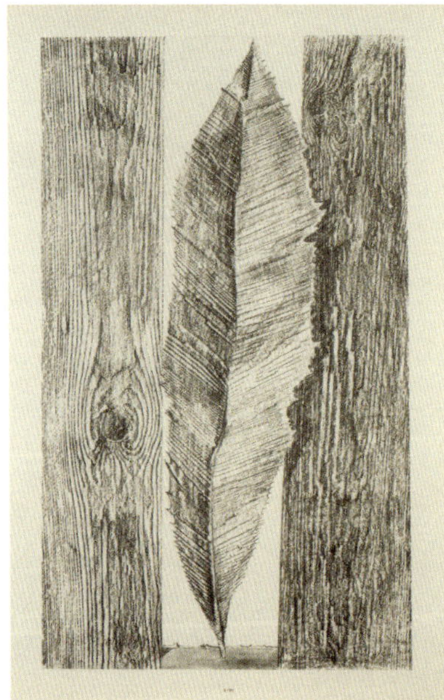

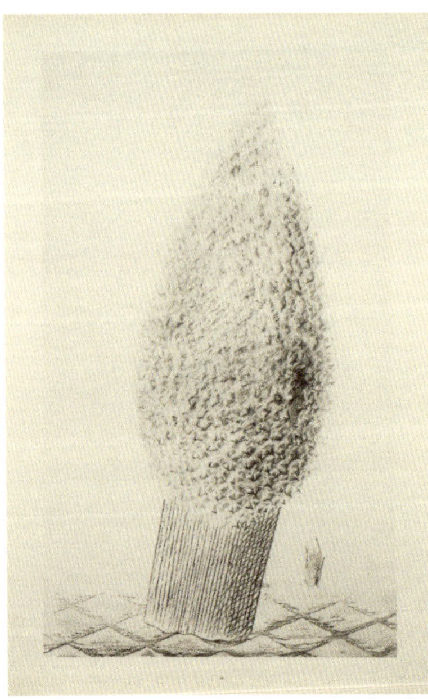

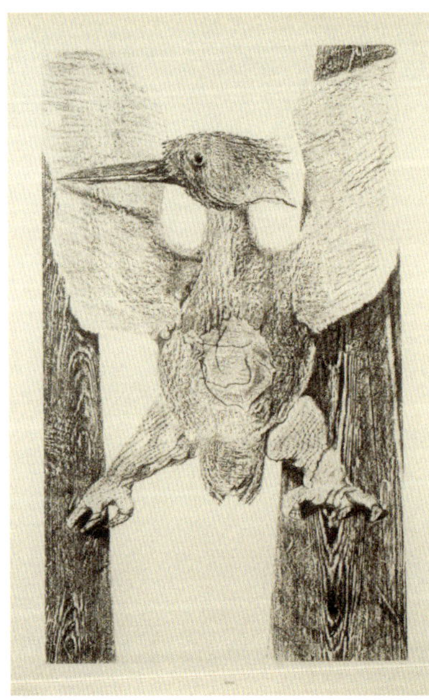

Max Ernst, a German painter, sculptor, graphic artist, and poet, was one of the primary pioneers of the Dada and Surrealist movements. Like his artistic colleagues working in the aftermath of World War I, Ernst shared an irreverent attitude toward conventional art and mores and experimented with a wide variety of automatic techniques, including automatic writing and drawing, collage, and decalcomania as means of complicating traditional expressions of authorial intention. On August 10, 1925, he discovered a new technique—what he described as frottage, or rubbing. It was after becoming fascinated by the grooves on floorboards that he decided to place sheets of paper "at random" on the floor and rub them with black lead:

> In gazing attentively at the drawings thus obtained … I was surprised by the sudden intensification of my visionary capacities and by the hallucinatory succession of contradictory images superimposed, one upon the other, with the persistence and rapidity characteristic of amorous memories.[1]

Ernst's reaction to the results of his technique highlights the Surrealists' emphasis on exploring the creative possibilities of altered and intensified states of mind as well as their belief in eroticism as a liberating force capable of yielding novel visual forms.

After this first experiment with his newfound technique, Ernst tried the technique on different surfaces:

> My curiosity awakened and astonished, I began to experiment indifferently and to question, utilizing the same means, all sorts of materials to be found in my visual field: leaves and their veins, the ragged edges of a bit of linen.... There my eyes discovered human heads, animals....[2]

His language echoes that of Leonardo da Vinci, whom he quotes, implying a continuity between the two artists, perhaps in an effort to offer a historical justification for his technique.[3] Like da Vinci, Ernst was mesmerized by the vitality and imagery of nature.

Also similar is Ernst's purportedly passive role in the creative process: "It is as a spectator that the author assists, indifferent or passionate, at the birth of his work and watches the phases of its development."[4] Yet Ernst was anything but passive in his execution of this newfound technique of frottage. He chose his surfaces and materials, he carefully combined rubbings, and he augmented the results in order to create coherent, if bizarre, compositions.

A limited-edition portfolio of thirty-four images, *Histoire naturelle* is Ernst's first and most inclusive cycle of frottages. Through precise selection, juxtaposition, control of texture, and some judicious additions, he built up surprising images of plant, animal, and human forms, many with strange titles (*The Vaccinated Bread, The Shawl with Flowers of Hoar-frost*). In *The Vaccinated Bread*, for instance, what looks like a loaf of bread on a table is made up of rubbings of at least four different surfaces denoting the table, wall, crust, and center of the bread.

The contrast between the indexical nature of Ernst's frottages and the imaginative ways in which he combined them parallels the disjunction between the title of this portfolio, which implies something rational and scientific, and its fantastical contents.

Like the many other techniques Ernst explored in his career—collage, decalcomania, and, later, grattage (the process of scraping wet or dried paint from a canvas)—the frottage method appealed to him as a means of cultivating his imaginative faculties and transforming what he found into bizarre combinations of recognizable parts meant to incite viewers to apply their own interpretive agency.

EH

NOTES

1. Max Ernst, "On Frottage" (1936), in his *Beyond Painting*, trans. Dorothea Tanning (New York: Wittenborn, Schultz, 1948), as cited by Herschel B. Chipp, *Theories of Modern Art: A Source Book by Artists and Critics* (Los Angeles: University of California Press, 1968), 429.

2. Ibid.

3. For further discussion of the connection between Max Ernst and Leondardo da Vinci, see Susan Laxton, "The Good Fairy Automatism," in this volume, 32–33.

4. Ernst, "On Frottage," 429.

André Breton
(French, 1896–1966)

Untitled, 1935
Ink transfer on paper, 10 x 12 3/4"

Oscar Dominguez
(Spanish, 1906–1957)

Untitled, 1936
Gouache on coated black paper, 8 x 9 11/16"
[top right]

Marcel Jean
(French, 1900–1994)

Untitled, c. 1936
Gouache on paper, 12 7/8 x 9 3/4"
[p. 34]

Salvador Dalí
(Spanish, 1904–1989)

Femme nue (*Nude Woman*), early 1930s
Gouache on paper, 9 15/16 x 7 15/16"
[bottom right]

Max Ernst
(German, 1891–1976)

L'Oeil du silence (*The Eye of Silence*), 1943–44
Oil on canvas, 43 1/4 x 56 1/4"
[below]

Developed as an artistic technique chiefly by Oscar Dominguez in 1935, and soon thereafter by Max Ernst and Hans Bellmer at the internment camp of Les Milles in France,[1] decalcomania (from the French "*décalquer*," or to transfer) involves covering a flat smooth surface such as glass or cardboard with a layer of paint and pressing it onto a surface, usually a canvas or a piece of paper. The resulting uneven areas of paint create a texture of organic designs and often a somewhat eerie sense of space, particularly evident in the decalcomanias by Marcel Jean and André Breton. The Surrealists understood the unlikely combinations of objects and images in terms of a liberating desire, or longing, that defies the restrictions of reason, and, like their previous experiments with automatism, invites viewers to participate in this erotic encounter. In an essay of 1936, André Breton described decalcomania as "a recipe within everybody's grasp," and as a means to "open one's window at will upon the most beautiful landscapes in this or any other world."[2]

Surrealists such as Salvador Dalí also experimented with a form of decalcomania that involves applying ink to one side of a piece of

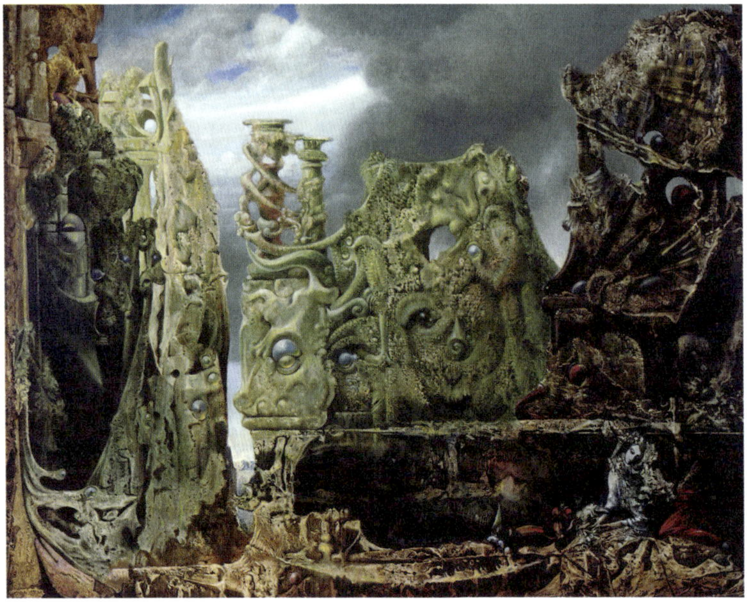

paper and folding it so the ink transfers to the other side, a technique similar to the Rorschach inkblot tests used by psychologists beginning in the early 1920s.[3] Overall, their decalcomanias range from the abstract to the figurative, and in neither extreme was artistic agency abandoned entirely. As with other Surrealist automatic techniques, in addition to choosing the dimensions and colors of a given piece, the artist would typically augment the initial unforeseen impression after the fact. In Dalí's *Femme nue*, for instance, the face, hair, and breasts appear to have been painted by the artist, and the clearly recognizable lion shape of Dominquez's haunting piece was created using a stencil.

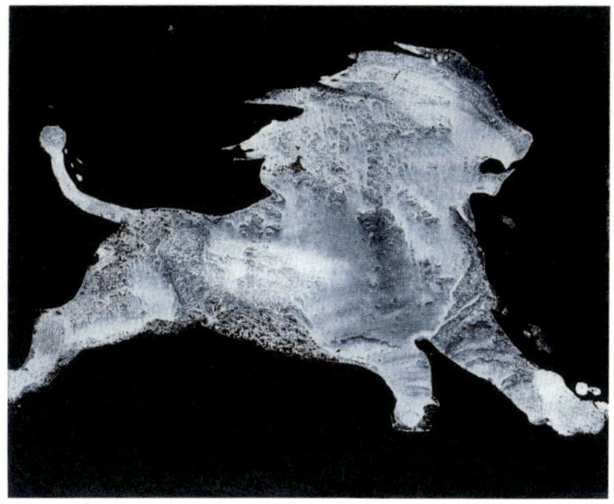

A particularly compelling example of decalcomania is Max Ernst's *L'Oeil du silence*, in which strange geological forms tower over a lake and a cavernous abyss. Created during World War II while Ernst was living as a political émigré in the United States, the painting presents a terrain made up of barely recognizable, seemingly morphing shapes—humans, animals, columns, grottoes, incongruously exposed stalactites and stalagmites, and even a profile of a bull (a reference to the Surrealists' signature Minotaur)—penetrated by eyelike orbs. This changing nature of forms that results from his technique, a phenomenon known as metamorphosis, creates a sense of transformation and volatility rather than an emphasis on fixed, unchanging forms directly rendered by the artist's hand.[4] In some of his works, however, Ernst merely imitated the effects of decalcomania by painting directly on to the canvas. Which method he used in *L'Oeil du silence* is a matter of dispute. The fact that he experimented with both highlights the tension between desire to use automatic techniques for unexpected results and interest in asserting control over the outcome of the composition.

EH

NOTES

1. For more on the sociopolitical context of Max Ernst's work during the war, see Sabine Eckmann, "Max Ernst in New York, 1941–45," in *Exiles + Emigrés: The Flight of European Artists from Hitler*, ed. Stephanie Barron and Sabine Eckmann (Los Angeles: Los Angeles County Museum, 1997), 158.

2. André Breton, "Oscar Dominguez: Concerning Décalcomania without Preconceived Object (Décalcomania of Desire)" (1936), reprinted in his *Surrealism and Painting*, trans. Simon Watson Taylor (New York: Harper & Row, 1972), 129.

3. The inkblot tests described by Swiss psychiatrist and psychoanalyst Hermann Rorschach were known to, and appealed to, the Surrealists. See Hermann Rorschach, *Psychodiagnostik: Methodik und ergebnisse eines warhrnehmungsdiagnostischen Experiments* (Bern: E. Bircher, 1921).

4. Eckmann points out that this metamorphic aspect, "by disrupting unitary forms of perception," has the effect of enacting a "cultural critique that undermines rationality": "By working with forcibly manipulated or dissociated visual perceptions, [Ernst] presented a generalized critique of civilization as he knew it." Eckmann, "Max Ernst," 161.

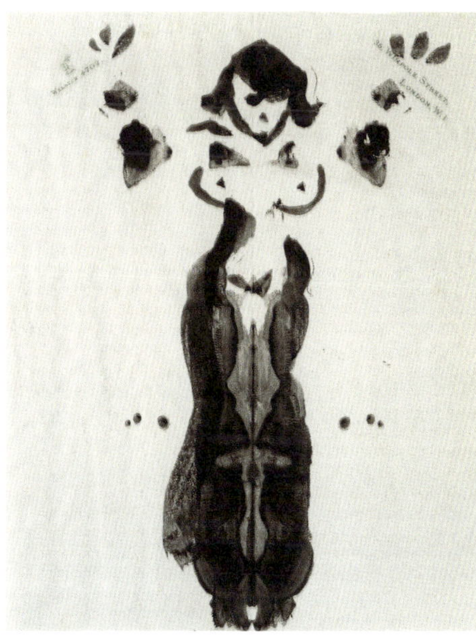

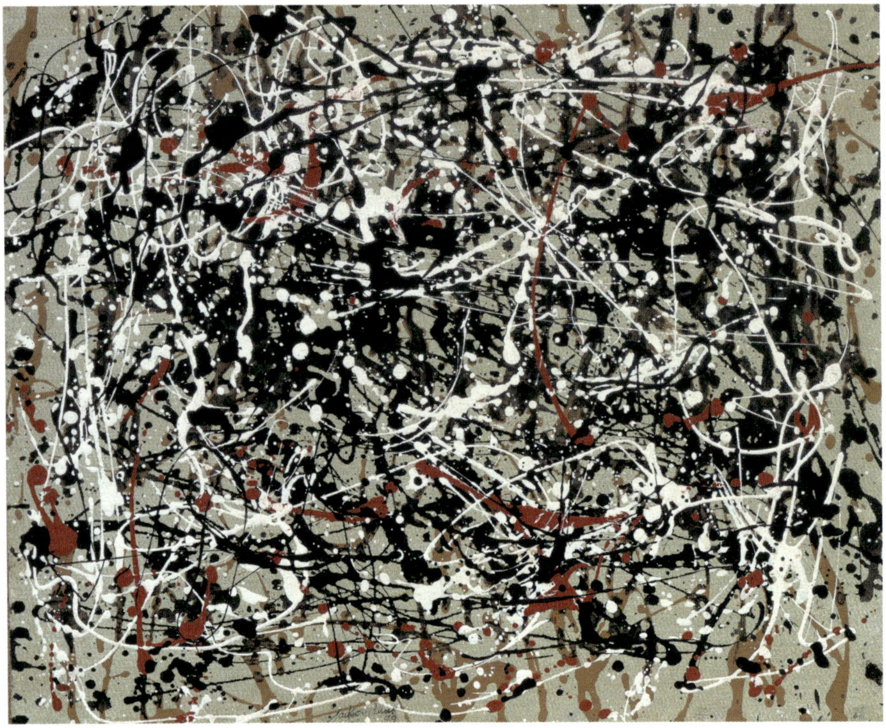

Jackson Pollock (American, 1912–1956)

Untitled, 1949
Oil and enamel on canvas mounted on masonite, 18 x 23"
[above]

Untitled, c. 1950
Ink on paper, 18 7/8 x 24 3/4"
[p. 15]

Few artists have experienced as profound a conflict with their own technique as Jackson Pollock, an artist whose name today is synonymous with spontaneity and the gesture. But a technique in which the artist must give over considerable control of the creative process to the medium itself was not an ideal match for one as crippled as Pollock was by anxiety, self-doubt, and paranoia that he would be revealed to the world as a "phony."[1] Pollock did not discover or invent the technique of dripping or pouring paint, and he was certainly aware that Max Ernst, Hans Hofmann, and the largely forgotten Janet Sobel had explored this territory before he made it part of the American postwar cultural landscape in the pages of *Life* magazine.[2] Pollock was, in a sense, the perfect storm of demographic and introverted machismo that the nation was looking for, a John Wayne to wrest the reins of the art world away from the European antagonist.

Whether it was or was not self-inflicted, the tremendous pressure under which Pollock found himself was unquestionably a major factor in his eventual wholesale rejection of the idea that anything in his work was arbitrary or a product of chance. His rhetoric in statements like "When I am *in* my painting ... I'm not aware of what I'm doing" from 1949 quickly changed to rebukes in 1950 aimed at suggestions of randomness, disorder, and unpredictability in his work, such as "I deny the accident," and the decidedly more vehement "NO CHAOS DAMN IT."[3]

While his protestations of control evoke an element of neurosis in his personality, there is little question that Pollock possessed a masterful facility with the medium, and that his control related not only to the manipulation of material but of space and density as well. A comparison of the oil painting on canvas, *Untitled* (1949), with the ink-on-paper drawing of 1950, for example, reveals his capacity to shift between densely layered compositions and open arrangements that evince a more calligraphic quality.

As with Robert Motherwell, Pollock's gestural technique was in part a response to Surrealist automatism in the work of André Masson, Roberto Matta, and other European artists in exile in the United States in the late 1930s. Additional inspirations for his groundbreaking process include the practices of Navajo sand painters that Pollock witnessed firsthand, the experimental painting techniques encouraged at the workshop of Mexican muralist David Alfaro Siqueiros that Pollock attended in New York in 1936, drawing techniques developed out of Jungian psychoanalytical sessions, Herbert Matter's experimental use of strobe lights and multiple exposures to capture motion in photography, and existentialist philosophy. Recent scholarship also points to Pollock's interest in the now-largely forgotten philosophy of vitalism, a "perhaps unlikely east / west fusion containing—among other influences—Aristotelian immanence, Zen Buddhism, Sufism, Hinduism, and [Gottfried] Leibniz" that purported to offer greater access to the forces and energies that flow through all living things.[4] But as successful and influential as Pollock was with his process of making paintings of "energy and motion made visible,"[5] he was also partially paralyzed by the significance of this process; despite a few experiments with different materials, his productivity dropped off severely during the last years of his life. Independent of the artist and his flaws, Pollock's aesthetic remains fascinating in its ability to defy and yet demonstrate order so effectively.[6]

BB

NOTES

1. Pollock used the word "phony" over and over during an infamously disastrous evening that followed the last day of Hans Namuth's shooting of a film about the artist at work. For details of Pollock's eruption that evening, see Steven Naifeh and Gregory White Smith, *Jackson Pollock: An American Saga* (New York: Clarkson N. Potter, 1989), 651–53.

2. See "Jackson Pollock: Is He the Greatest Living Painter in the United States?," *Life*, August 8, 1949, 42–45.

3. Pollock's assertion of "I deny the accident" was made during a radio interview with William Wright in 1950. For a transcript of the interview, see Pepe Karmel, ed., *Jackson Pollock: Interviews, Articles, and Reviews* (New York: Museum of Modern Art, 1999), 20–23. "NO CHAOS DAMN IT" was written by Pollock in a telegram to the editor of *Time* in response to the magazine's article "Chaos, Damn It!," which quoted a healthy portion of Bruno Alfieri's essay "A Short Statement on the Painting of Jackson Pollock," published in *L'Arte Moderna* (June 8, 1950). See *Jackson Pollock: Interviews*, 68–71. For an extended discussion of control in Pollock's work, see Michael Leja, *Reframing Abstract Expressionism: Subjectivity and Paintings in the 1940s* (New Haven, CT: Yale University Press, 1997), 276–83.

4. Jonathan D. Katz, "Jackson Pollock's Vitalism: Herbert Matter and the Vitalist Tradition," in *Pollock Matters*, ed. Ellen G. Landau and Claude Cernuschi (Chestnut Hill, MA: McMullen Museum of Art; Chicago: University of Chicago Press, 2007), 59–71.

5. Jackson Pollock, from a handwritten statement on the back of a photograph in the collection of the Museum of Modern Art, reprinted in *Jackson Pollock: A Catalogue Raisonné of Paintings, Drawings, and Other Works*, vol. 4, ed. Francis V. O'Connor and Eugene Victor Thaw (New Haven, CT: Yale University Press, 1978), 253.

6. Recent use of the sophisticated mathematics of fractal geometry to look for patterns and other evidence of organization in the seemingly chaotic system of Pollock's process only serves to reinforce how closely the mysteries and vast complexities of nature are reflected in his paintings. See Claude Cernuschi and Andrzej Hercynski, "Cutting Pollock Down to Size: The Boundaries of the Poured Technique," in *Pollock Matters*, 82–84; and Claude Cernuschi, Andrzej Hercynski, and David Martin, "Abstract Expressionism and Fractal Geometry," in ibid., 91–104.

Robert Motherwell (American, 1915–1991)

Twenty-four works from the *Lyric Suite*, 1965

Ink on rice paper, 11 x 9" or 9 x 11" each

[right; frontispiece]

The influx of European Surrealists into the United States in the late 1930s and early 1940s was a watershed in the development of American art and a pivotal ingredient in the rise of American Abstract Expressionist painting that would soon follow. Escaping the spread of fascism across Europe, leading Surrealists André Breton, Max Ernst, Yves Tanguy, Salvador Dalí, André Masson, and Roberto Matta brought with them innovative approaches and techniques for generating an art through which they sought to fuse psychology with the creative process. Among the young American artists who benefited most from the presence of these Surrealists in exile was Robert Motherwell, who, at the behest of his professor Meyer Schapiro, abandoned his pursuit of a doctorate in art history at Columbia University in 1941 to explore his potential as an artist. It was Schapiro who introduced him to the Surrealists, and the work of Matta in particular, which was instrumental in forming Motherwell's deep interest in psychic automatism.[1] In his subsequent paintings and collages, Motherwell would distinguish himself from the Surrealists with a gestural spontaneity that revealed a tremendous depth of feeling, yet was tempered by an understanding of compositional structure gleaned from Cubism.[2]

Politically motivated and intensely literate, Motherwell became an authoritative spokesman for the Abstract Expressionist movement. Over and above his vital presence as a leader of the New York School, he also demonstrated his fluency in a wide range of twentieth-century art styles as the editor of the Documents of Modern Art series and the acclaimed anthology *The Dada Painters and Poets.*[3] Like many of his fellow Abstract Expressionists, Motherwell distanced himself from the automatist procedures of the Surrealists in that he relinquished some control over the media, not for the purpose of revealing a repressed psychic content within the mark, but to directly communicate a concept or feeling through the idiom of the spontaneous gesture. Motherwell called this technique "plastic automatism," a concept based on the idea that expression is located in the "spontaneous interaction of the artist with his material environment."[4]

Nowhere is this more evident than in the subtly moving *Lyric Suite*, a series of nearly six hundred small drawings Motherwell made using a watercolor brush and various inks on Japanese rice paper.[5] A virtuoso exercise in automatic drawing, Motherwell produced between ten and fifty of these drawings a day during April and May 1965, most requiring only seconds to execute, though they were far from finished when Motherwell's brush left the paper. Motherwell described the process: "Unable to control spread of ink ... never know what one would set as, until 'set'; *each picture would change before my eyes after I had finished working on it*, sometimes for hours—as the ink spread, like a spot of oil."[6] Unique for Motherwell in their small scale, these drawings represent the artist at his most willing to allow material interactions to determine the outcome of the work of art. Like Jackson Pollock, Motherwell questioned the role of the "accident" in the creative process, although unlike Pollock's insistence on his ultimate control over the medium, Motherwell defended the accidental insofar as it suited his needs: "I don't exploit so-called 'accidents' in painting," he noted in a 1962 conversation, "I accept them if they seem appropriate. There is no such thing as an 'accident' really; it is a kind of casualness: it happened, so let it be, so to speak."[7] While the *Lyric Suite* closed far short of Motherwell's intended one thousand drawings (the artist

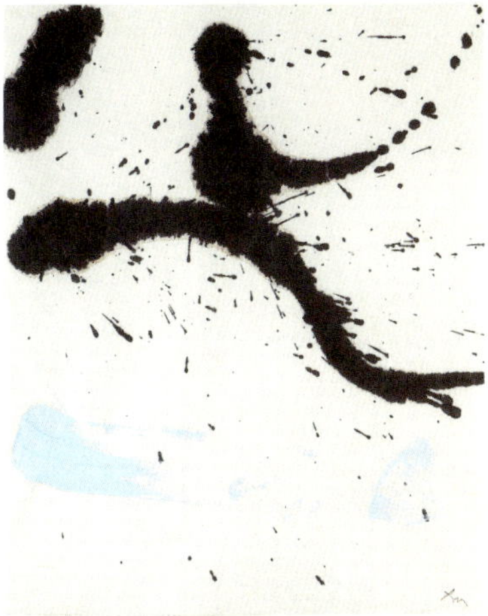

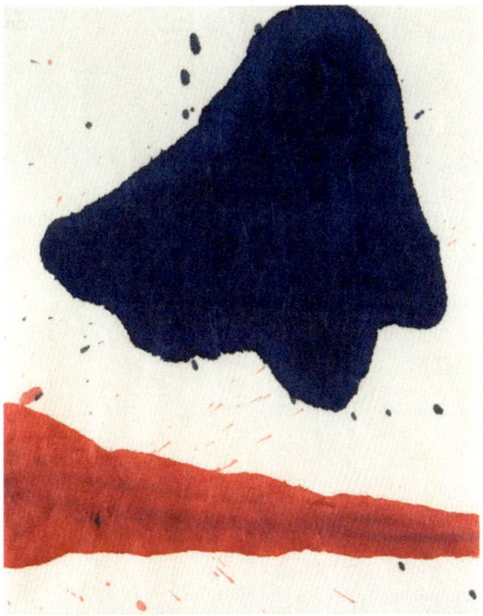

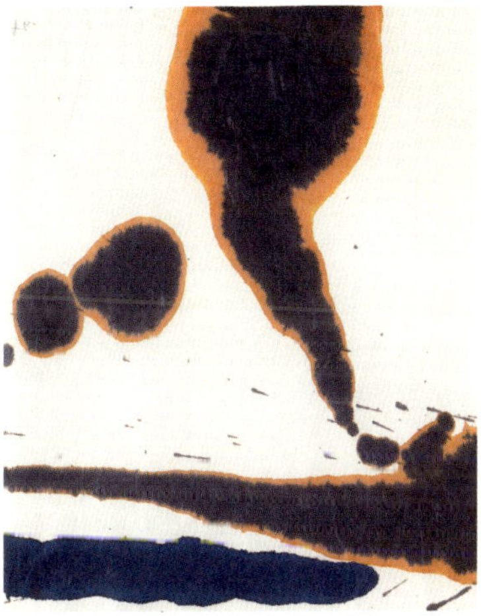

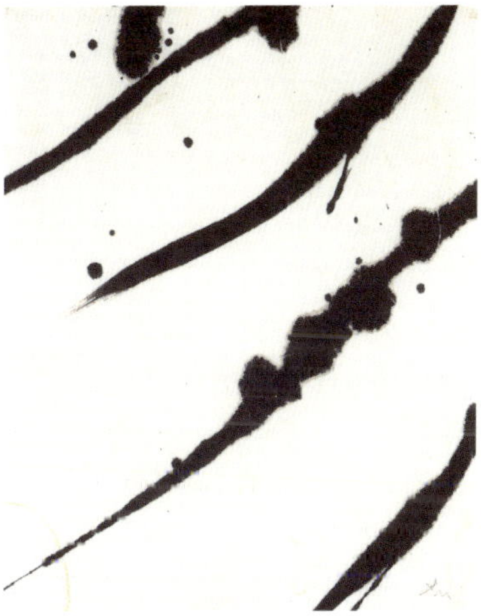

ceased producing them following the death of his close friend, sculptor David Smith, on May 23, 1965), the freedom and unselfconsciousness they express attest to his conviction that the act of drawing or painting is a partnership between artist and media.

BB

NOTES

1. Motherwell described his beginnings as an artist and his introduction to automatism at length in an interview conducted by art historian Sidney Simon in January 1967, reprinted in *The Collected Writings of Robert Motherwell*, ed. Stephanie Terenzio (Oxford: Oxford University Press, 1992), 155–68.

2. Motherwell gave several lucid descriptions of his painting and collage processes in an interview conducted by Charles Chetham in November 1962, and in his essay "A Process of Painting" (1963), both reprinted in *Collected Writings*, 134–41.

3. Robert Motherwell, *The Dada Painters and Poets: An Anthology* (New York: Wittenborn, Schultz, 1951).

4. Daniel Belgrad, *The Culture of Spontaneity: Improvisation and the Arts in Postwar America* (Chicago: University of Chicago Press, 1998), 77–78, 135.

5. *Lyric Suite* was named in part after a string quartet by Alban Berg (see *Collected Writings*, 170–71). The rice paper used in the work was purchased by Motherwell on an impulse, reiterating the artist's desire to exploit intuition.

6. Robert Motherwell, "Addenda to The Museum of Modern Art *Lyric Suite* Questionnaire—From Memory with Possible Chronological Slips" (1969), reprinted in *Collected Writings*, 172.

7. Motherwell, interview with Chetham, 136.

Guy Debord (French, 1931–1994)
Asger Jorn (Danish, 1914–1973)

Fin de Copenhague: Conseiller technique pour le détournement, 1957
Artist's book, 10 1/16 x 7 x 3/8"

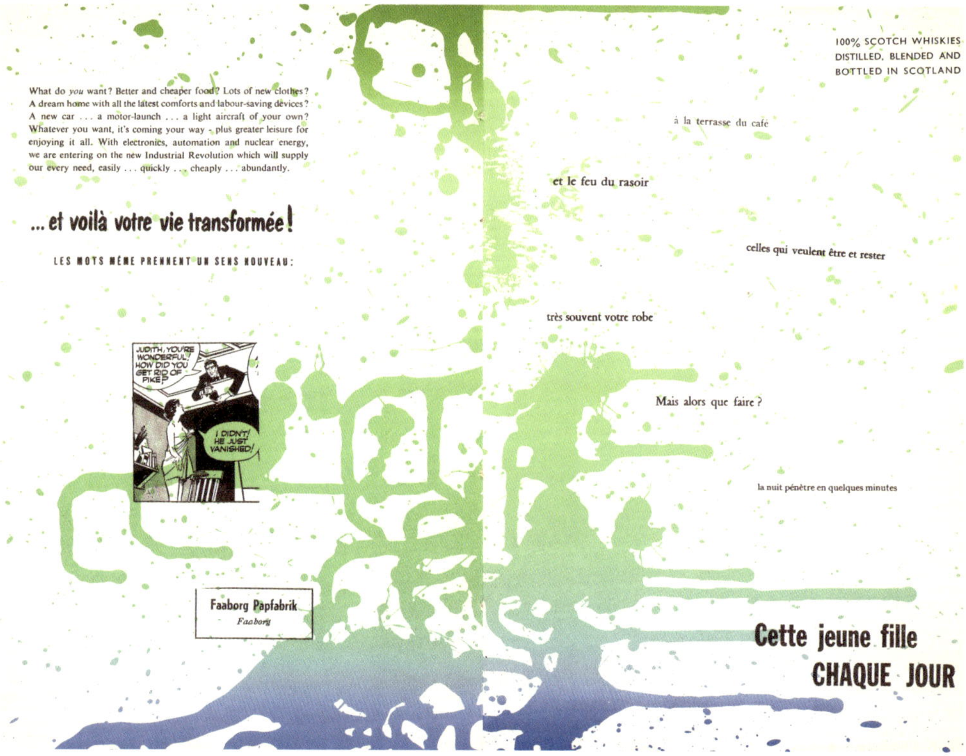

Fin de Copenhague (End of Copenhagen) is the result of a frenzied collaboration between Danish artist Asger Jorn, French activist Guy Debord, and the printers Permild and Rosengreen in Copenhagen in 1957. Spontaneously created over a twenty-four-hour period, this artist's book consists of snippets of text and images taken from a vast assortment of national and international newspapers and magazines found at a Danish newsstand—including small maps, images of Danish products, and copious references to alcohol—collaged and overlaid with brightly colored splatters of ink. The book, which has no apparent narrative structure, ultimately presents through oblique references a satirical picture of Jorn's life in Denmark, while at the same time serving as a clever critique of the experience of modernity, attacking both popular and high culture through the technique known as *détournement*. This collage-like method involves the appropriation of preexisting elements (the French term connotes theft or plagiarism), diverting, decontextualizing, and subsequently reassembling them into new ensembles.

As founding members of the Situationist International (SI), a revolutionary cultural organization formed in 1957 by artists, writers, and activists, Debord and Jorn advocated a complete transformation of everyday life as means for the necessary reconstruction of modern society as a whole.[1] Their critique was driven by a Marxist reading of the inherent conditions of modernity within advanced capitalism: uneven abundance of consumption, reduction of life to a spectacle, and repressive urbanism. *Détournement*, what the SI described as a "parodic-serious" operation, offered a means of transgressing the rules of consumerism by redistributing products, images, and rhetoric.[2] The principle behind this practice underscores Debord's whole conception of society: all the elements necessary for a new life were already available; they merely needed to be modified in their meaning and organized differently. A section of text from *Fin de Copenhague* asks the reader: "What do *you* want? Better and cheaper food? Lots of new clothes? A dream home with all the latest comforts and labour-saving devices? A new car ... a motor-launch ... a light aircraft of your own? Whatever you want, it's coming your way." This unattributed, overtly positivist assertion is immediately called into question, diverted by subsequent phrases that read as a sarcastic parody of the promises of capitalism: "And voilà, your life is transformed! Words take on a new sense!"

In addition to the texts, the vibrant, acid-colored splatters appearing across the pages of *Fin de Copenhague* add a further layer of cultural critique. To create these spills, Jorn dropped lithographic ink from the top of a stepladder onto folios laid on the floor, letting the paint splash and run in all directions. This act directly recalls Jackson Pollock's drip method, yet Jorn's work takes it to a new extreme, removing the artist notably further than Pollock's process did from control over the final image. Jorn's incorporation of chance reveals Pollock's process in contrast to be a rather elegant and personalized gesture that refers to nothing outside of the artist's performance, and thus a failed act of communication. Jorn's photolithographed splatters (a gesture twice removed) intentionally undermine the rhetoric of transparency, authenticity, and transcendence attributed to Pollock's practice. By asserting that the heroic artistic gesture is always mediated, both by the artist and in the viewer's reception of it, Jorn's work emphasizes what was for him the primary social nature of the artwork.[3]

MM

NOTES

1. The SI was founded at Cosio d'Arroscia in northern Italy out of the union of two preexisting avant-garde groups, the International Movement for an Imaginist Bauhaus and the Lettrist International.

2. See "Le Détournement comme négation et prélude" (1959), reprinted in *Situationist International Anthology*, ed. and trans. Ken Knabb (Berkeley: Bureau of Public Secrets, 1981), 56. In addition to the use of *détournement*, the SI also championed the practice of *dérive*, or spontaneous drifting, to achieve a similar sense of disorientation in contrast to the habitual, repetitive activities of everyday life in a consumer society. Unlike the Surrealist excursions organized by André Breton in the 1920s, the drift emphasized a sort of conscious aimlessness, displacing the notion of poetic, aestheticized experience with political action designed to enrich everyday life.

3. For a thorough discussion of Jorn's parodic artistic practice, see Karen Kurczynski, "Ironic Gestures: Asger Jorn, Informel, and Abstract Expressionism," in *Abstract Expressionism: The International Context*, ed. Joan Marter (New Brunswick, NJ: Rutgers University Press, 2007), 108–24.

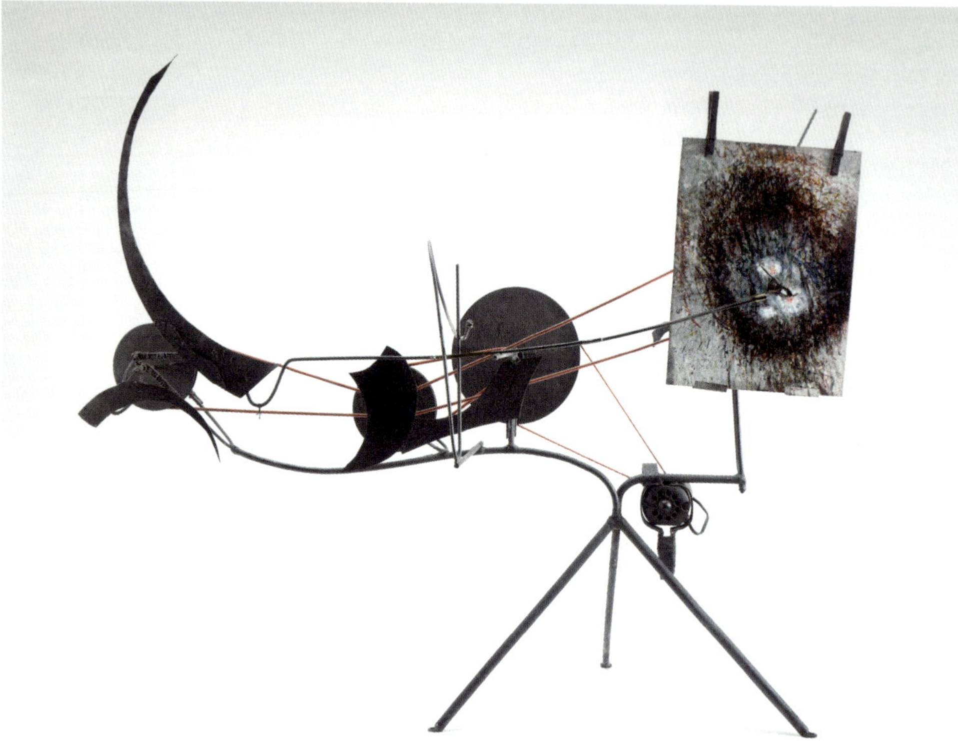

Jean Tinguely (Swiss, 1925–1991)

Metamatic No. 9, 1958

Round rubber belt, steel rods, painted sheet metal, wire wooden pulleys, two clothes pins, and electric motor, 35 1/2 x 56 5/8 x 14 1/4"
[above]

Metamatic drawings from *Metamatic No. 9*, 1959

Seven ink on paper drawings, 12 3/4 x 9 3/4" each
[right; p. 56]

Swiss artist Jean Tinguely, perhaps best known for his self-destroying assemblages such as *Homage to New York*, which randomly shook, banged, and burned itself to pieces at the Museum of Modern Art's Sculpture Garden in 1960, was a member of the Paris-based group of artists known as the Nouveaux Réalistes. Many of the Nouveaux Réalistes, including Arman, Niki de Saint Phalle, and Daniel Spoerri, engaged in works that challenged conventional definitions of art and its production by incorporating everyday objects, chance, and audience participation as key elements of their artistic practice—Tinguely chief among them.

Assembled from objects found in the junkyards of Paris and animated by secondhand electronic motors, Tinguely's *Metamatics* were typically composed of scrap metal, along with a series of disks, rubber bands, a small board to which paper was secured, and a metal arm with a clip used to hold a marker or pen. Once a piece of paper was attached to the given board and a pen secured in its fastener, the entire machine shook violently, emitting cacophonous sounds and producing "unique" abstract drawings. Tinguely described his *Metamatics* as "anti-machine machines," noting how the abstract drawings they produced were always different because the motors were constructed in such a way that the machines were incapable of producing "that dull repetitive action so typical of ordinary machines."[1] By removing the direct trace of the artist's hand and replacing it with the workings of his chaotic machines, Tinguely's sculptures were widely recognized as a sarcastic critique of both the spontaneous gestures and the heroic posturing of practitioners of postwar abstraction.

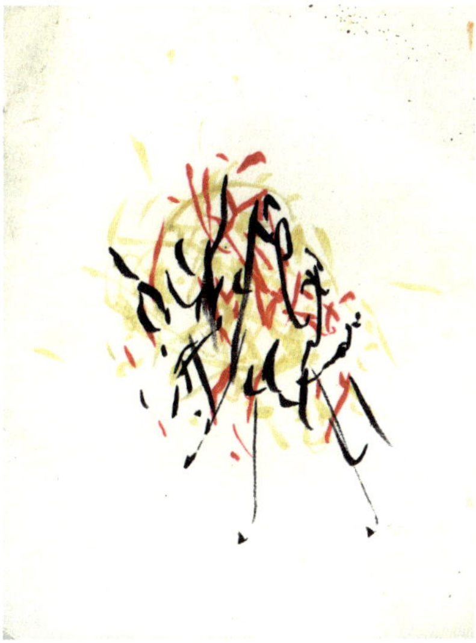

While his perverse mechanization of the artistic process supplanted traditional notions of artistic genius with that of the modern *bricoleur* and the practical joker, it also revealed his critical engagement with social concerns and anxieties specific to the postwar period—namely, the effects of automation and serialized industrial production on modern daily life. The title *Metamatic*, with its play on the word "automatic" and its definition as a machine that operates autonomously, conjures up images of self-service and commercial vending machines. Indeed, when exhibited at the Iris Clert Gallery in Paris in 1959, coin slots were fitted to each of the machines and visitors had to pay to play them as if at an arcade. Instead of a signature, the works produced were stamped: "Painting executed in collaboration with Tinguely's méta-matic No. __." Although nominally unique, each painting was thus always recognized as part of a series originating from Tinguely's *Metamatics*.[2]

By brazenly blurring the boundaries between art and mass-produced commodities, Tinguely humorously reveled in the paradox of automatic production. While human energy is saved from carrying out excessively repetitive tasks, the individual is deprived of the possibility of contributing something truly personal to the final product.[3] Tinguely promoted consumption by offering participants a variety of secondary features to "personalize" a given work, such as choice of color and duration and speed of execution, but the style of the work was ironically predetermined by the arbitrary movements of his unstable machines. Severely restricting human mediation in the actual production of a drawing to a few habitual acts and nominal selections, Tinguely's *Metamatics* wittily demonstrate how the supposedly liberatory elements of chance and choice can all too easily become tools of commodification and instrumentality.

MM

NOTES

1. Jean Tinguely, as quoted in John Rydon, "Mr. Tinguely Puts on a Show of Self-Propelled Art," *Daily Express* (London, October 14, 1959), n.p.

2. Only a few days before the opening of the exhibition at the Iris Clert Gallery, Jean Tinguely applied for an industrial patent for his *Metamatics*. According to the explanatory text, the machines could be applied to a variety of uses: as a toy, for the realization of abstract drawings and paintings capable of being exhibited and preserved, and for the continuous decoration of rolls of paper or cloth.

3. Jean Baudrillard's observations in *The System of Objects* (1968) regarding the modern notion of models and series of consumer products is particularly useful in analyzing the ways in which personalization through choice works in Tinguely's machines. Baudrillard notes that no serially produced industrial object appears on the market as a single type, but with a range of inessential differences that create the illusion of choice.

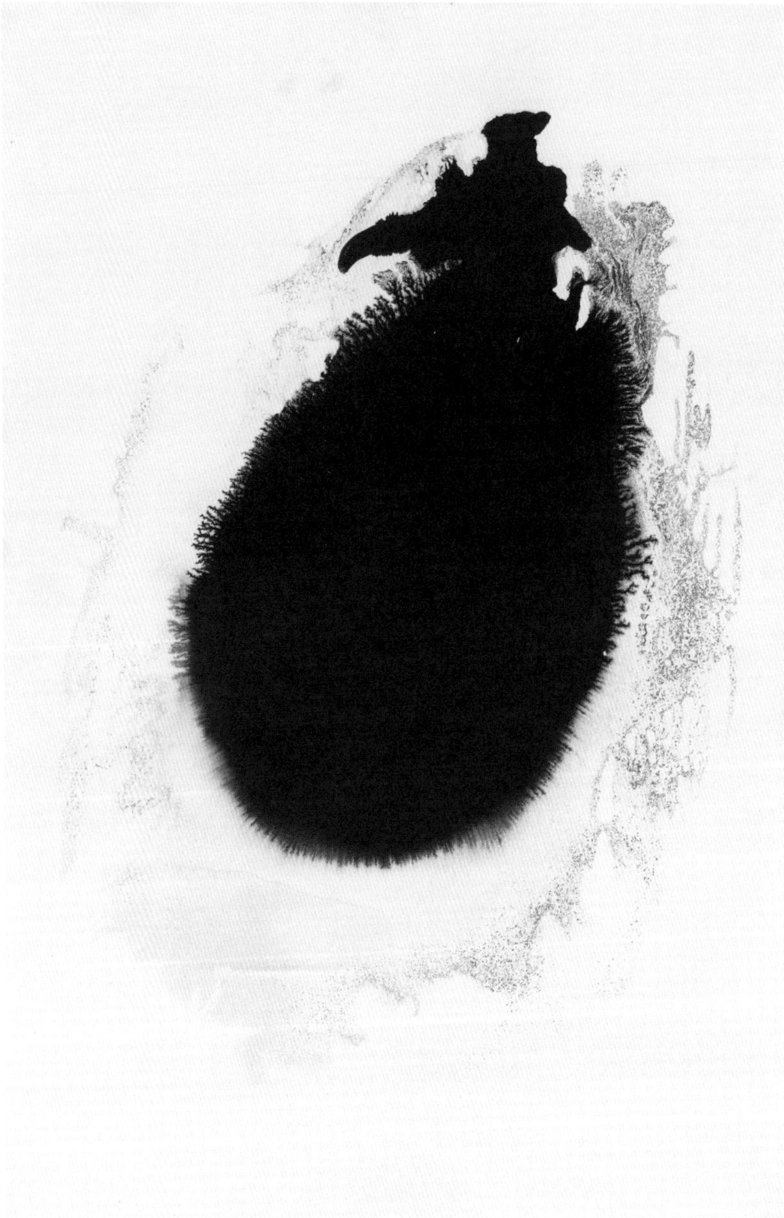

George Maciunas (American, 1931–1978)

Hydrokinetic-Osmotic Painting, 1961
Ink on paperboard on wood, 30 1/16 x 20 1/16"

George Maciunas is best known as the leader of the international Fluxus movement. Until his death in 1978, he organized festivals, designed publications, and theorized about the collective social identity and political ideology of Fluxus. Marcel Duchamp's radical democratization of the art object and John Cage's rule-based chance operations and indeterminate compositional techniques offered Maciunas two important models concerning the de-emphasis of authorial control and the commitment to alternative methods of artistic production. Anything could be art and anyone could make it. While his main role was as a designer, arranger, and promoter of Fluxus, Maciunas's output was profuse and eclectic. To create his *Hydrokinetic–Osmotic* paintings, he dropped india ink on wet paper, letting it puddle and seep into the paper. Unlike Surrealist automatism, Maciunas's rejection of conscious compositional control had little to do with liberating the unconscious from its rational restrictions. Rather, as made evident by his references to kinetic movement and osmosis in the work's title, his interest lay in the indeterminate course of natural events.

Smaller versions of his *Hydrokinetic-Osmotic* paintings were to be included in a deluxe version of Maciunas's planned *Flux No. 2 Western European Yearbox*. The standard edition of the box was to be issued in one thousand copies containing mainly reproducible sheets or printed matter. The "luxus-fluxus" edition was to include the standard edition along with what Maciunas described as "original solid-nonreproducible works: films, pieces of 2 dimensional or 3 dimensional art, 'ready-mades,' 'found objects,' junk, records."[1] A series of boxes were planned, but only the first, FLUXUS I, was produced.[2] Around 1969, the idea of a kinetic-osmotic work would resurface as *Kinesthesis Slides* and *Kinetics Nos. 1 to 3*. The former involved the use of a hollow glass slide into which living organisms (cockroaches, worms, flies, and caterpillars) were inserted. The slide was then projected on a wall, allowing viewers to watch the movements of the organism contained inside. The latter project also involved the use of hollow glass slides, but instead of highlighting the movement of insects, the kinetic events of osmosis (a drop of India ink in water or oil paint in turpentine), diffusion (alka seltzer in water), and crystallization (barium chloride in sulfuric acid) were projected as part of planned Fluxus film and slide shows.[3]

These works underscore the concept of temporal flow and process-oriented production implied by the word "fluxus" while also demonstrating Maciunas's intent to, as stated in his 1963 manifesto, "purge the world of dead art, imitation, artificial art, abstract art, illusionistic art," promoting instead "living art, anti-art ... NON ART REALITY to be grasped by all peoples, not only critics, dilettantes and professionals."[4] He favored a particular notion of "concretism," which he equated with the real or the ready-made, versus artificial abstraction and illusionism.[5] According to Maciunas, a true concretist rejects artificial human contrivances completely, allowing nature, "either in the form of an independent performer or indeterminate-chance compositional methods," to complete the work independently of the artist, resulting in a closer affinity with and understanding of reality.[6]

MM

NOTES

1. Jon Hendricks, *Fluxus Codex* (Detroit: Gilbert and Lila Silverman Fluxus Collection; New York: Harry N. Abrams, 1988), 103, 124.

2. In 1961 and early 1962, Maciunas planned an ambitious series of Fluxus anthologies, or yearboxes, which grew directly out of La Monte Young's *An Anthology* [Cat., p. 136]. FLUXUS I appeared in 1964. Tentative plans for six more boxes were drawn up but never realized. See Jon Hendricks, "Introduction to the Exhibition," in *Fluxus: Selections from the Gilbert and Lila Silverman Collection*, ed. Clive Phillpot and Jon Hendricks (New York: Museum of Modern Art, 1988), 20–21.

3. See Hendricks, *Fluxus Codex*, 362–63.

4. George Maciunas, "Fluxus Manifesto" (1963), reprinted in *In the Spirit of Fluxus*, ed. Elizabeth Armstrong and Janet Jenkins (Minneapolis: Walker Art Center, 1993), 24.

5. While distinct from the concrete art promoted by Theo Van Doesburg and, later, Max Bill, Maciunas's definition of "concretism" did share some of the central principles of concrete art, especially an emphasis on anti-individualism and the use of visual, verbal, and musical elements derived from reality as opposed to subjective compositional strategies.

6. George Maciunas, "Neo-Dada in Music, Theater, Poetry, Art" (1962), reprinted in *In the Spirit of Fluxus*, 156.

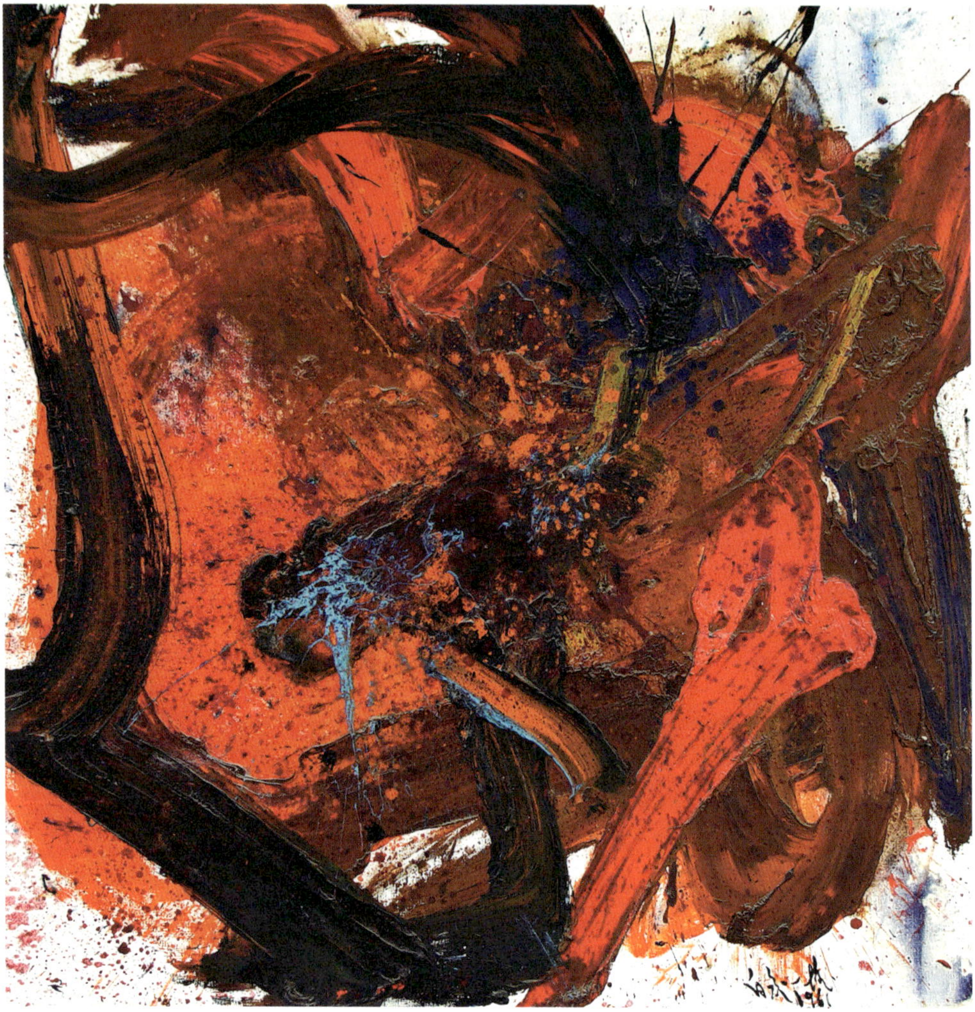

Kazuo Shiraga (Japanese, b. 1924)

Dragons Emerging from the Forest, 1961
Oil on canvas, 51 1/2 x 51 1/4"

As a key member of the Gutai Art Association founded in Osaka, Japan, in 1954 under the leadership of Jiro Yoshihara, Kazuo Shiraga carried out innovative artistic experiments, incorporating performative events and unorthodox materials that defied traditional notions of art making. Gutai, which literally means "concreteness," emerged at a time when the Japanese avant-garde was struggling to rediscover its voice after being silenced by state repression in the years before and during World War II.[1] Gutai artists emphasized the role of process over product, rejecting the creation of representational objects in favor of presentational modes of action that extended the boundaries of painting into real time and space. In the "Gutai Manifesto," published in 1956, Yoshihara wrote:

> Gutai Art does not alter the material.
> Gutai Art imparts life to the material.
> Gutai Art does not distort the material.
> In Gutai Art, the human spirit and the material shake hands with each other, but keep their distance.... To make the fullest use of the material is to make use of the spirit. By enhancing the spirit, the material is brought to the height of the spirit.[2]

For Yoshihara, art was the direct reflection of the liberated self in the temporal here and now, as expressed through the chance collaboration between physical action and material. The members' use of their bodies as material and the introduction of natural elements and everyday objects such as mud, sand, lightbulbs, and smoke were aimed at reinvesting matter with spirit. In its approach, Gutai shared certain affinities with action painting and *art informel*, a mode of gestural abstraction that became prevalent in Europe during the postwar period, which were both derived in part from Surrealist automatism.[3] Yet members of the Gutai group were intentionally disinterested in the formalist arguments of modern Euro-American abstract art, and were averse to the use of art as political activism or nationalist propaganda.

Shiraga was among the most enterprising of the group, and his action event *Challenging the Mud* (1955), in which he jumped on top of a mud pile and kicked and wrestled with it, remains one of Gutai's most iconic works. Shiraga's foot paintings, which he began shortly before joining Gutai in 1955, also earned him widespread recognition. To create a work such as *Dragons Emerging from the Forest*, the artist would swing back and forth from a rope attached to the ceiling and push wet oil paint with his feet across unstretched canvas placed on the floor. In 1955, Shiraga described the origin of his technique:

> When I first discovered what seemed to be my own talent—when I decided to be "naked," to shed all conventional ideas—forms flew out the window and techniques slipped off my painting knife and shattered. In front of me lay an austere road to originality. Run forward, I thought, run and run, it won't matter if I fall down.... Let me do it with my hands, with my fingers. Then, as I ran, thinking that I was moving forward, it occurred to me: Why not feet? Why don't I paint with my feet?[4]

Made without a brush or any of the usual tools of painting, this work evinces how Shiraga largely abandoned creative control to the caprices of chance while translating his bodily actions into painting. The finished work stands as a record of his unfettered spins, thrashes, and slips—pure bodily expression enacted, in part, as a response to the awareness of humanity's fragility in the aftermath of the destruction of the war.

MM

NOTES

1. Gutai lasted until 1972, the year of Yoshihara's death, but its most fervent period of activity was in the late 1950s and early 1960s.

2. Jiro Yoshihara, "The Gutai Manifesto" (1956), as quoted in Alexandra Munroe, ed. *Japanese Art after 1945: Scream against the Sky* (New York: Harry N. Abrams, 1994), 84. Originally published in Japanese as "Gutaibijutsu sengen," in *Geijutsu shincho* 7, no. 12 (December 1956).

3. Jackson Pollock's all-over drip compositions, with their brute materialism, were recognized as catalysts for the group as a whole. French critic Michel Tapié was introduced to Gutai during a trip to Japan in fall 1957. He commended the group for its affinities with *art informel* and became a conduit between the Japanese group and the Western art world. Allan Kaprow later characterized Gutai action events as forerunners to Happenings.

4. Kazuo Shiraga, "Only Action," *Gutai* 3 (October 20, 1955): 22, as quoted in Munroe, *Japanese Art after 1945*, 372–73.

William Anastasi (American, b. 1933)

Untitled (V. Dwan 10.4.67), 1967
Untitled (Sol LeWitt 11-19-69), 1969
Untitled (12-4-69 Angelo Savelli), 1969
Pencil on paper drawings, 7 1/2 x 11 1/2" each
[p. 39]

Untitled (one gallon of industrial high-gloss enamel, poured), 1966 / 2009
Enamel paint, variable dimensions
[below]

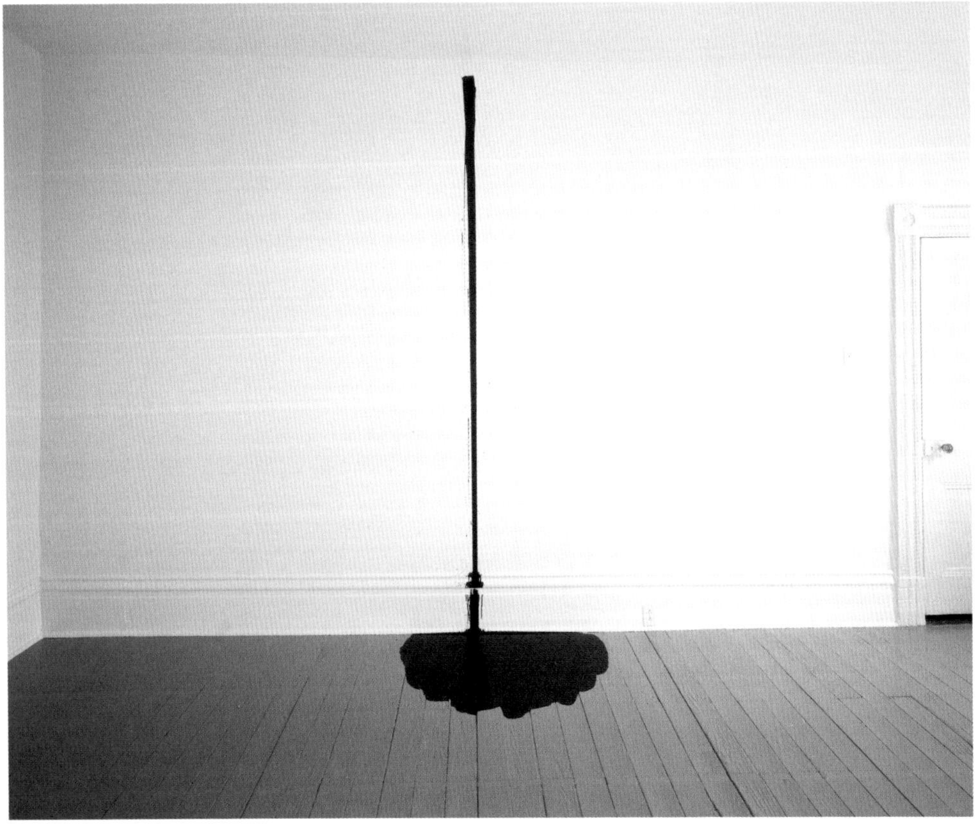

In the 1960s, conceptual artist William Anastasi began a series of "unsighted" works—blind drawings, pocket drawings, and subway drawings—which aimed to bypass artistic control by submitting the graphic process to chance. Inspired by composer John Cage's systematic use of chance as a compositional principle, Anastasi established situations that depend on a combination of accident and predetermined limitations. To create his series of subway drawings, which is still ongoing today, the artist takes a seat on a train (in the 1970s, this often took place on the way to a weekly chess game with Cage), places a sketchpad on his lap, takes a pencil in each hand, rests the points on the paper, holds his elbows stiffly at a 90 degree angle, is careful not to let his back touch the seat, and closes his eyes. He also wears firing-range headphones to block out all sound, transforming a cacophonous situation into an almost meditative one.[1] By giving up control of his hands and the use of his eyes, Anastasi lets the movement of his body, dictated by the rocking of the subway, determine the composition of each drawing. While his rejection of conscious compositional control can be compared to Surrealist automatism, the artist claims no psychological goals, favoring instead an emphasis on physicality and phenomenology. His body becomes in essence a device to absorb and record subtle movements over a given period of time. The resultant drawings are all similar in appearance—composed of two clusters of scrawls, scratches, and scribbles—yet each one reveals subtle variations: the markings appear thicker or more scattered depending on the length of the artist's subway ride and the twists and turns of a given route. When, paradoxically, Anastasi expresses dismay over the fact that there are imitation subway drawings in circulation, we are reminded of how difficult abandoning the self really is.[2]

In his installations originating from the same period as his subway drawings, Anastasi follows the same basic principle of making: the production of an indeterminate result is contingent upon the establishment of specific parameters and arbitrary limits set in advance. To create *Untitled (one gallon of industrial high-gloss enamel, poured)*, for instance, Anastasi pours one gallon of paint down a wall, starting as close to the top of the wall as possible, letting gravity take over as the pigment forms a puddle on the floor. In a sister piece also first created in 1966, the parameters are similar but the paint is thrown against a wall rather than poured. Anastasi's process of pouring and throwing paint, which he spells out in the subtitles of his artworks, wittily subverts the rhetoric of heroic individualism and authentic mark making associated with high-modernist abstraction. The literalness of Anastasi's physical, task-based drawings, combined with his willingness to abdicate authorial responsibility for his art, resonates strongly with the tactics employed by Marcel Duchamp as well as those of numerous conceptual and process-driven projects undertaken throughout the 1960s and 1970s.

MM

NOTES

1. In a 1995 interview with Anne Barclay Morgan, Anastasi stated: "I wear these headphones that make it very quiet, and it could be a train full of people, but once I close my eyes, I am able, for a couple of minutes... not to be there, and to not be there in art, to be somewhere else, away from the artist in me." William Anastasi, interview with Anne Barclay Morgan, *Art Papers* 19, no. 6 (November / December 1995): 25.

2. William Anastasi, conversation with author, December 18, 2008, New York City.

Robert Morris (American, b. 1931)

Untitled, 1967–68
Felt, 180 x 72 x 3/8"

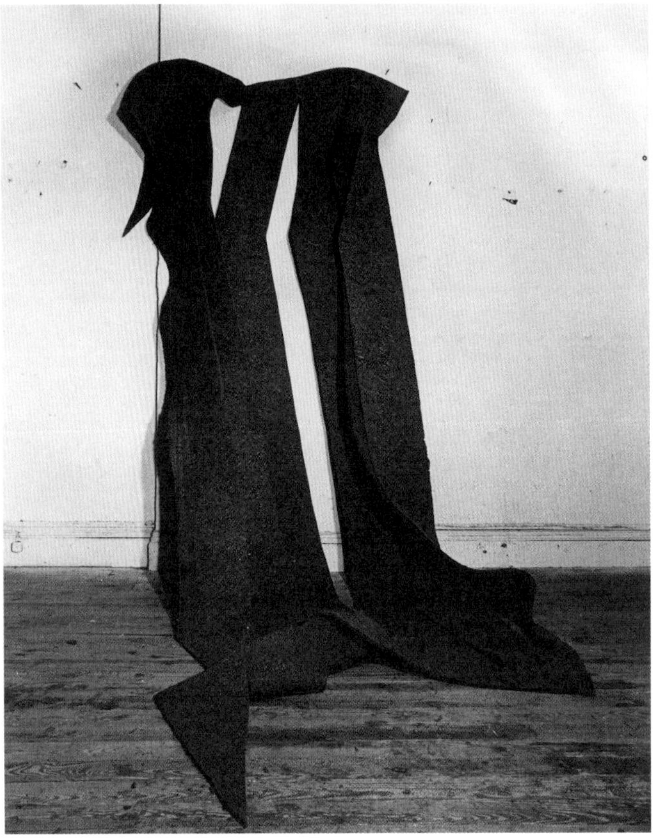

Robert Morris began his career exploring gestural abstraction in San Francisco in the late 1950s, during which time he also began investigations into dance and improvisational theater. Like many artists of his generation who found themselves charged with the reconciliation (or conflation) of Jackson Pollock's process-driven formalism and neo-Dadaist conceptualism via the rediscovery of Marcel Duchamp by avant-garde artists in the late 1950s, Morris sought to bridge elements of formalism and conceptualism. In his case, he turned toward an aesthetic program in which the relationship between process and product, determined in part by the nature of the materials, would be clearly evident. Oscillating between extremes of media and presentation, Morris aggressively confronted the art world with radical reconstructions of sculpture, dance, performance, conceptual art, and film.

After relocating to New York in 1961, Morris was briefly involved with Fluxus and the Judson Dance Theater, both of which were heavily indebted to the work of John Cage, with whom Morris also established a relationship.[1] Following a period of producing objects that directly engaged with Duchamp's propositions regarding chance and the readymade, Morris embarked on his first major critique of formalism with the austere geometry of Minimalist objects and installations. With these simplified objects he called "unitary forms," Morris sought to extend the arguments against the arbitrary subjectivity of the Greenbergian formalism that Jasper Johns and Frank Stella had initiated through the use of predetermined forms and systematic approaches to painting, respectively. In opposition to modernist principles, Morris's Minimalist columns and L-beams demonstrate his desire to "construct instead of arrange," or to replace form with action.[2]

Following several years of producing sculpture and theoretical texts fundamental to the development of Minimalism, Robert Morris quickly changed directions in the late 1960s toward the exploration of a modified aesthetic approach he designated "anti-form." In these works, Morris used flexible materials such as rubber, rope, and heavy yet pliable industrial felt to emphasize the effects of gravity that resulted from hanging, piling, or scattering them in the gallery space. In *Untitled*, he segmented a large sheet of felt with several parallel, lengthwise slices and cut through one end completely, leaving one end hanging and the other lying on the floor. Virtually guaranteed to be unique with every subsequent reinstallation, *Untitled* exemplifies how anti-form maintains the simplified, industrial aesthetic of Minimalism, and continues to eschew the formalist preference for the subjective gesture through the Postminimalist exploitation of natural forces such as gravity. Maintaining the connotations of labor and manufacture that he sought to express through his earlier Minimalist objects, Morris's industrial-grade felt sculptures continued his critique of formalism just as his rectilinear Minimalist counterparts had done, but now with an even more diminished emphasis on causal arrangement. In sculptures like *Untitled*, the ephemeral replaces modernist permanence: "Random piling, loose stacking, hanging, give passing form to the material. Chance is accepted and indeterminacy is implied."[3] Through anti-form, Morris revisited automatism vis-à-vis Abstract Expressionism and repositioned it in the new category of automation, which "serves to remove taste and the personal touch by co-opting forces, images, and processes to replace a step formerly taken in a directing or deciding way by the artist."[4]

Following his experiments with felt sculptures, Morris pursued further measures to critique formalism and the institutional complex of the museum. Later attempts at approaching an art characterized by formlessness included a gallery filled with randomly scattered thread waste material and jets of steam situated outdoors that visually dematerialized in the air.[5] Extending his explorations into process and chance procedures into the 1970s, Morris sought to realize Duchamp's commonly cited edict that the work of art is incomplete until it is received by the spectator. His eponymous exhibition at the Tate Gallery in 1971 is a case in point: viewers were invited to participate in basic activities, such as hauling forms up steel ramps with ropes, kicking a wooden ball around a circular track, or negotiating various tightropes, balance beams, and vertical surfaces for climbing, each of which resulted in a continuous reorganization of space based in processes beyond the control of the artist.[6]

BB

NOTES

1. For more on Robert Morris's relationship to Fluxus, see Maurice Berger, *Labyrinths: Robert Morris, Minimalism, and the 1960s* (New York: Harper & Row, 1989), 28. For more on the relationship between Morris and John Cage, see Branden W. Joseph, "Robert Morris and John Cage: Reconstructing a Dialogue," *October* 81 (Summer 1997): 59-69.

2. Robert Morris, "Some Notes on the Phenomenology of Making: The Search for the Motivated," *Artforum* 8 (April 1970): 62–66, reprinted in *Continuous Project Altered Daily: The Writings of Robert Morris*, (Cambridge, MA: MIT Press, 1993), 91. No editor given.

3. Robert Morris, "Anti Form," *Artforum* 6 (April 1968): 33–35, reprinted in *Continuous Project*, 46.

4. Morris, "Some Notes," 87.

5. For a criticism of anti-form as both recognizably formal and playing into institutional practices, see Allan Kaprow, "The Shape of the Art Environment: How Anti Form Is Anti-Form?," *Artforum* 6 (Summer 1968): 32–33.

6. See Berger, *Labyrinths*, 121-23.

GAMES AND SYSTEMS OF RANDOM ORDERING

The implementation of randomizing systems in artistic creation has held a sustained allure for the avant-garde as a way of redefining the work of art, the self, and the nature of representation.

MARCEL DUCHAMP
VICTOR BRAUNER
JACQUES HÉROLD
VIOLETTE HÉROLD
YVES TANGUY
ANDRÉ BRETON
JACQUELINE LAMBA
RAOUL UBAC
JOHN CAGE
ELLSWORTH KELLY
GEORGE BRECHT
LA MONTE YOUNG
GEORGE MACIUNAS
RAY JOHNSON
NAM JUNE PAIK
BEN VAUTIER
DANIEL SPOERRI
ALISON KNOWLES
FRANÇOIS MORELLET
ÖYVIND FAHLSTRÖM

Tossing coins, rolling dice, playing cards, drawing from a hat, and using random numbers to determine compositional choices are just a few of the techniques that artists have employed to diminish personal bias in the selection and placement of formal elements. These practices rely not on pure chance (a complete absence of intention or cause), but on mechanical procedures and the laws of probability to guarantee the production of unforeseen outcomes. Random systems have been applied to the selection and arrangement of sounds by composers, movement and pace by dancers, linguistic elements by poets, form and color by painters, and three-dimensional form by sculptors.

Marcel Duchamp's notion of "canned chance," describing processes that depend on chance yet paradoxically attempt to somehow fix or standardize it, and experimental composer John Cage's rigorous implementation of "chance operations" provide two key touchstones in this section. To determine the organization of sound events within a time structure, for example, Cage often listed in a chart all of the elements—pitch, duration, instrumentation, volume—that he wanted to use. He then threw dice in order to determine their characteristics and order, sometimes consulting the Chinese *I Ching* (*Book of Changes*). His rigorously systematic practice subsequently motivated a wide range of conceptual projects in which artists stipulate a work's parameters but leave the results to circumstance.

Since chance used in this way necessitates a program of operations that can become impossibly complicated, many artists employing such randomizing methods have confined themselves to a vocabulary of simple geometric forms. In the work of French artist François Morellet and American artist Ellsworth Kelly, for instance, chance and system are brought together through the use of charts, grids, and random numbers. The recourse to aleatory processes to determine the form, distribution of components, and placement of color within their abstract compositions recasts the artist in the role of manager, following a predetermined premise to its logical conclusion. Random ordering then becomes both the subject of the work and its means of production.

The exploration of games of chance is another popular variation of generative systems. For the Surrealists working in the 1920s and 1930s, creative collaboration through games was among the many automatist strategies employed to liberate the unconscious from its rational restrictions, unleashing the marvelous or the irrational. The fascination with the capacity of play and games to free the mind of critical control and foster metaphorical and analogical combinations of words and images took various forms. Among the most celebrated of these ludic strategies was the collaborative drawing and writing game, the *cadavre exquis* (exquisite corpse), in which multiple players make contributions without seeing those of the other participants. While the rules remain the same, each round yields a different result, testifying to the game's ability to open up new modes of creation and representation from within the bounds of the system.

The post-World War II period witnessed a renewed interest in play and games on the part of artists and theorists alike, as evidenced by the wide translation in the late 1940s of Johan Huizinga's sociological study *Homo Ludens: A Study of the Play-Element in Culture* and the appearance of French philosopher Roger Caillois's *Man, Play, and Games* in 1958.[1] Intrigued by the effects of chance, rules, competition, and amusement that games engender, Fluxus artists working in the 1960s devised puzzles, game boxes, and event scores that invited open interpretation and viewer participation. According to George Maciunas, the founder of Fluxus, the group's primary objectives were social; games provided a kind of framework for interaction and for the production of indeterminate outcomes, a device that appeared especially subversive in comparison with the homogeneity of postwar spectacle culture. For some artists, the focus on ludic experience rather than object-based art was a means of liberating art from the demands of the market. For others, participatory games were designed to democratize the creative act, deemphasizing the artist's role as author and giving agency to the viewer instead. In George Brecht's *Water Yam* (1963), for instance, cards with brief instructions direct play; the artist merely provides the concept or method by which a diversity of forms are then created or enacted by an outside participant. Indeterminacy is in this case introduced, not through compositional method, but through each performer's subjective choices, thus presaging a shift toward the radical open-endedness of reception-based meaning in the arts.

NOTES

1. Benjamin Buchloh notes the importance of play in the 1950s and its link to consumer culture. During the 1950s, he writes, "a theory of games would reemerge as a cultural project at the very moment of an ever-increasing instrumentalization of libidinal desire through consumer culture." Benjamin H. D. Buchloh, "Robert Watts: Inanimate Objects—Inanimate Subjects," in Benjamin H. D. Buchloh and Judith F. Rodenbeck, *Experiments in the Everyday: Allan Kaprow and Robert Watts, Events, Objects, Documents* (New York: Columbia University, Miriam and Ira D. Wallach Art Gallery, 1999), 25 n4.

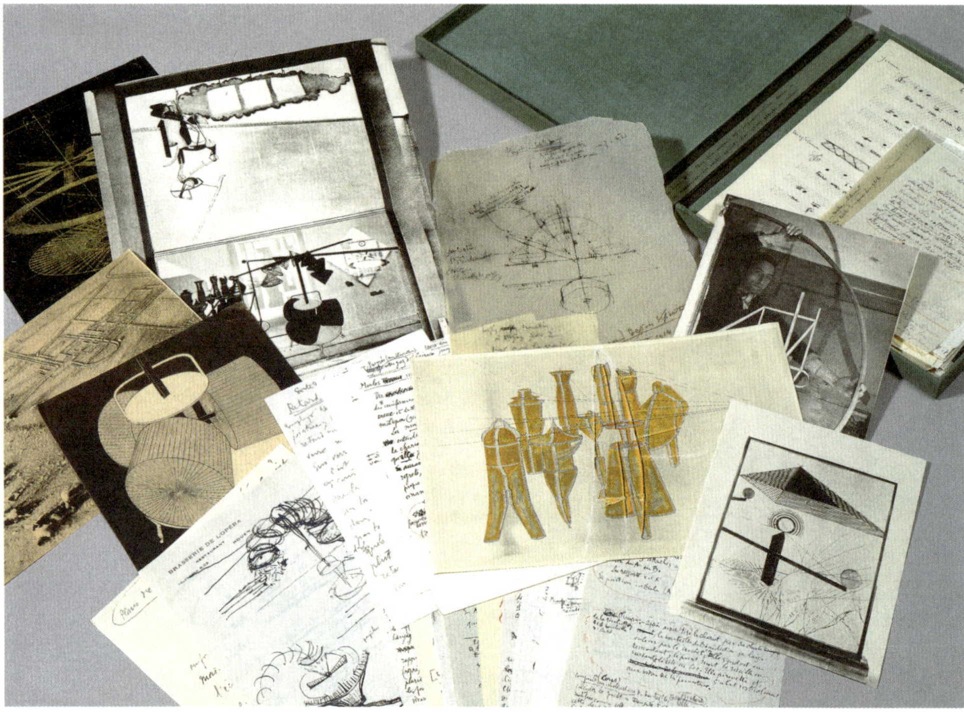

Marcel Duchamp

(American, born France, 1887–1968)

Three Standard Stoppages, 1964 (replica of 1913–14 original)
Thread on canvas attached to glass, wood sticks, enclosed in wood croquet case, 51 x 11 1/8 x 9" (case)
[p. 10]

La Mariée mise á nu par ses célibataires même (La Boîte verte) (The Bride Stripped Bare by Her Bachelors, Even [The Green Box]), 1934
Ninety-four facsimile documents in a green suede box, 13 1/16 x 11 1/8 x 1"
[above]

Just as Marcel Duchamp demonstrated with his introduction of the readymade that virtually any object selected by an artist could be understood as a work of art, so too did his groundbreaking inauguration of chance procedures in art establish that any force could be a creative one if specifically chosen by the artist to act in such a capacity. With the introduction of the element of chance, Duchamp could distance himself from the creative process, circumventing the insertion of his own judgment or taste. Duchamp called this process in which the parameters are defined by the artist and the outcomes are controlled by outside forces or determinants "canned chance," the best known and most influential example of which is arguably his *Three Standard Stoppages* from 1913–14.

During a period of intense productivity beginning in 1913 and gradually waning toward 1923, Duchamp executed what many consider his most important work, *The Bride Stripped Bare by Her Bachelors, Even* (known as *The Large Glass*), a complex object of oil, varnish, lead foil, wire, and dust on two glass panels that he left "definitively unfinished" in 1923. His notes for *The Large Glass*, which were intended to serve as a textual analog to its visual manifestation, along with notes for numerous other projects, were collected by the artist in 1934 in *The Bride Stripped Bare by Her Bachelors, Even (The Green Box)*, which became known simply as *The Green Box*. Carefully reproduced on scraps of paper torn to mimic the original notes, the written materials in *The Green Box* are arranged in no particular order, leaving the viewer free to leaf randomly through these unbound sheets. The notes that comprise *The Green Box* contain instructions for chance operations inspired by the proto-Surrealist language games of Duchamp's early hero, the French poet Raymond Roussel, as well as Duchamp's own unique understanding of advancements in contemporary mathematics. *The Green Box* also contains a facsimile of *Erratum Musical*, Duchamp's 1913 musical score created entirely through chance procedures, including the artist and his two sisters drawing "as many notes out of a hat as there were syllables in the dictionary definition of the word '*imprimer*' ('*empreinte*'), picked up by chance."[1] The seventy-five musical notes were inserted in the order chosen for three voices, but with no instructions for how the work should be performed.

Another note in *The Green Box* reads "3 Standard Stops = canned chance—1914," a reference to a note in Duchamp's *Box of 1914* that lays out the procedure through which he created the *Three Standard Stoppages*. Dropping three horizontal strings one meter in length from a height of one meter onto a horizontal plane, to which they were immediately attached with varnish to maintain their respective shapes, Duchamp enacted the course of action that would result in the melding of pseudo-science ("playful physics," in Duchamp's words), mathematics, and chance that formed the foundation of *The Large Glass*. The *Stoppages* subsequently became the model for other works derived from *The Large Glass* that incorporated chance and gravity, such as the photograph *Dust Breeding* of 1920, in which Duchamp and his frequent collaborator Man Ray photographed the lower portion of *The Large Glass* horizontally positioned and covered in months worth of dust. As a critique of the notion of standardized measurement, it is worth noting that the *Stoppages* was created shortly after Duchamp was asked to withdraw his *Nude Descending a Staircase, No. 2* (1912) from the Salon des Indépendents.[2] An embittered Duchamp could have intended the *Stoppages* as a critique of all standards, including notions of taste and quality in art. "In itself it was not an important work of art," Duchamp told Katharine Kuh in an interview, "but for me it opened the way—the way to escape from those traditional methods of expression long associated with art.... For me the *Three Stoppages* was a first gesture liberating me from the past."[3]

BB

NOTES

1. Marcel Duchamp, as quoted in Ecke Bonk, *Marcel Duchamp: The Box in a Valise*, trans. David Britt (New York:Rizzoli,1989), 10. According to Arturo Schwarz, the notes were likely derived from a cut-up piano score. This type of procedure was anticipated by Lewis Carroll, the tala and raga systems in Indian music, and even by Mozart. See Arturo Schwarz, ed., *The Complete Works of Marcel Duchamp*, third edition, (New York: Delano Greenridge, 1997), 187.

2. On the relationship of the *Stoppages* to non-Euclidean geometry and the French standard meter, see Linda Dalrymple Henderson, *Duchamp in Context: Science and Technology in* The Large Glass *and Related Works* (Princeton, NJ: Princeton University Press, 1998), 61–63.

3. Marcel Duchamp, in Katharine Kuh, "Marcel Duchamp," in her *The Artist's Voice: Talks with Seventeen Artists*, (New York: Harper & Row, 1962), 81.

Victor Brauner
(Romanian, 1903–1966)

Jacques Hérold
(Romanian, b. 1910)

Yves Tanguy
(French, 1900–1955)

Exquisite Corpse, c. 1932
Graphite and collage on paper,
10 1/2 x 7 7/8"

André Breton
(French, 1896–1966)

Jacqueline Lamba
(French, 1910–1993)

Yves Tanguy
(French, 1900–1955)

Untitled "Cadavre exquis" ("Exquisite Corpse"), 1938
Collage on graph paper,
10 15/16 x 5 1/2"
[right]

Victor Brauner
(Romanian, 1903–1966)

Jacques Hérold
(Romanian, 1910–1987)

Violette Hérold

Yves Tanguy
(French, 1900–1955)

Raoul Ubac
(Belgian, 1910–1985)

Untitled "Cadavre exquis" ("Exquisite Corpse"), 1938
Graphite and collage on paper,
10 3/8 x 8 1/16"
[p. 37]

In 1925, the Surrealists began creating what they called "exquisite corpse" texts and images. Based on parlor and children's games, the technique for making these bizarre compositions involves the collective and random creation of a text or figure according to a set of rules. In the written version of the game, each collaborator adds to a composition in sequence, either by writing a series of predetermined classes of words (adjective, noun, verb, et cetera) or by responding to the last word or phrase written by the previous participant. Founding member André Breton explained that the goal of this technique was "to provide the most paradoxical confrontation possible between the elements of speech, so that human communication, diverted thus initially from its logical path, should impart the greatest possible sense of adventure to the mind recording it."[1] The name the Surrealists gave to this playful process comes from a phrase that resulted from one of the first sentences they produced in this way: "The exquisite corpse will drink the new wine" ("Le cadavre exquis boira le vin nouveau").

The visual version of the game involves the first player drawing a head (or a head-shaped form), then folding the paper over so that what has been drawn cannot be seen by the second person, who draws the next portion of the body, folds the paper again and passes it along to another, and so on until the figure is complete. Often participants drew objects that stand in for body parts, creating a hybrid figure made up of incongruous pieces that require the viewer to use his or her imagination to interpret the results. In the 1930s, the Surrealists refined this game by including collage techniques. For example, a piece by André Breton, Jacqueline Lamba, and Yves Tanguy is made up of cutouts of drawings. A hot air balloon turned upside-down serves as the head with a cup and saucer and two birds for ears, while a carrot (or some other root vegetable) functions as the neck and a shoe forms one of the figure's shoulders. However, the end product was not entirely coincidental. As with the group's automatic writings and drawings, the Surrealists often added to their exquisite corpse images.

The aleatory and communal characteristics of this method appealed to the Surrealists, who valued its de-emphasis on skill and single authorship as well as the seemingly endless number of combinations it could generate. Although the more advanced works of the 1930s indicate the degree to which the technique had been adapted over the years, they also bear witness to the Surrealists' broader interest in the continued manipulation of the creative potential of a game with rules to generate unforeseen results.

EH

NOTES

1. André Breton, "The Exquisite Corpse, Its Exaltation" (1948), in his *Surrealism and Painting*, trans. Simon Watson Taylor (New York: Harper & Row, 1972), 288.

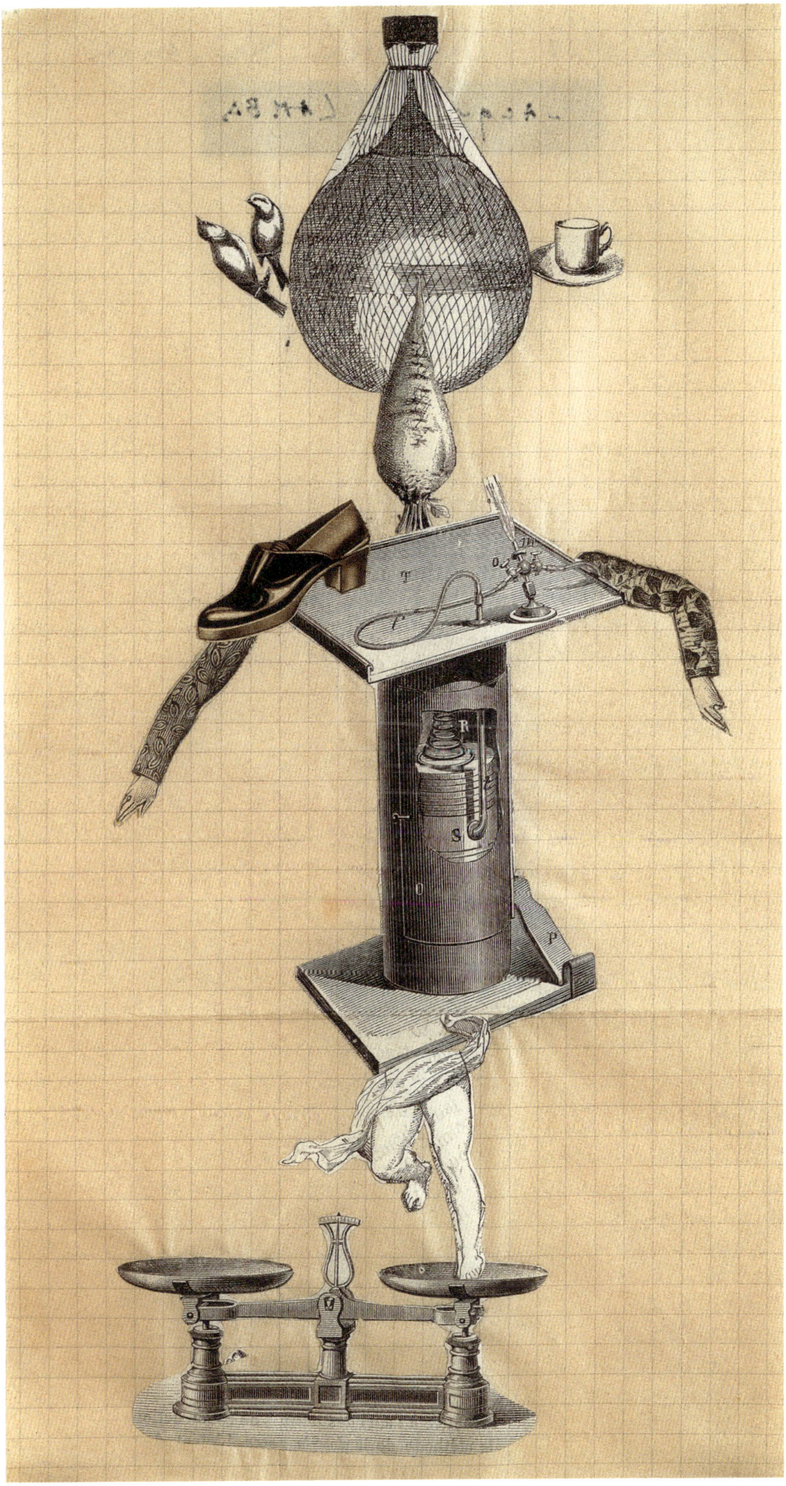

John Cage (American, 1912–1992)

Score for *Music of Changes*, 1951

© Henmar Press Inc., 1961
Sheet music, 11 11/16 x 8 7/8"

Score for *Fontana Mix*, 1958

© Henmar Press Inc., 1960
Sheet music on mylar, variable dimensions
[right]

While Marcel Duchamp's experiments with aleatory music may have preceded John Cage's by several decades, Cage remains the composer most immediately associated with the exploration of what he called "chance operations" in the composition and performance of music. In the 1930s, Cage studied with a succession of avant-garde composers, most notably Arnold Schoenberg, one of the pioneers of atonality, or music composed without the use of a traditional tonal or key structure, often resulting in chord progressions that may sound random or dissonant. In numerous instances, however, Cage contended that the most profound influence on his work was Marcel Duchamp, whose efforts to undermine traditional ideas of aesthetic judgment in creative art, as well as his use of chance and found objects, continued to challenge and drive Cage toward work of an increasingly progressive and uncompromising nature.[1] Other influences included a mixture of Indian philosophies via Gita Sarabhai and Ananda Coomaraswamy, Zen Buddhism, the fourteenth-century mystic Meister Eckhardt, avant-garde composer Morton Feldman's use of graph paper to notate sounds numerically, Merce Cunningham's revolutionary incorporation of everyday movements into dance, Robert Rauschenberg's *White Paintings* (1951), and, perhaps the most significant of all, the ancient Chinese oracular text the *I Ching*, or *Book of Changes*.[2] In turn, Cage himself became an extraordinarily influential figure through his compositions and lectures as well as his courses at Black Mountain College and the New School for Social Research, which were formative in the development of both Happenings and Fluxus.

The key to Cage's approach to writing music was discontinuity, or the elimination of any subjective or conscious arrangements of sound in a composition by employing procedures through which "sounds would be made to follow each other in a manner indeterminate of the other sounds in the sequence."[3] Few of Cage's compositions exemplify discontinuity better than the groundbreaking solo piano piece, inspired by processes described in the *I Ching*, titled *Music of Changes*, his first work based wholly on chance operations, wherein each decision regarding "his selection of pitches, nonpitched percussive sounds, durations, amplitude, tempo, and other variables are not dictated by conscious choice ... but rather are derived from the tossing of coins, which in turn refer to a carefully prepared list of possibilities."[4]

Indeterminacy, by which subjectivity is removed from both the composition and the performance of the work, often taking advantage of "non-intentional" sounds, is at the heart of Cage's *Fontana Mix* (1958), the score for which consists of ten transparencies with points, ten opaque paper sheets with six different types of lines, a graph, and a line (the latter two on transparencies), all to be used to plot out a composition.[5] The score for *Fontana Mix* contains no music, only the means by which a composer can arrange six different classes of sounds or actions based on the interactions of the lines, points, and the graph. While Cage used prerecorded environmental and artificial (man-made) sounds in *Fontana*

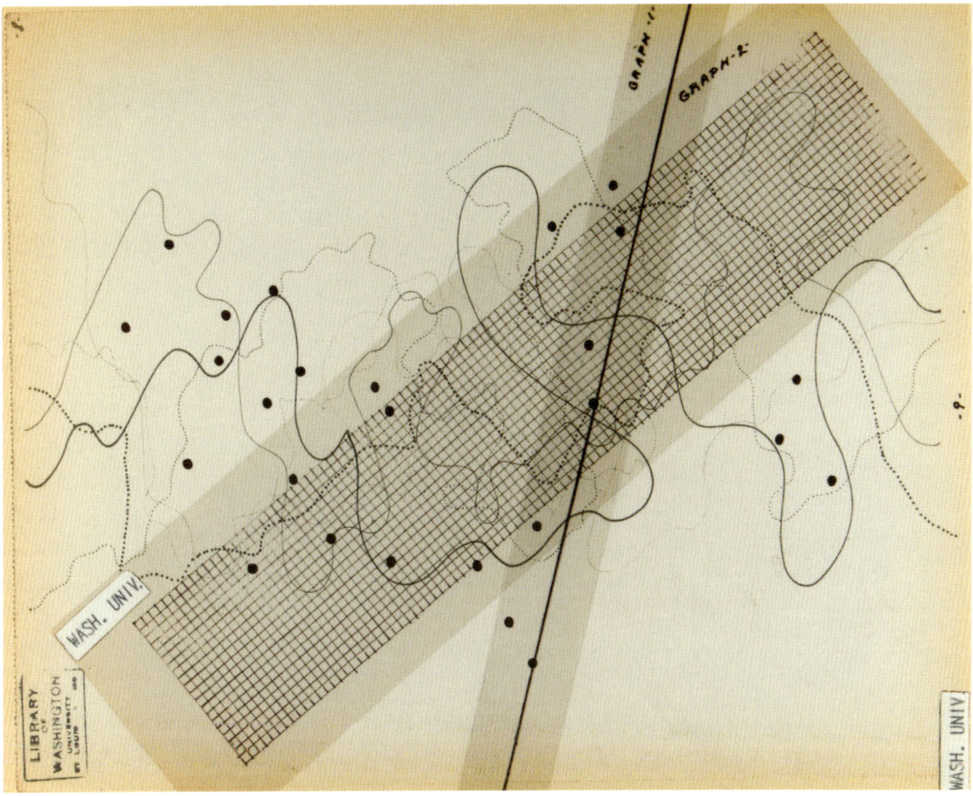

Mix to create an eponymous sound collage of spliced, multichannel audiotape (as well as numerous other compositions in the ensuing years), he indicated in the score that the material "may be used freely for instrumental, vocal and theatrical purposes."[6] Scores such as *Fontana Mix* may offer the impression that Cage used both chance operations and indeterminacy to avoid making any choices. For Cage, however, the critical choices ("composing," in the traditional sense) are already made prior to the implementation of the procedure—or, as the composer himself said: "My choices consist in choosing what questions to ask."[7]

BB

NOTES

1. See Margorie Perloff, "'A duchamp unto my self': 'Writing through' Marcel," in *John Cage: Composer in America*, ed. Marjorie Perloff and Charles Junkerman (Chicago: University of Chicago Press, 1994): 100–101.

2. The *I Ching* has been used for centuries to predict trends and shifts in the universe through interpreting the results of chance procedures such as coin tosses with the sets of diagrams provided.

3. Branden W. Joseph, "Robert Morris and John Cage: Reconstructing a Dialogue," *October* 81 (Summer 1997): 63.

4. Elliott Schwartz and Daniel Godfrey, *Music since 1945: Issues, Materials, and Literature* (New York: Schirmer Books, 1993), 71.

5. For more on Cage's distinction between chance and indeterminacy, see John Cage, "Composition as Process: Indeterminacy," in his *Silence* (Middletown, CT: Wesleyan University Press, 1961), 35–40.

6. John Cage, score for *Fontana Mix* (New York: Henmar Press, 1960), n.p.

7. John Cage, as quoted in Constance Lewallen, "Cage and the Structure of Chance," in *Through John Cage's Music, Poetry, and Art*, ed. David W. Bernstein and Christopher Hatch (Chicago: University of Chicago Press, 2001), 235.

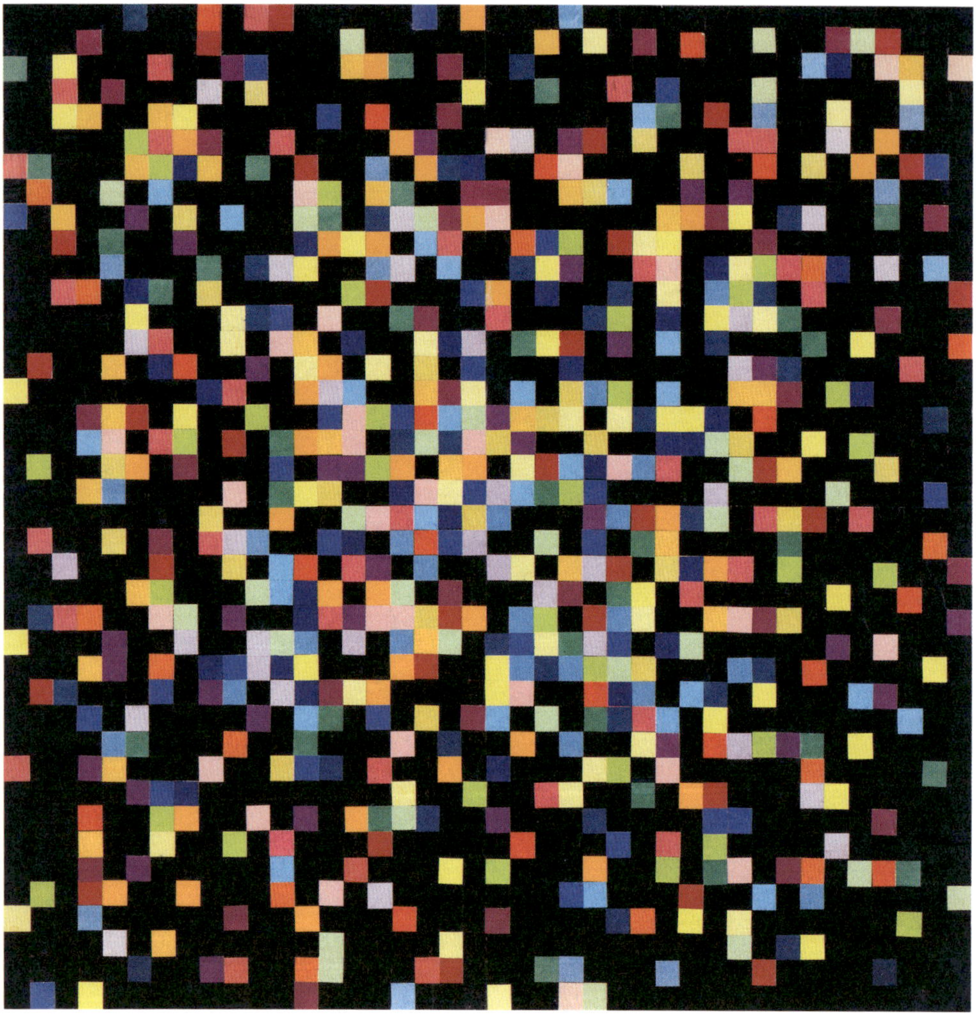

Ellsworth Kelly (American, b. 1923)

Spectrum Colors Arranged by Chance V, 1951
Collage on paper, 39 x 39"

Spectrum Colors Arranged by Chance V, one of eight in a series of collages Ellsworth Kelly composed during his time in France (1948–1954), marks a turn in his work toward a more systematic approach to chance methodologies than his earlier experiments with techniques such as collage and various modes of automatism.[1] Throughout his experiments with chance, Kelly, much like his Dada and Surrealist predecessors, struggled to strike an acceptable balance between chance and control, artistic intuition and systems of determination. With his turn to the grid in 1951, such as in his cut-up drawings and *Spectrum* series, he began a more comprehensive examination of this fundamental opposition.

The origins of the *Spectrum* series can be traced to an earlier drawing by Kelly, *Study for Seine* (1950). In this piece, Kelly drew a grid, within which he penciled in squares systematically. He would start on either end and pencil in an increasing number of squares—from one to forty—in each column as he advanced toward the center. The vertical placement of the squares, however, was random, determined by numbers he drew from a hat. This playful compositional technique was the basis of Kelly's black and white painting, *Seine* (1951), and of his *Spectrum* series, to which the artist added another variable: color.[2]

For the *Spectrum* collages, Kelly cut out multiple squares of paper in many (approximately eighteen to twenty) colors, arbitrarily assigning a number to each color.[3] He then plotted the numbers onto a large gridded piece of paper according to various pseudo-mathematical systems he had devised.[4] Finally, he methodically arranged the squares according to the location determined by their numbers, placing all squares of one color at a time, so that the final composition was not apparent until the very end.[5] The grid became Kelly's means of balancing determination and chance, as it provided a structure upon which his random systems could be registered as such.[6]

The introduction of color posed a challenge to the original system Kelly devised for *Seine*, as it raised the possibility that unintended color patterns and even figures might emerge, interfering with the balanced, if random, arrangement he sought.[7] Obeying the rules he established for the *Spectrum* series, Kelly accepted the results as a part of the game he had created for himself. His ultimate lack of control over the outcome, however, may explain why he chose to turn only one of these compositions into a painting.[8] Among Kelly's last explorations of the creative potential of chance, the *Spectrum* collages mark a critical moment in his career. Upon completion of the series, he began working with fewer colors and focusing on more controlled experimentations with form.

EH

NOTES

1. See the catalog entries in this volume on Ellsworth Kelly's *Children's Leftovers Arranged by Chance* and *Brushstrokes Cut into Forty-Nine Squares and Arranged by Chance* (p. 82); *Glass Roof Pattern, Charenton* (p. 80); and *Automatic Drawing* (p. 100).

2. While the first collage in the series mimics the composition and rectangular shape of *Seine*, the rest of the works are square, measuring just over three feet square (they range from 37 1/2 inches square to 44 inches square).

3. Kelly most likely chose the word "spectrum" in the title to emphasize the detached, objective nature of the piece.

4. Kelly worked out calculations and numerical progressions in his graph paper notebooks in advance, altering the systems as needed to yield a suitable result. The size of each unit of the grid (and thus each paper square) was determined by the dimensions of the overall composition. In *Spectrum Colors Arranged by Chance V*, he divided the dimensions of the piece (39 inches square) by the number of rows and columns he wished to include (forty), so that each square is a little less than one inch square. See Jack Cowart, "Method and Motif: Ellsworth Kelly's 'Chance' Grids and His Development of Color Panel Paintings," in *Ellsworth Kelly: The Years in France, 1948–1954*, ed. Yve Alain-Bois, Jack Cowart, and Alfred Pacquement (Washington, DC: National Gallery of Art; Munich: Prestel-Verlag, 1992), 45 n26.

5. In the first four collages, the colors are clustered toward the center, first against a white ground and then a black ground. Beginning with *Spectrum Colors Arranged by Chance V*, the squares are increasingly evenly distributed throughout the composition, until in the final two works there is no sense of a background at all.

6. See Yve-Alain Bois, *Ellsworth Kelly: The Early Drawings, 1948–1955* (Cambridge, MA: Harvard University Art Museum; Winterthur, Switzerland: Kunstmuseum Winterthur, 1999), 25.

7. See Yve-Alain Bois, "Ellsworth Kelly in France: Anti-Composition in Its Many Guises," in *Ellsworth Kelly: The Years in France*, 26; and Cowart, "Method and Motif," 43.

8. The painting, *Spectrum Colors Arranged by Chance* (1951–53), is based on *Spectrum VI*.

George Brecht (American, 1926–2008)

Chance Painting, 1957

Ink-stained bed sheet, 70 7/8 x 86 5/8"
[right]

Chance-Imagery, 1957 / 1966

Artist's pamphlet, 8 3/8 x 5 5/16"
[below]

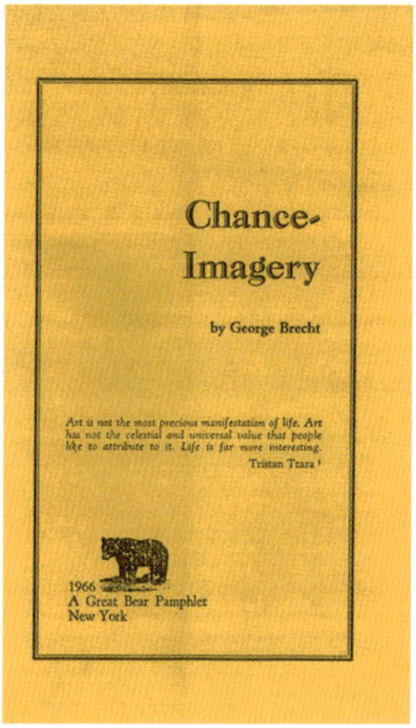

Even before he joined Allan Kaprow, Al Hansen, Dick Higgins, Jackson Mac Low, and Robert Whitman in John Cage's weekly class on experimental music at the New School for Social Research in 1958, George Brecht had already investigated a series of chance procedures that an artist could use to avoid "the biases engrained in our personality by our culture and personal past history" in his seminal essay of 1957, *Chance-Imagery*.[1] Following a summary of the advancements in chance operations employed by the artists of the Dada and Surrealist movements and an acknowledgment of the model of Zen Buddhism, in this essay Brecht went on to position Jackson Pollock's automatic painting technique as the most significant advancement in the use of chance. "Pollock achieved a profound, sustained and irrational synthesis of all the principles which had preceded him in Dada," Brecht wrote of the artist. "His paintings seem much less manifestations of one of a group of techniques for releasing the unconscious (as the Dada experiments seemed), than they do of a single, integrated use of chance as a means of unlocking the deepest possible grasp of nature in its broadest sense."[2]

Chance-Imagery was written while Brecht was engaged with a variety of experiments with chance techniques, including his *Chance Paintings*. To produce these seemingly expressive paintings, Brecht used "a bed sheet altered with blotted ink and marble, bunched up and left to dry in all kinds of 'expressive' ways, none of which were produced, directly, by the hand of the artist."[3] By reconstructing an Abstract Expressionist painting through artificial, systematic, and repeatable means, Brecht effectively deconstructed and demystified the process of 1950s action painting to the extent that the painting, devoid of soul searching or exploration of the unconscious mind, becomes entirely conceptual.

As a scientist as well as an artist (he worked for several years as a chemist for Johnson & Johnson), Brecht was able to meld the intuitive chance procedures he found already in use in the art world with what he termed "randomness," a more empirical, mathematical process, such as random number generation, the aim of which, when combined with other chance procedures into "compound chance events," was to completely eliminate personal bias. Brecht was not only trained in this kind of structured, experimental approach, he soon came to favor

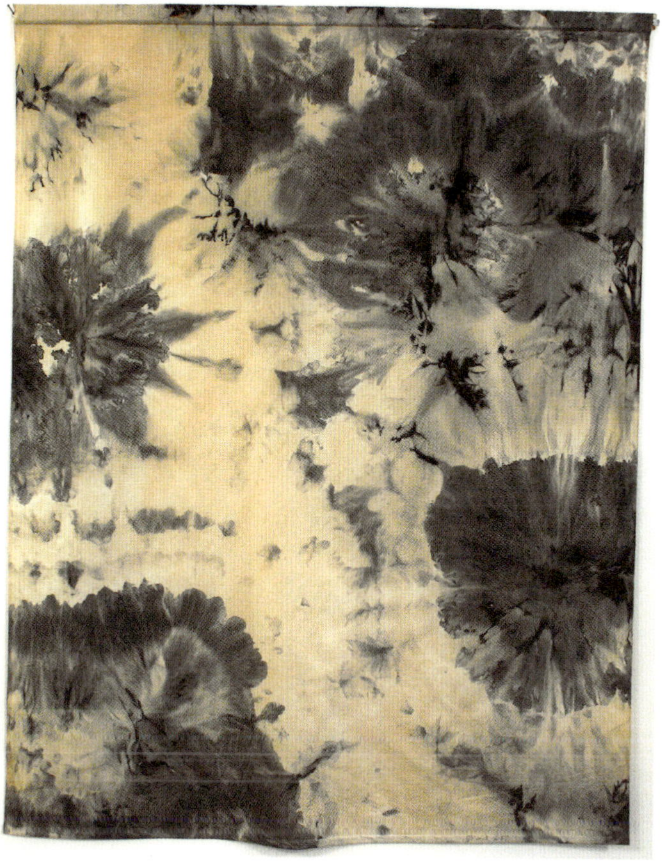

the underlying empiricism of projects like Marcel Duchamp's *Three Standard Stoppages* [Cat., p. 126] and Cage's *I Ching*-inspired coin flips [Cat., p. 130] over the intuitive subjectivity of automatist painting. In a 1965 addendum to *Chance-Imagery*, Brecht wrote: "In 1957 I had only recently met John Cage and had not yet seen clearly that the most important implications of chance lay in his work rather than in Pollock's. Nor could I have foreseen the resolution of the distinction between choice and chance which was to occur in my own work."[4] This latter distinction of "chance and choice" was fundamental to the development of his pioneering new medium, the event score, a remarkable and radical re-envisioning of Cage's "found sound" into a process that would require performers of the score to make decisions over which Brecht exercised no control, thus allowing the artist greater freedom to focus on the parameters of the event rather than specifics of how each action was to be carried out.[5]

BB

NOTES

1. George Brecht, *Chance-Imagery* (1957), reissued with an addendum by the artist (New York: Great Bear Pamphlet / Something Else Press, 1966), 14.

2. Ibid., 6.

3. Julia Robinson, *George Brecht: Events, A Heterospective*, ed. Alfred M. Fischer (Cologne: Walther König, 2005), 28.

4. Ibid., 15.

5. For more on Brecht's event scores, see Julia Robinson, "The Brechtian Event Score: A Structure in Fluxus," *Performance Research* 7, no. 3 (September 2002): 110–23.

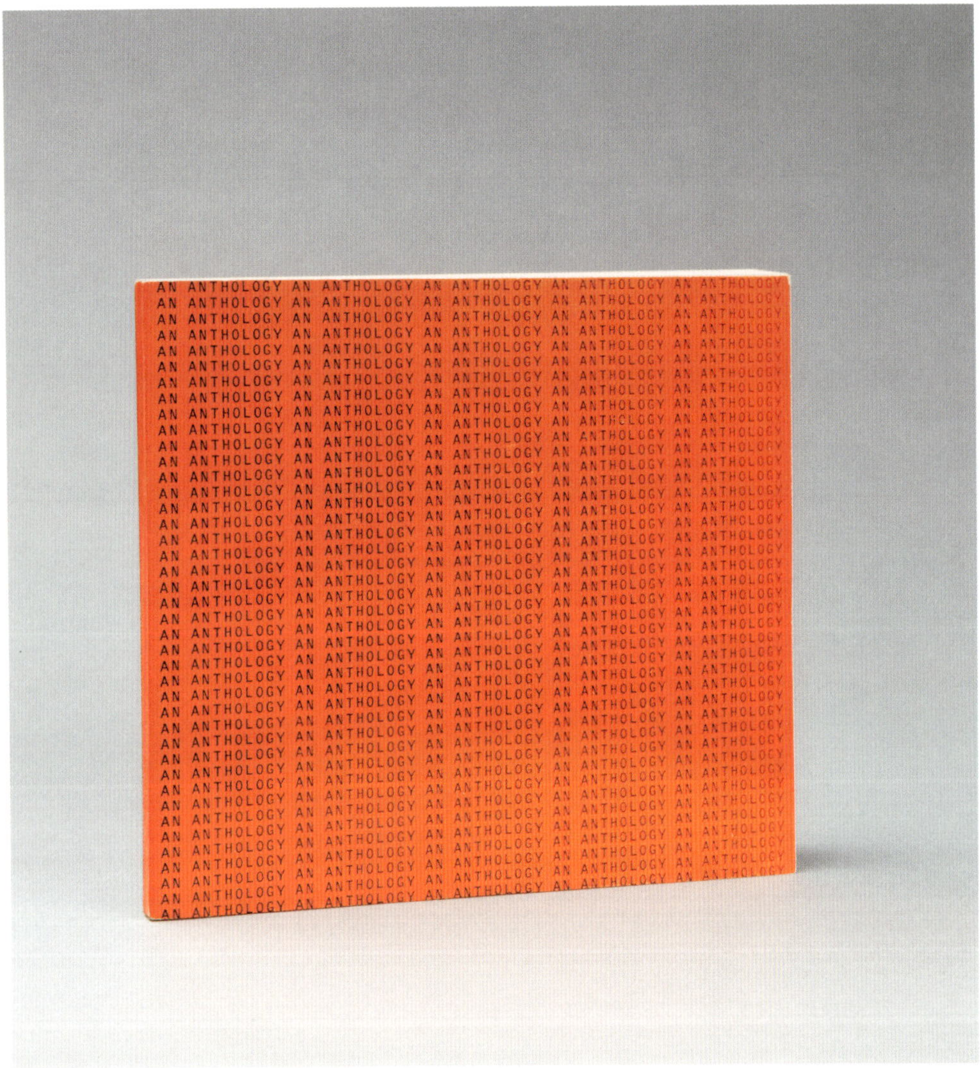

La Monte Young (American, b. 1935)
George Maciunas (American, 1931–1978)

An Anthology, 1963
Artist's book, 8 1/8 x 9 1/16"
Published by Jackson Mac Low and La Monte Young, New York

The first of many compendia offered by the group of international artists, writers, and musicians forming the core of Fluxus, *An Anthology of Chance Operations: Concept Art, Anti-art, Indeterminacy, Improvisation, Meaningless Work, Natural Disasters, Plans of Action, Stories, Diagrams, Music, Poetry, Essays, Dance, Constructions, Mathematics, Compositions* (generally called *An Anthology*) is a collection of music scores, concrete poetry, choreography, event scores, essays, proposals for projects, songs, and other materials from twenty-six contributors. The book begins with George Brecht's *Motor Vehicle Sundown (Event)*, a virtual symphony of motion, light, and sound produced by and within an ensemble of automobiles, with the duration of each action determined by chance. Like Brecht's event score (which was dedicated to John Cage), many of the entries were created by, or intended to be performed using, one or more chance procedures, through which the artist, composer, or choreographer, after setting the parameters of the action, cedes control over the artwork or performance to the viewer or performer. Jackson Mac Low, for example, included a score titled *Thanks: A Simultaneity for People*, the instructions for which describe a cacophonous sound collage of "utterances," defined as anything from a sentence to "any other sounds produced in the mouth, throat or chest." Walter de Maria's *Surprise Box*, one of his several proposals for artworks, consists of a box in which the participant removes the object found therein and replaces it with a new object. The book concludes with La Monte Young's compositions that clearly reflect the influence of Cage's *4'33"*, calling for notes of virtually limitless duration, feeding the piano hay and water, and pushing the piano against the wall to the point of exhaustion on the part of the participant.

The works within *An Anthology* provide classic examples of the ways in which Fluxus artists structured events and other performances, such that the indeterminacy of the result of the actions was dependent upon the individual choices of the participants, which cannot be controlled by the artist or composer. Prefiguring the collectivist *Flux Year Boxes* and *Fluxkits* assembled by founding Fluxus artist George Maciunas [Cat., p. 146], *An Anthology* began as a journal called *Beatitude East*, intended to be the East Coast equivalent of the West Coast avant-garde music magazine, *Beatitude West*.[1] Edited by composer La Monte Young, with the assistance of writer and artist Jackson Mac Low, and designed by Maciunas, *An Anthology* is often listed among the official Fluxus publications. While the book does not contain the word "Fluxus" anywhere, it was advertised in Fluxus publications, included in larger Fluxus anthologies, and sold by the *European Mail-Order Warehouse / Fluxshop*.[2]

BB

NOTES

1. See Hannah Higgins, *Fluxus Experience* (Berkeley: University of California Press, 2002), 2.

2. See Jon Hendricks's comprehensive chronology of Fluxus art and events, *Fluxus Codex* (Detroit: Gilbert and Lila Silverman Fluxus Collection; New York: Harry N. Abrams, 1988), 40.

Ray Johnson (American, 1927–1995)

Year, c. 1960–61

Cardboard box with approximately 120 envelopes containing cut cardboard collage fragments, many with color and all perforated, 10 x 13 9/16 x 16 5/16"

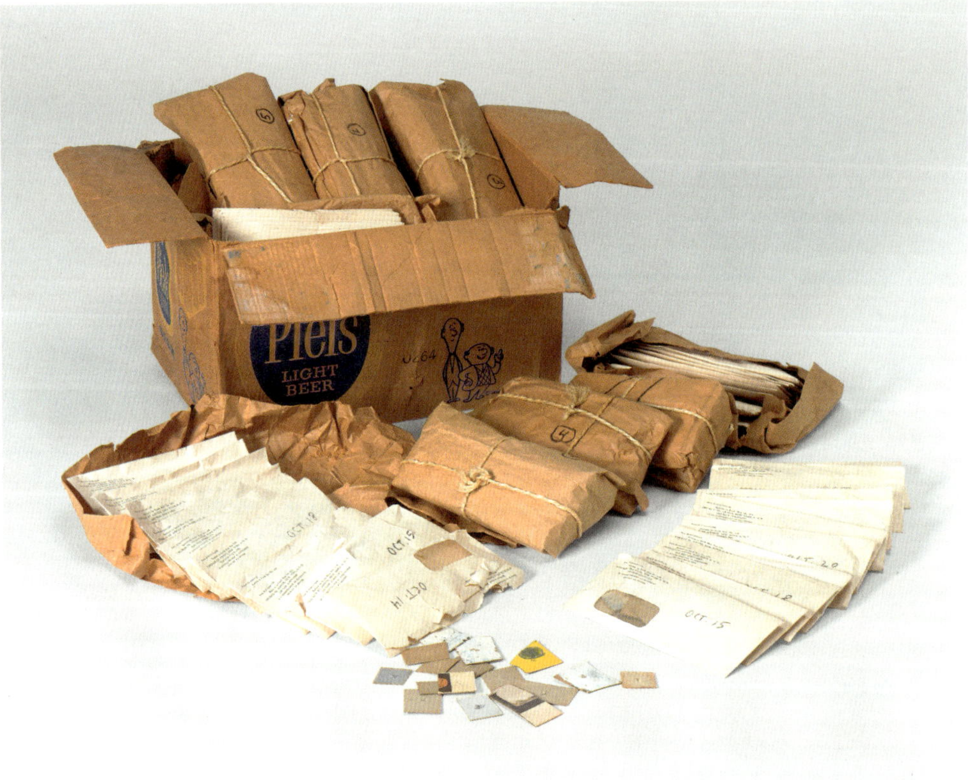

Throughout his career, American artist Ray Johnson experimented with extra-institutional art practices that adopted a nonlinear approach and engaged with random and unpredictable outcomes. In the mid-1950s, he began sending out drawings, collages, newsletters, and even fictional gallery announcements, initiating what came to be known as the New York Correspondence School, an international mail art network.[1] This collective, which has continued in altered form into the twenty-first century and is composed of an ever-expanding number of correspondents, depends not on the commercial art market but on the postal system to circulate postcards, collages, zines, and various other creative efforts (free of charge). Its formation was in part a reaction against the notion of authentic originality, autonomy, and heroic individualism associated with American Abstract Expressionist painters. By using the postal system, the collective attempted to create an alternative venue of exchange, one based on the erratic vicissitudes of social networks rather than the institutional system of galleries and museums that was burgeoning in the postwar years.

Collage—a combinational, often collaborative medium—was a fundamental strategy in Johnson's practice. The artist spent most of his career working primarily in this medium, drawing from a vast and expanding archive of newspaper and magazine clippings, letters and collages he received from other mail artists, his own compositions, and other found materials, which he often augmented with pencil, paint, gouache, and crayon. He combined materials in ways that seem somewhat cryptic and open-ended, encouraging viewers to draw out formal as well as political (and often comical) correspondences. Art critic David Bourdon said of Johnson's collages that they "are the equivalent of Rorschach inkblot tests that can be interpreted in almost as many ways as there are individuals to examine them."[2] Johnson himself called his collages "moticos," a word that originated from an anagram for "osmotic," suitably reflecting his conviction that his collages, as he once put it, "continually change, like the news in the paper or the images on a movie screen."[3] He made his collages on a daily basis, sending most of them away to correspondents in his mail art network as gifts.

In the late 1950s and into the 1960s, Johnson began using discarded cardboard components such as those included in *Year*, a work sent to American composer La Monte Young as a birthday gift. *Year* consists of a large cardboard box filled with packages of envelopes wrapped in brown paper and twine. Each envelope is dated covering a time span of about three months. The envelopes hold cardboard cutouts, some of which are colored, and each one has a hole punched through it. *Year* invites interaction, as individual pieces can be arranged as a two-dimensional puzzle or as a three-dimensional installation, with each piece, for instance, threaded on a string. Most of Johnson's collages have an evolving quality to them, but works like this one relate specifically to John Cage's notion of indeterminacy, according to which the author, or composer, establishes certain parameters, but allows the audience, or performer, to determine the final outcome.[4] As Johnson once explained in reference to his collages: "Every time they're shown, they're reshuffled and become a different story."[5] *Year* effectively democratizes the creative process, relinquishing authorial control by inviting the collaboration of whoever assembles its pieces. It also exemplifies how Johnson resisted the notion of a work of art as a single, unchanging entity in favor of a multitude of meanings and a lively network of visual communication and social interaction.

EH

NOTES

1. The formation of this group was influenced by the rise of numerous antiformalist tendencies in New York such as Fluxus, performance art, Happenings, and improvisational dance.

2. David Bourdon, as quoted in Donna De Salvo, "Correspondences," in *Correspondences*, ed. Donna De Salvo and Catherine Gudis (Columbus, OH: Wexner Center for the Arts; New York: Flammarion, 1999), 27.

3. Ray Johnson, as quoted in ibid., 21.

4. In the 1940s, Johnson attended Black Mountain College, where he studied with Joseph Albers and John Cage. While Albers's teaching offered his students a discipline and control over materials, Cage opened up ways of working that accepted spontaneity and randomness as valid aesthetic processes.

5. Ray Johnson, as quoted in Henry Martin, "Should an Eyelash Last Forever? An Interview with Ray Johnson" (introduction to interview), in *Correspondences*, 185.

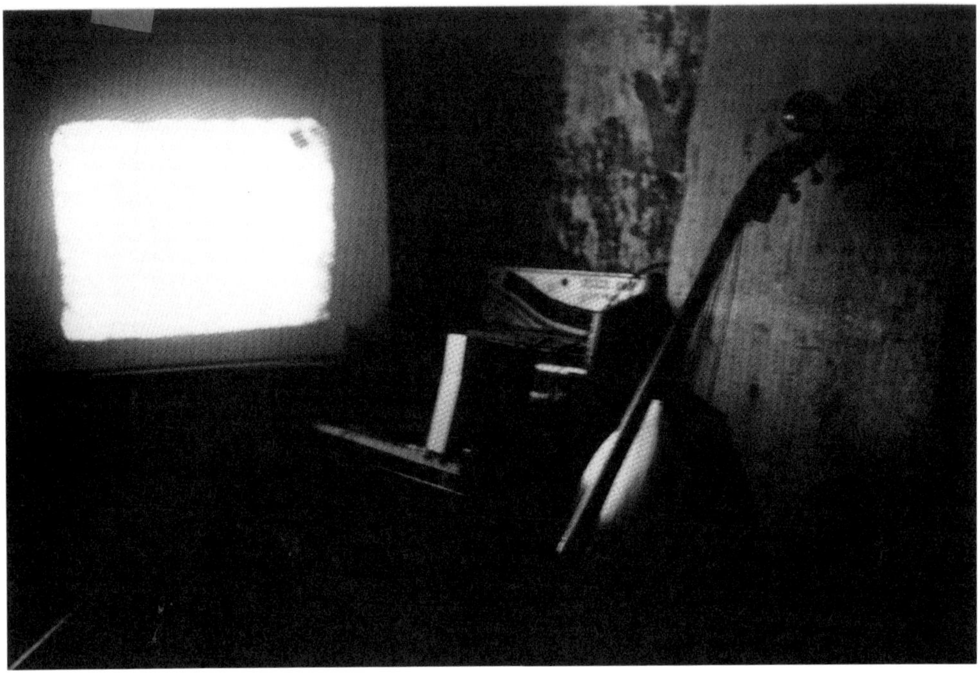

Nam June Paik (South Korean, 1932–2006)

Zen for Film, 1962–64 / 2009
Unexposed 16mm film, looped
Installation shot, Fluxus Concerts, Fluxhall / Fluxshop, New York, 1964
Photo by Peter Moore © Estate of Peter Moore / VAGA, New York, NY

On May 8, 1964, at the Fluxhall on Canal Street in New York City, Nam June Paik presented the first public screening of *Zen for Film*, a work consisting of nothing more than a roll of 16mm clear leader projected as a film.[1] No images were seen, just the scratches, dirt, and dust particles that accumulated on the leader over time. New "content" was introduced with subsequent screenings, and the film was visibly altered by each screening. The product of Duchampian appropriation, Cagean indeterminacy, and a desire to circumvent the standard technologies of production and postproduction, *Zen for Film* negates the indexical character of cinema in favor of a concrete immediacy.[2]

Paik graduated from the University of Tokyo in 1956, wrote a dissertation on composer Arnold Schoenberg, and participated in various Fluxus productions from the group's founding around 1961 through leader George Maciunas's death around 1978. In the early 1960s, Paik became one of the earliest practitioners of video art, experimenting with television as a new artistic medium by manipulating its content so as to fulfill its potential as a truly interactive interface. John Cage's Zen-inspired credo of art as an open field of experiential immediacy and his innovative democratization of sound articulated a radical critique of rationalized modes of composition, one that provided an important model for Paik and his fellow artists associated with Fluxus and Happenings.[3] Indeed, *Zen for Film* can be understood as a visual nod to Cage's "silent" composition *4′33″* (1952) in which only the duration of the piece (four minutes and thirty-three seconds) is dictated. Just as the unintentional sounds and noises of the environment emerge as the listening experience in Cage's piece, Paik's blank projection visually exposes the presence of dust particles in the environment as well as the silhouetted form of individuals moving between the projector and the screen.

Cage was himself inspired to compose his "silent" work after seeing Robert Rauschenberg's *White Paintings* (c. 1951), a series of canvases devoid of any imagery yet constantly changing due to environmental conditions—the accumulation of dust and the registration of shadows as light moves across their smooth surfaces. He saw in Rauschenberg's blank canvases how the unfolding of site, process, and time could constitute a work of art.[4] While seemingly similar in concept, Cage noted important distinctions between his project and those of Rauschenberg and Paik:

> In the music, the sounds of the environment remain, so to speak, where they are, whereas in the case of the Rauschenberg painting, the dust and the shadows, the changes in light and so forth, don't remain where they are but come to the painting. In the case of the Nam June Paik film, which has no images on it ... what you see is the dust that has collected on the film. I think that's somewhat similar to the case of the Rauschenberg painting, though the focus is more intense.[5]

In *Zen for Film*, what initially appears empty and devoid of content becomes full as the piece remains open to natural processes outside of itself. The stripping down of the medium to its bare essentials is enacted, not as a reduction toward the essence of film, but rather as a means of incorporating the temporally changing, non-art realm. The unpredictable interaction between the perceiver, the object perceived, and the surrounding environment offers a diversity of experience that ranges from boredom to intense immersion in endless variation.

MM

NOTES

1. Conceived in 1962, the work was not publicly presented until two years later when, at the invitation of George Maciunas, Paik took part in a six-week Fluxus Concerts series.

2. For more on formative influences on Paik's filmic work, see Bruce Jenkins, "Fluxfilms in Three False Starts," in *In the Spirit of Fluxus*, ed. Elizabeth Armstrong and Janet Jenkins (Minneapolis: Walker Art Center, 1993), 136-37. *Zen for Film* exists in two Fluxus versions: a long version suitable for theater screenings and a boxed edition containing a small loop of leader and sold as a multiple. See Jon Hendricks, *Fluxus Codex* (Detroit: Gilbert and Lila Silverman Fluxus Collection; New York: Harry N. Abrams, 1988), 438

3. Many artists working in the 1950s and 1960s exhibited an interest in Zen Buddhism as a productive strategy for creating a new aesthetic program. Zen's emphasis on detachment, spontaneity, and the elimination of hierarchies was of crucial formal interest to artists in the West. For more on the mediated use of Zen philosophy in artistic practice, see Alexandra Munroe, "Buddhism and the Neo-Avant-Garde: Cage Zen, Beat Zen, and Zen," in *The Third Mind: American Artists Contemplate Asia, 1860-1989*, ed. Alexandra Munroe (New York: Solomon R. Guggenheim Museum, 2009), 199–215.

4. Branden Joseph's study of Robert Rauschenberg draws important links between John Cage's Zen-inspired practices and Henri Bergson's theories of duration and change. See Branden W. Joseph, *Random Order: Robert Rauschenberg and the Neo-Avant-Garde* (Cambridge, MA: MIT Press, 2003), 25–72.

5. John Cage, "On Nam June Paik's 'Zen for Film'" (1968), reprinted in *Nam June Paik: Video Time—Video Space*, ed. Toni Stooss and Thomas Kellein (New York: Harry N. Abrams, 1993), 117.

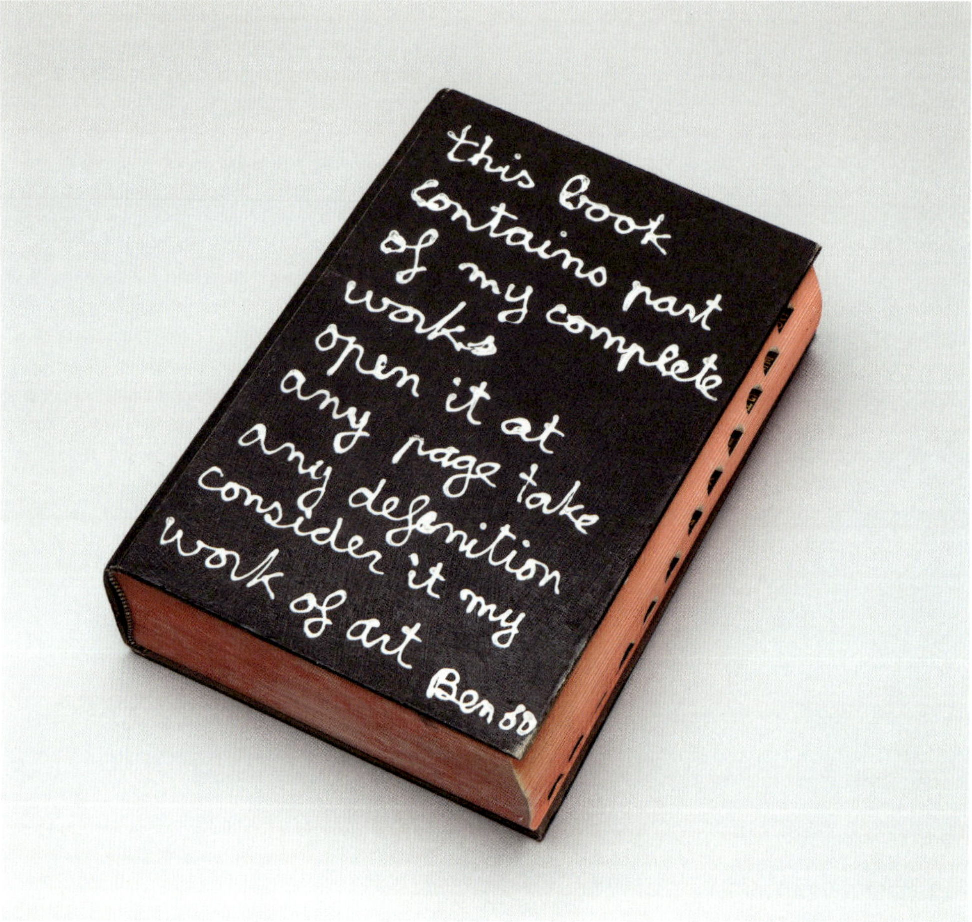

Ben Vautier (French, b. Italy, 1935)

Flux Catalogue, 1960 / 1968
Dictionary with the concept for the work handwritten by the artist on the cover,
10 x 7 x 4" (approximate)
Prototype for proposed Fluxus Edition

Ben Vautier (known simply as "Ben") was one of several artists in the late 1950s through the 1970s developing a concept of "total art," or an art that could encompass all things, entities, and concepts through appropriation. A prolific and dedicated member of Fluxus, Ben established Fluxus South (one of the two French Fluxus satellites) in Nice at his record shop and gallery, Laboratoire 32 (later renamed Galerie Ben Doute de Tout), which he owned and operated until 1973.[1] Ben also performed with Fluxus artists in New York in 1963, and a significant number of his objects were incorporated into the various *Fluxboxes* and *Fluxkits* organized by Fluxus leader George Maciunas [Cat., p. 146]. Maciunas championed Ben, whose French background helped to broaden the spectrum of nationalities that comprised what Maciunas envisioned as an antinationalist collective, though he repeatedly chided Ben for an insufficient effort to de-Europeanize as a show of solidarity with the antinationalist leanings of the group, as well as for the blatant anticollectivist self-referentiality of his work.[2]

Ben's larger program of total appropriation is exemplified by his *Flux Catalogue*, one of his many *Écritures*, or painted phrases. For *Flux Catalogue*, Ben took a copy of a Larousse dictionary and wrote inside, in his distinctive looping script, the phrase "this book contains part of my complete works open it at any page take any definition consider it my work of art," followed by his omnipresent signature "Ben" at the lower right. By signing volumes such as dictionaries and encyclopedias, which signify authority and comprehensive understanding, Ben demonstrated the absolute nature of his agenda. Moreover, the artwork invites the viewer to become involved in the charade, playfully goading the participant to select an entry at random and survey what the artist has claimed as part of his "complete works," referring not to his actual body of work, but rather to a Cagean understanding of everything as one's total environment. As Ben indicated about the "complete works": "It could be the notion of 'Everything' more as an idea than a publication."[3]

As with the Dadaists and many of his Fluxus cohorts, paramount to Ben is the game, whether between himself and the art world or himself and the viewer. Ben's instructions to the viewer / participant on the *Flux Catalogue* recall the myth surrounding the selection of the name Dada, which was allegedly chosen at random from a dictionary. Likewise, the game with which Ben is engaged in his *Flux Catalogue* is entirely conceptual—it does not matter which definition the participant chooses because the result will always be subsumed under Ben's all-encompassing rubric. It is at this point that Ben's program comes dangerously close to coming unbound, as the boundlessness of his conceptual program negates any potential for randomness. Through the repeated act of applying his signature to appropriated reference texts, Ben reveals the underlying futility (and hubris) of the attempt to sign (possess) everything. As art historian Ina Blom wrote: "The world or 'totality' will not be conquered: for every space covered by Ben's handwriting one is reminded of all the millions of spaces into which his hand does not reach. Ben's point is precisely that the world will resist total appropriation."[4]

BB

NOTES

1. After Ben closed the shop, it was purchased by the Musée National d'Art Moderne and reconstructed at the Centre Pompidou as *Magasin* (*Store*). See Owen Smith, "Developing a Fluxable Forum: Early Performance and Publishing," in *The Fluxus Reader*, ed. Ken Friedman (New York: Academy Editions, 1998), 10.

2. Maciunas wrote in a letter to Vautier in 1964: "Curb & eliminate your ego entirely (if you can) don't sign anything—don't attribute anything to yourself—depersonalize yourself! That's the true Fluxus collective spirit. De-europeanize yourself!" Gilbert and Lila Silverman Fluxus Collection (Inv. 01038), as quoted in Thomas Kellein, *Fluxus* (London: Thames and Hudson, 1995), 14.

3. Ben Vautier, as cited in Jon Hendricks, *Fluxus Codex* (Detroit: Gilbert and Lila Silverman Fluxus Collection; New York: Harry N. Abrams, 1988), 502. Ben's pursuit of totality is not unlike Piero Manzoni's in his *Socle du Monde* (1961), an upside-down pedestal upon which Manzoni placed the world as his found object. Both Ben and Manzoni were inspired by Yves Klein.

4. Ina Blom, "Boredom and Oblivion," in *The Fluxus Reader*, 85–86.

Daniel Spoerri (Swiss, b. Romania, 1930)

Topographie anécdotée du hasard (An Anecdoted Topography of Chance), published 1962

Artist's book, 7 1/4 x 5 5/16"

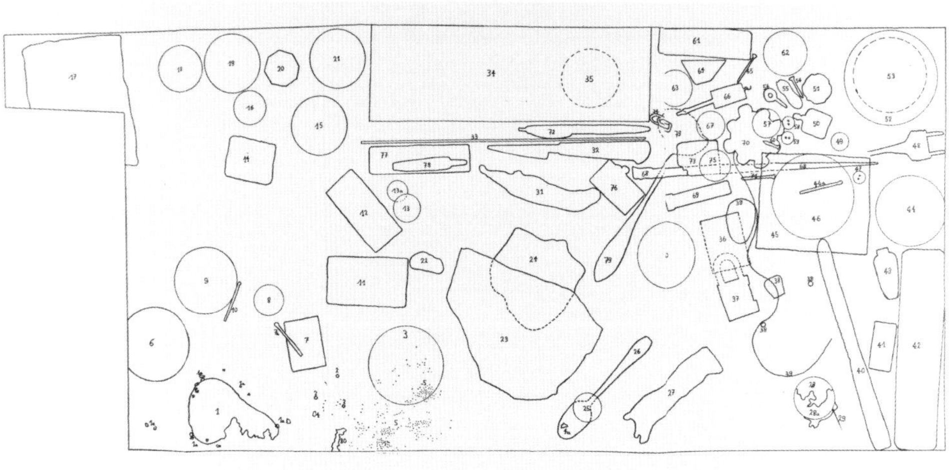

Daniel Spoerri's *An Anecdoted Topography of Chance* tells the story of a random assortment of everyday objects found on a table in the artist's hotel room in Paris on October 17, 1961, at 3:47 pm. On the first page of the slim book, the artist describes his process: "I have set out here to see what the objects on a section of this table ... might suggest to me, what they might spontaneously awaken in me in describing them." In addition to the text, which consists of entries about each item, Spoerri attached a topographic map to the end of the book denoting the exact position and shape of each object found on the table. Readers are invited to play the game of matching up the shapes on the map to their textual descriptions. With this book, Spoerri attempted to meticulously lay out the fortuitous directions of a life as revealed through the presence of various items—including a bent nail, several grains of salt, a jar of Nescafé, a pack of blue toilet paper, a red stapler, some curry powder, and a wine stain—in his room at a precise, yet completely arbitrary, moment in time.

This booklet was first published in February 1962 in lieu of a catalog for an exhibition of the artist's *tableaux-pièges*, or snare pictures, at the Gallery Lawrence in Paris [Cat., p. 86]. Since its original publication, the book has gone through numerous editions and translations. Each edition presents an increasingly complicated system of footnotes, as anecdotes are added by Spoerri and his friends, creating a work ostensibly open to endless adaptations and digressions.

A productive tension between structured experimentation and the arbitrariness of chance informs Spoerri's *Topography*. While emulating the methodical practices of detectives, historians, or archeologists in his disciplined mapping of the scene in his hotel room, Spoerri generated his anecdotes unsystematically, following the ambiguities of personal experience and memory. Although his anecdotes may appear plain to the point of obviousness, they are forever veering off into unexpected idiosyncrasies. For instance, object 8 is described as:

> A pepper shaker of transparent plastic, which contained 20 grammes of white pepper, almost empty, Dipac brand, price I franc 20 centimes. This pepper shaker has changed position many times since the evening meal and probably isn't in its original place. The meal in question was a stew made with goat's neck, which I looked forward to very much but after three hours of cooking the meat was still uneatable, and I had to throw it out.

Spoerri's *Topography* depicts a world that is both banal and unexpected. The various items referenced in the book reflect not only the private and public spaces of the artist's life, but also the larger sociocultural context through which they move. What was merely a plastic case for an electric razor becomes a protagonist. Reading the description of object 31, we understand that this particular case belongs to a new Philips razor bought the same day that Spoerri decided to make a snare picture out of a board on which his old razor was lying among a pile of other things. He goes on to describe his purchase of the razor as part of a sale in which he received a 5-franc reduction; however, if he had bought it a day earlier he would have received a 10-franc discount. We then learn that the snare picture made with the original razor was almost stolen when Spoerri stopped in Lyon on his way to Nice with fellow Nouveau Réaliste Raymond Hains. Someone forced open the car door, panicked when he couldn't lift the razor or any of the other objects glued to the board, and made off with one of Hains's shirts instead, which we are told was bought at the House of 100,000 Shirts in Paris.

Spoerri's intense attention to everyday objects and chance encounters unquestionably resonates with contemporary anxieties concerning how one might negotiate a life within a postwar society defined by a massive shift toward American-style consumerism. The *Topography* is above all a provocation designed to jolt the reader out of traditional patterns of perception. Sidestepping heroic or spiritual ideals, Spoerri chose to investigate the minute and the particular, inviting individuals to stop and look anew at the random proliferation of objects defining their daily existence.

MM

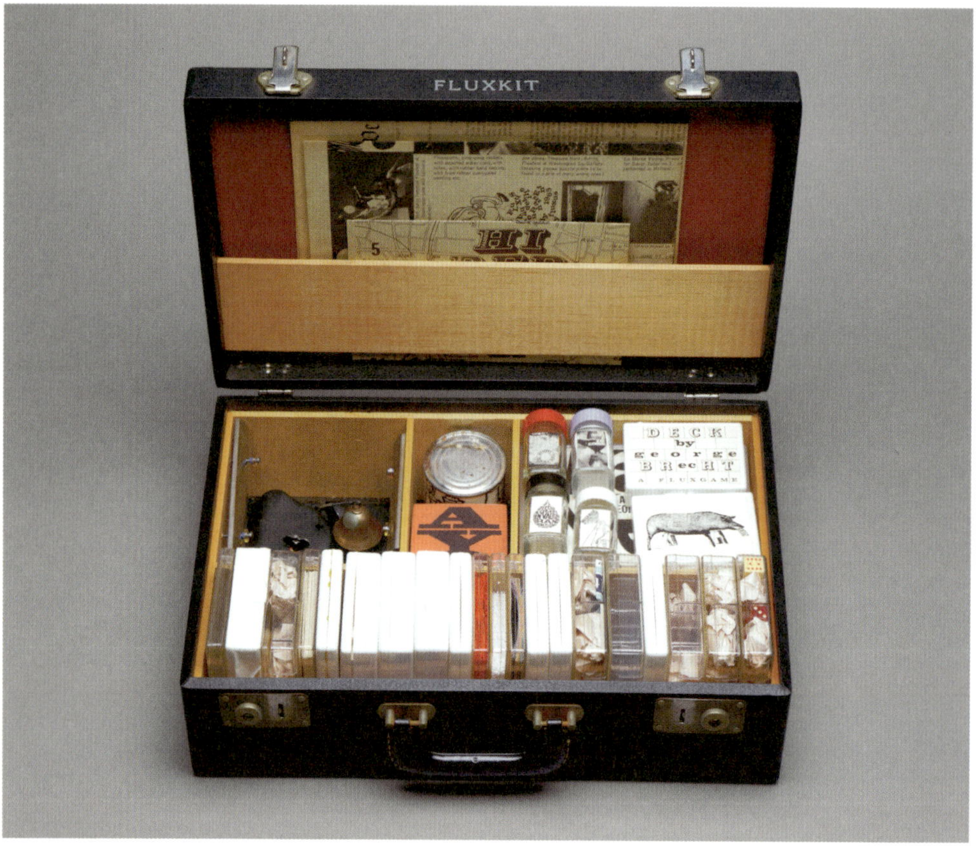

George Maciunas (American, 1931–1978)

Fluxkit, 1966–67
Mixed media, 11 1/4 x 17 3/8 x 5 3/4"

As an aesthetic and political reaction against bourgeois modernist tastes, the Fluxus movement sought to undermine every tenet of modernism, from the preciousness of the object to its hierarchizing approach to media.[1] True to the neo-Dadaist principles of artistic nihilism and commitment to concrete realities, many Fluxus artists took maximum creative advantage of the chance procedures pioneered by Marcel Duchamp and John Cage, whether applied to musical compositions, outdoor public performances, poems, music and event scores, photographs, films, or, especially, games. The game as a format was ideal for Fluxus artists, as it has inherent connotations of fun and frivolity, is generally small in scale and both easy and cheap to produce, and invites active participation on the part of the viewer. Moreover, many of the games developed by Fluxus artists had rules or instructions that could not logically be followed with the materials or playing pieces provided, inviting the participant to question whether the presentation was ironic, absurd, or some combination of the two. With play as a foundation for Fluxus art, games were also well suited to a rejection of the high seriousness of modernism in favor of the often mundane but verifiable reality of the everyday.

With an international roster of artists (George Brecht, Nam June Paik, Dick Higgins, Robert Watts, Alison Knowles, Geoffrey Hendricks, Ay-O, Daniel Spoerri, Ben Vautier, Yoko Ono, and Emmett Williams, to name just a few) producing an extraordinary variety of materials, Fluxus leader George Maciunas took it upon himself to figure out how to collect, reproduce, and distribute the games, boxes, event scores, and other miscellanea that he solicited from the artists.[2] With a remarkable aptitude for organization and promotion, balanced by a sense of humor and affinity for the absurd, Maciunas created several different anthology collections, all of which were highly tactile, interactive displays of objects housed in some form of handheld container. The second anthology box, first assembled in 1964, was the *Fluxkit*. With the goal of maintaining the collective spirit, Maciunas filled a vinyl briefcase with Fluxus items and publications intended to engage the widest range of sensorial experience, organized in a nonhierarchical fashion.[3] The *Fluxkit* was undoubtedly a nod to Marcel Duchamp's random arrangement of notes in his *The Green Box* [Cat., p. 126], which invites the viewer to survey the contents of the box directly, as well as to Duchamp's portable museum, the *Boîte-en-valise*, a case that contains a career retrospective by means of miniature versions and reproductions of Duchamp's body of work.

Among the boxes, decks of cards, and other games found in the *Fluxkit*, which changed over the years as objects and materials were added and removed, is George Brecht's *Water Yam*, the boxed edition of the artist's event scores first manufactured by Maciunas in 1963. Intended to heighten one's awareness of the simple, generally marginalized actions of everyday life, the event scores in *Water Yam* (cards with phrases or instructions printed on them) range from the simple and straightforward, such as turning a light on and off, to the evocative and nearly poetic, such as the oft-performed *Drip Music* ("A source of dripping water and an empty vessel are arranged so that the water falls into the vessel"). More confounding is Brecht's *Name Kit*, which challenges participants to spell out their names with dice and other small, randomly selected objects with the benefit of no instructions other than "spell your name." With no legend or key to translate the objects into characters or other form of text, Brecht underscores the often arbitrary nature of language and its seemingly incoherent relationship to concrete realities.

In addition to games and event scores, another regular feature of the *Fluxkit* was Ben Vautier's *Flux Mystery Food*, comprised of identically sized cans of food whose contents remain unknown until consumed. In order to decipher the contents of the can, all of the senses must be utilized and in full engagement with each other, as sight is translated into texture, smell into taste. Indeed, the contents of the *Fluxkit* are attuned to inviting participants to engage with the senses and the intellect in unexpected and often perplexing ways, through what are initially perceived as mundane or meaningless exercises, but are actually designed to make them perceive their everyday environment and activities with the same attention they would normally give to works of art.

BB

NOTES

1. For more on Fluxus and modernism, see Stephen C. Foster, "Historical Design and Social Purpose: A Note on the Relationship of Fluxus to Modernism," in *The Fluxus Reader*, ed. Ken Friedman (New York: Academy Editions, 1998), 166–71.

2. George Maciunas's leadership of Fluxus did not please all members, and he was also accused by some of megalomania. In 1963, Maciunas issued *News-Policy Letter No. 6*, which called for Fluxus to engage in overtly radical, seemingly anarchic, activities, causing Robert Morris, Walter de Maria, Daniel Spoerri, and Joseph Beuys to distance themselves from the group, and all but ending the Fluxus movement in Europe. See Thomas Kellein, *Fluxus* (London: Thames and Hudson, 1995), 12.

3. For more on the *Fluxkit* and its appeal to the senses, see Hannah Higgins, *Fluxus Experience* (Berkeley: University of California Press, 2002), 33–58.

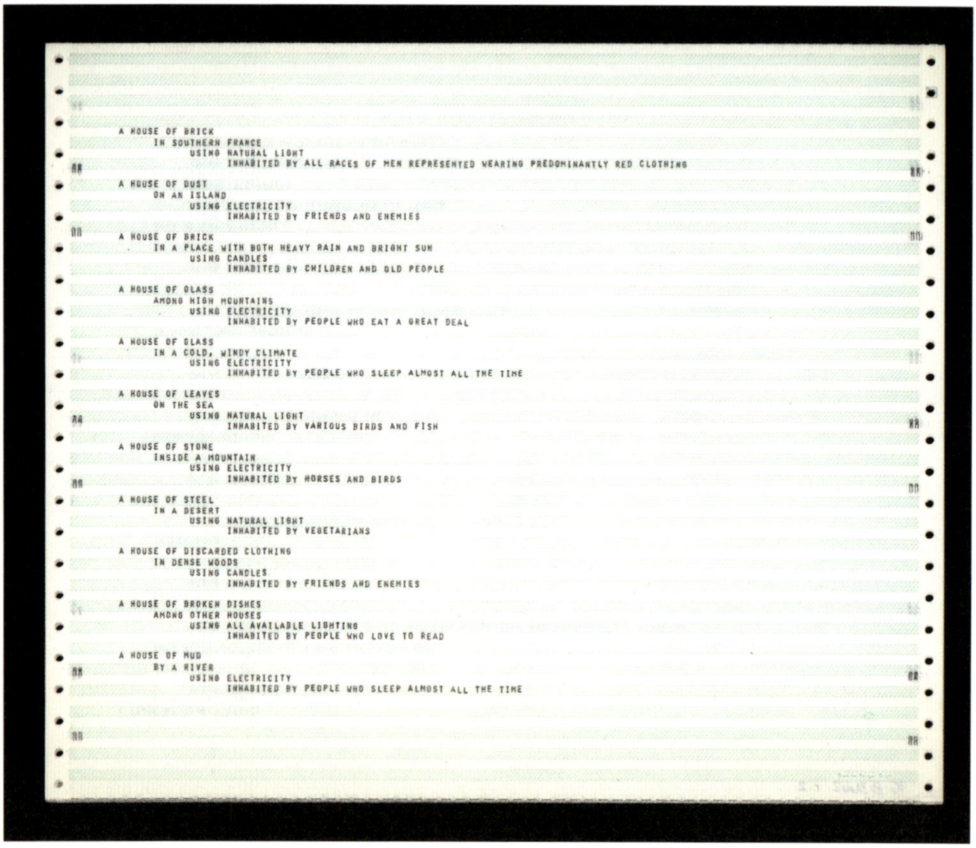

Alison Knowles (American, b. 1933)

A House of Dust, 1968
Ink on paper, variable dimensions

As was the case with many of her Fluxus colleagues, for Alison Knowles it was John Cage's radical scoring practices and his concept of programmatic indeterminacy that provided the impetus for her incorporation of duration and experience into the conception of the work of art. Knowles employed indeterminacy to great effect in her event scores—short instruction-like texts that bring the form of the score from music into the visual arts. For instance, in *Proposition #1: Make a Salad* (1962), the reader is given the simple directive to "make a salad"—a singular instruction that allows for an incredible amount of freedom in its realization. Similarly, in *Proposition #6: Shoes of Your Choice* (1963), members of an audience are invited to describe a pair of shoes that they may or may not be wearing, in both objective and subjective terms, including where they were purchased, their size and color, what is appealing about them, and so on. While Knowles determined the initial parameters of all of her event scores, these parameters act as mere catalysts toward action that occurs beyond her control. Anyone can use the structure she lays out to produce new interpretations, creating new pieces and thereby effectively blurring the boundary between author and interpreter. In addition to her event scores, Knowles also produced interactive objects, such as her experimental book *The Bean Rolls* (1963), which is comprised of a can filled with a few dried beans and several small scrolls on which are printed what appears to be arbitrary material about beans in songs, recipes, stories, cartoons, advertisements, and more.[1] In order to "read" *The Bean Rolls*, one must overturn the can, dump out its contents, and select a scroll at random.

Five years later, Knowles produced *A House of Dust*, an early example of computerized poetry that extends the virtually unlimited potential for variety and random juxtapositions inherent in her earlier work, giving it a decidedly more high-tech edge. The project resulted from Knowles's participation in a workshop taught by the American electronic composer and computer engineer James Tenney. Tenney wanted to introduce artists and writers who were advancing a Cagean aesthetic of chance operations and aleatory permutations to the use of the computer.[2] To create *A House of Dust*, Knowles produced four word lists that were then translated into a computer language and organized into quatrains according to a random matrix. Each of the four lists consists of a series of terms that describe an aspect of a house: materials, location, lighting, and inhabitants. When the words are randomly arranged into syntax via the computer program, the transaction imposes a nonrational ordering of subjects and ideas, generating rather charming phrasing and imagery:

> A house of dust, in a hot climate, using all available lighting, inhabited by all races of men represented wearing predominantly red clothing. A house of steel, in a deserted factory, using candles, inhabited by friends and enemies. A house of broken dishes, on the sea, using natural light, inhabited by vegetarians. A house of tin, in dense woods, using all available lighting, inhabited by friends and enemies.

While hundreds of "houses" could be produced if all the permutations of the program were exhausted, each version of the book contains only around twenty pages. Printed on perforated tractor-feed paper (common to the dot matrix printers of the time), the pages are presented as a long scroll that is then folded like an accordion and placed in a plastic pouch. A seemingly endless number of different printouts is possible, as every version of the poem begins and ends with a different set of quatrains. As with George Brecht's early experiments with *Chance Paintings* [Cat., p. 134], which resulted not from the spontaneous expression of a human gesture but from a more mechanical, depersonalized system of actions, Knowles used the computer to do with language what Brecht did with the gesture: reveal the underlying arbitrariness of the word or mark itself, which is not suffused with meaning, but rather acquires meaning through structural relationships and shifting context.

MM, BB

NOTES

1. For an insightful discussion of Knowles's work along this vein, see Julia Robinson, "The Sculpture of Indeterminacy: Alison Knowles's Beans and Variations," *Art Journal* 63, no. 4 (Winter 2004): 96–115.

2. Cage also turned to the computer at this time. In 1969, he collaborated with Lejaren Hiller to make HPSCHD, a musical piece consisting of fifty-one computer-generated sound tapes and seven solo harpsichord parts. The composers used a computer program that approximated the *I Ching*'s chance operations to assemble some of the solos and the fifty-one sound tapes. In his *Diary: How to Improve the World (You Will Only Make Matters Worse)*, Cage humorously noted: "It took six weeks to teach the computer how to toss three coins six times. Somewhat worried, I tossed the coins manually to discover from the *I Ching* how the *I Ching* felt about being programmed. It was delighted." John Cage, as cited in *Writings through John Cage's Music, Poetry, and Art*, ed. David W. Bernstein and Christopher Hatch (Chicago: University of Chicago Press, 2001), 190.

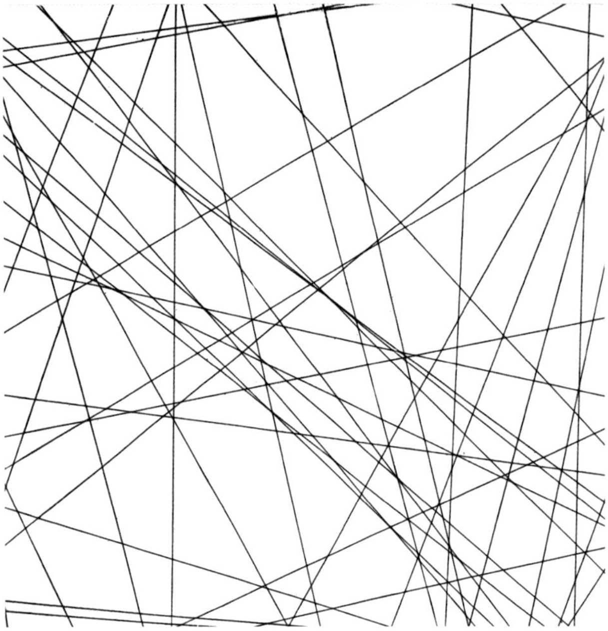

François Morellet (French, b. 1926)

50 lignes au hasard, 1967

Adhesive on Plexiglas, 45 11/16 x 45 11/16"
[above]

40,000 carrés, 1971

Portfolio of eight serigraphs, edition Galerie Denise René, 31 1/2 x 31 1/2" each
[right]

Since the early 1950s, French artist François Morellet's paintings have been characterized by a lack of interest in the arbitrariness of subjective compositional choices and personal taste and by the presence of simple, obvious systems. His initial turn to abstraction derived from his discovery of the work of Swiss artist Max Bill in Brazil in 1950. Bill favored a highly systematic and programmed art, also known as concrete art, in which structure and order were the primary characteristics through which the ideal of a universal language (freed from individual idiosyncrasies) would ostensibly be achieved. In 1958, Morellet took a definitive step away from the rigidity of Bill's rationalist approach and adopted chance as the principal means of organizing his compositions.[1] This measure was taken in order to further offset the arbitrariness of subjective choice that even the most determined systems can not entirely suppress. As stated by the artist, his turn to chance provided a means of reawakening "those of my systems which lay dormant, resting on their laurels. I loved the irritations, the accidents caused by programmed chance and not by the subjectivity of my own arbitrary decisions."[2] Morellet's most renowned works in this vein include his 1961 painting, *Random Distribution of 40,000 Squares Using the Odd and Even Numbers of a Telephone*

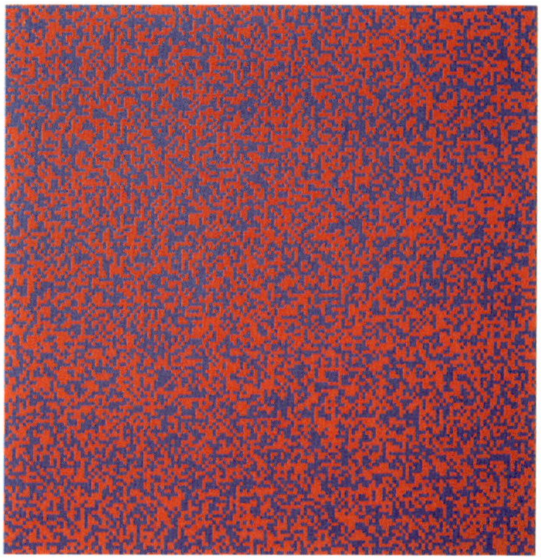

Directory, and the subsequent series of silkscreens titled *40,000 carrés* (40,000 Squares).[3] To make the initial painting from which the silkscreens derive, Morellet traced two hundred horizontal lines and two hundred vertical lines on a canvas, producing a grid of forty thousand squares. He then enlisted his wife and children to read to him in the evenings a series of numbers from the telephone book. As his family read off the digits, Morellet gave each square a number. If a number came up even he would mark the square with a cross, and if the number came up odd he would leave it blank. He then painted all the squares with a cross blue and all those without red. This meticulous process took the better part of a year to complete.

By imposing as little of himself as possible in his programmed art, Morellet also sought to open a space for the spectator to become an essential partner in the interpretation of a work's meaning. The notion that the viewer should become a collaborator directly evokes the practice of Marcel Duchamp, whom Morellet met in 1951. Morellet understood Duchamp's readymades as a stance against the notion of an "arbitrary artisan-creator," and he particularly admired Duchamp's complete elimination of the artisan element in their manufacture.[4] *50 lignes au hasard*, like *40,000 carrés*, employs dual strategies of system and chance; however, two important changes mark this project as distinct: Morellet gave up the brush and canvas for tape and Plexiglas, and an assistant was employed to execute the entire work for the artist. *50 lignes au hasard* was produced while Morellet was a member of GRAV (Groupe de recherche d'art visuel), a collective of artists based in Paris who took a scientific approach to art making, experimenting with the use of non-art materials and technological methods. As with the other members of GRAV, Morellet felt that conventional notions of painting were obsolete; he employed unorthodox materials such as stainless steel, aluminum, neon, and, in the case of *50 lignes au hasard*, Plexiglas and black industrial tape. After delineating a square made up of twenty-five units on each side, Morellet began at the top left and continued along the four sides, numbering each unit in order from 0 to 99. From an arbitrarily selected page in the telephone book, he chose the last four digits in a series of telephone numbers and then used these numbers as coordinates, which he plotted and connected by a straight line. As part of a larger series of works (*5 lignes au hasard, 20 lignes au hasard*, et cetera), *50 lignes au hasard* represents just one of the boundless possibilities this self-generating system suggests. Employing straightforward titles, comprehensible number series, and randomizing systems, Morellet wittily attempts to banish subjective decision making and demystify the creative act.

MM

NOTES

1. See Yve-Alain Bois's precise and insightful discussion of Morellet's repudiation of the tradition of geometric abstraction, "François Morellet / Sol LeWitt: A Case Study," in *Artistic Exchange: Acts of the 28th International Congress of Art History, Berlin, July 15-20*, ed. Thomas Gaehtgens (Berlin: Akademie Verlag, 1993), 311. The artist's turn to aleatory procedures was also influenced by Jean (Hans) Arp, whom Morellet met in 1958, and by American artist Ellsworth Kelly, who entered into an intense investigation of chance-based compositional strategies in the early 1950s in Paris.

2. François Morellet, as quoted in Stéphanie Jamet, "Chronology," in *Morellet* (Kunzelsau: Museum Würth, 2002), 251.

3. In 1971, Morellet, in collaboration with the Denise René Gallery, produced an album of eight silkscreen prints based on the original work. Following the painting, each print juxtaposes two colors, including blue / red (after the original). In each, Morellet chose colors with similar value to achieve an optical vibration.

4. See François Morellet, "The Choice in Present-Day Art," in *DATA: Directions in Art, Theory, and Aesthetics*, ed. Anthony Hill (Greenwich, CT: New York Graphic Society Ltd., 1968), 237.

Öyvind Fahlström (Swedish, born Brazil, 1928–1976)

Sitting ... Dominoes, 1966

Color silkscreen on vinyl, magnets, metal, and Plexiglas, 40 3/8 x 28 1/4 x 11/16"

[p. 40]

C. I. A. Monopoly (small), 1971

Acrylic and india ink on magnets and vinyl, 25 3/8 x 35 1/2"

[below]

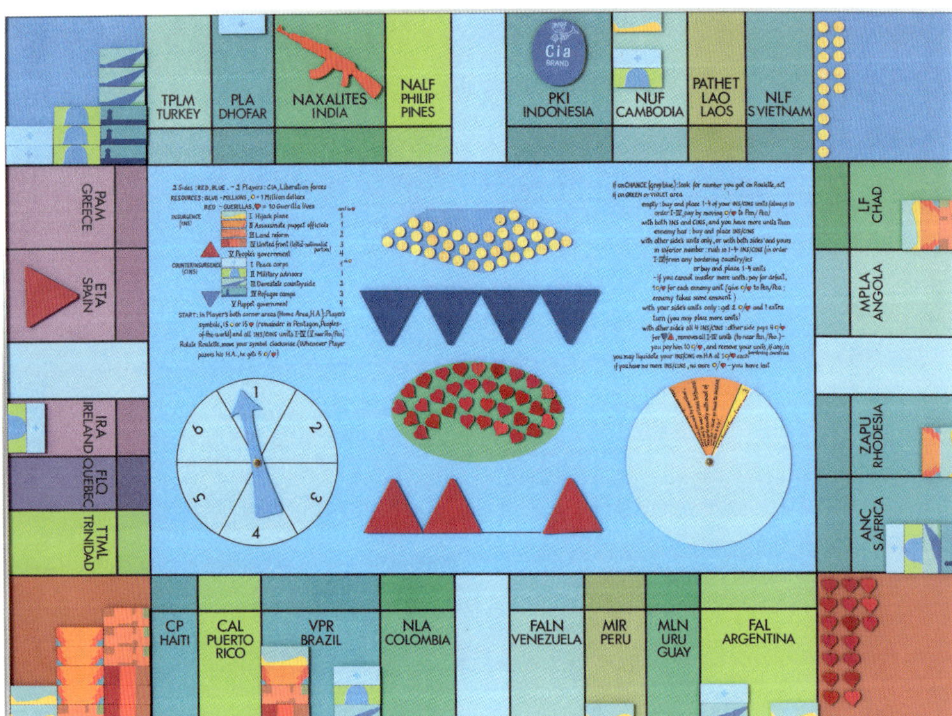

Swedish artist Öyvind Fahlström became a significant presence in the international art scene in the early 1960s with his production of variable paintings—works consisting of multiple pieces that, with the aid of magnets, could be moved across the picture's surface, enhancing the spatial and temporal aspect of the works—and his successful forays into film and performance.[1] The majority of his variable paintings, including the series *Sitting ... Dominoes*, are stocked with figures derived from comics and other popular culture sources, and follow a gamelike structure with preset conditions or rules as material for numerous variations.[2] The meaning of each individual element, what Fahlström termed "character-signs," is forever alterable as it changes with every new arrangement. Unlike the irrational games that fascinated the Surrealists, such as the multiplayer exquisite corpse, Fahlström's variable paintings have more in common with the type of transformability inherent in John Cage's indeterminate musical compositions. For Fahlström, the spectator played the role of performer, negotiating the conflict between the rigidity of given rules and the potential for infinite variability found within the predetermined structure:

> Without manipulating the works of art you do not realize the fantastic nature of the astronomical freedom of choice and the enormous rigidity in the appearance of the parts.... After this fundamental fact comes the brittle rigidity of the game—rules—like our conventions and agreements: the border between the Congo and Angola, the numbers in the telephone book, the buttoning of jackets. There the tension lies in the possibility of breaking against the rigidity—as it does in my game models.[3]

Fahlström's work is very much a product of the Cold War climate of political intrigue and game theory, a branch of applied mathematics arising in the postwar period that was used to study complex social relations. The artist was particularly drawn to the psychological analysis of human interrelations as presented, for example, by pop psychologist Eric Berne in his bestselling book *Games People Play* (1965). Rather than producing fantasy games detached from political and social reality, Fahlström directly engaged the world of modern science, technology, politics, and journalism in his art in order to affect the passivity of people and to expose the injustice and deception of global politics. This is most readily evidenced in his series of Monopoly boards created in the early 1970s.[4] *C. I. A. Monopoly* pits the Central Intelligence Agency against Third World liberation. As a sharp parody of this classic game of capitalism, the work consists of a painted metal game board complete with a list of rules and over two hundred magnetic pieces. As stated by Fahlström: "By choosing sides and strategies, the player will be involved in a miniature political psychodrama. The game can be played intensively in an hour with two to four participants. Or by one person, for months."[5] While the structure of the game provides a predictable rhythm (an assertion of stability that runs counter to the dynamism of chance), each identically regulated round of the game yields a different result depending on who the players are, and is thus forever transformed. Intended for mass production as an editioned multiple available at low cost to a large audience, Fahlström's Monopoly boards never materialized beyond the prototype stage.

MM

NOTES

1. Fahlström was born in Brazil and spent most of his youth in Sweden before relocating to New York City in 1961.

2. The original title of the series was to be *Sitting Like Pat, with a Bat in Her Hat*, a nonsense phrase that references both a hat that Pat Oldenburg once wore to a party and material from Batman comics. See Manuel Borja-Villel et al., *Öyvind Fahlström: Another Space for Painting*, (Barcelona: Museu d'Art Contemporani de Barcelona, 2001), 141. While Fahlström's use of comics and references to popular culture loosely link his works to Pop art, he always exhibited a strong interest in issues of narration and included overt political content. In the 1960s, he was affiliated with Narrative Figuration, an association of European artists who saw art as an instrument of social transformation and put issues of contemporary society and its images at the heart of their work.

3. Öyvind Fahlström, "Hot Dogs and Tweezers—A Running Commentary" (1966), reprinted in *Another Space for Painting*, 175–74.

4. Other works in the series include *World Trade Monopoly, World Politics, U.S. Monopoly*, and *Indochina*.

5. Öyvind Fahlström, "On Monopoly Games" (1971), reprinted in *Öyvind Fahlström* (New York: Solomon R. Guggenheim Museum, 1982), 82.

CHECKLIST OF THE EXHIBITION

Alphabetical by artist within each section

COLLAGE, ASSEMBLAGE, AND THE FOUND OBJECT

Arman
Claes Oldenburg's Refuse, 1970–71
Plexiglas box with refuse, 47 1/4 x 23 5/8 x 23 5/8"
Gilbert and Lila Silverman, Detroit
© 2009 Artists Rights Society (ARS), New York / ADAGP, Paris
Photography, R. H. Hensleigh

Jean (Hans) Arp
Objets placés selon les lois du hasard III: Configuration symétrique (Objects Arranged according to the Laws of Chance III: Symmetrical Configuration), 1931
Oil on wood, 10 1/8 x 11 3/8 x 2 3/8"
San Francisco Museum of Modern Art
Purchase
© 2009 Artists Rights Society (ARS), New York / VG Bild-Kunst, Bonn

Jean Dubuffet
Tête barbue (Bearded Head), 1959
Driftwood with barnacles, 11 1/8 x 8 1/2 x 4"
Mildred Lane Kemper Art Museum, Gift of Florence S. Weil, 1982
© 2009 Artists Rights Society (ARS), New York / ADAGP, Paris

Marcel Duchamp
Hat Rack, 1964 (4th version of 1917 original)
Wood, 8/8, 9 7/16 x 17 5/16 x 13"
Indiana University Art Museum: Partial gift of Mrs. William H. Conroy
© 2009 Artists Rights Society (ARS), New York / ADAGP, Paris / Succession Marcel Duchamp

Raoul Hausmann
Fmsbwtözäu, 1918
Photomechanical reproduction with typography on brown paper, 12 13/16 x 19"
Centre Pompidou, Paris, Musée national d'art moderne / Centre de création industrielle
© 2009 Artists Rights Society (ARS), New York / ADAGP, Paris

Ellsworth Kelly
Children's Leftovers Arranged by Chance, 1950
Collage on paper, 15 3/4 x 10 1/4"
Collection of the artist
© Ellsworth Kelly

Ellsworth Kelly
Glass Roof Pattern, Charenton, 1950
Pencil and ink on paper, 8 1/4 x 59 1/4"
Collection of the artist
© Ellsworth Kelly

Ellsworth Kelly
Brushstrokes Cut into Forty-Nine Squares and Arranged by Chance, 1951
Cut-and-pasted paper and ink, 13 3/4 x 14"
The Museum of Modern Art, New York. Purchased with funds given by Agnes Gund, 1997
© Ellsworth Kelly

Mimmo Rotella
La Dernière Marilyn, 1966
Décollage on canvas, 53 1/2 x 37 1/4"
Private collection, courtesy of Fondazione Mimmo Rotella, Milan, and Knoedler & Company
© 2009 Artists Rights Society (ARS), New York / SIAE, Rome

Dieter Roth
Kleiner Sonnenuntergang (Small Sunset), 1968
Sausage on paper in plastic bag, 16 15/16 x 12 9/16"
Dieter Roth Foundation, Hamburg

Dieter Roth
Small Landscape, 1969
Pressing, soft cheese on emery paper, in plastic sleeve, 12 5/8 x 30 15/16"
Dieter Roth Foundation, Hamburg

Dieter Roth
Big Cloud, 1971
Felt pen and mayonnaise on white paper, 29 1/2 x 39 13/16"
Dieter Roth Foundation, Hamburg

Niki de Saint Phalle
Grand tir-séance Galerie J, 30 June–12 July 1961
Plaster, paint, wire mesh, string, and plastic, 56 5/16 x 30 5/16"
Niki Charitable Art Foundation

Daniel Spoerri
Le Tiroir de ma mère, 1960
Objects on wood, 15 7/16 x 15 x 5 1/8"
Niki Charitable Art Foundation

Daniel Spoerri
Meal Variation No. 2 Eaten by Marcel Duchamp, c. 1967
Glass-covered photo-laminated tabletop mounted on wood with metal pedestal and four rubber spacers, 28 3/4 x 25 x 21 1/8"
Publisher: Fluxus Edition, New York
Fabricator: George Maciunas, New York
The Museum of Modern Art, New York. The Gilbert and Lila Silverman Fluxus Collection Gift, 2008

Photography, R.H. Hensleigh

Tristan Tzara, Richard Huelsenbeck, and Marcel Janco
"L'Amiral cherche une maison à louer," 1916
Simultaneous poem published in *Cabaret Voltaire*, no. 1 (1916)
Research Library, The Getty Research Institute, Los Angeles
Research Library, The Getty Research Institute, Los Angeles, California (85-S714)

Jacques Villeglé
Rue de Crimée, 28 novembre 1969, 1969
Décollage on canvas, 39 1/4 x 28 3/4"
Courtesy of Alan Koppel Gallery

AUTOMATISM

William Anastasi
Untitled (one gallon of industrial high-gloss enamel, poured), 1966 / 2009
Enamel paint, variable dimensions
Courtesy of the artist

William Anastasi
Untitled (V. Dwan 10.4.67), 1967
Untitled (Sol LeWitt 11-19-69), 1969
Untitled (12-4-69 Angelo Savelli), 1969
Pencil on paper drawings, 7 1/2 x 11 1/2" each
Collection of the artist

André Breton
Untitled, 1935
Ink transfer on paper, 10 x 12 3/4"
The Museum of Modern Art, New York. Purchase, 1969

Salvador Dalí
Femme nue (Nude Woman), early 1930s
Gouache on paper, 9 15/16 x 7 15/16"
Collection of Timothy Baum, New York

Guy Debord and Asger Jorn
Fin de Copenhague: Conseiller technique pour le détournement, 1957
Artist's book, 10 1/16 x 7 x 3/8"
Research Library, The Getty Research Institute, Los Angeles

Oscar Dominguez
Untitled, 1936
Gouache on coated black paper, 8 x 9 11/16"
Collection of Timothy Baum, New York

Max Ernst
Histoire naturelle, 1926
Portfolio of photogravures, 19 5/8 x 12 3/4"
Published by Jeanne Bucher, Paris
Department of Special Collections, Washington University Libraries, St. Louis

Max Ernst
L'Oeil du silence (The Eye of Silence), 1943–44
Oil on canvas, 43 1/4 x 56 1/4"
Mildred Lane Kemper Art Museum, St. Louis, University purchase, Kende Sale Fund, 1946

Marcel Jean
Untitled, c. 1936
Gouache on paper, 12 7/8 x 9 3/4"
Collection of Timothy Baum, New York

Ellsworth Kelly
Automatic Drawing, 1950
Pencil on paper, 12 3/8 x 17 5/8"
Collection of the artist

George Maciunas
Hydrokinetic–Osmotic Painting, 1961
Ink on paperboard on wood, 30 1/16 x 20 1/16"
The Museum of Modern Art, New York. The Gilbert and Lila Silverman Fluxus Collection Gift, 2008

André Masson
Untitled, 1926
Pen and black ink on off-white laid paper, 16 13/16 x 12 1/2"
University of Michigan Museum of Art, Museum Purchase

André Masson
Figure, 1926–27
Oil and sand on canvas, 18 1/8 x 10 1/2"
The Museum of Modern Art, New York. Gift of William Rubin, 1973

Robert Morris
Untitled, 1967–68
Felt, 180 x 72 x 3/8"
Collection of the artist, courtesy of Leo Castelli Gallery

Robert Motherwell
Twenty-four works from the *Lyric Suite*, 1965
Ink on rice paper, 11 x 9" or 9 x 11" each
Dedalus Foundation, Inc., New York

Benjamin Péret and Yves Tanguy
Dormir, dormir, dans les pierres, 1927
Limited edition book with cover and title illustrations by Yves Tanguy, 9 x 7"
Collection of Timothy Baum, New York

Francis Picabia
La Sainte-Vierge (The Blessed Virgin), 1920
Ink blot on paper, published in *391*, no. 12 (March 1920)
Research Library, The Getty Research Institute, Los Angeles

Jackson Pollock
Untitled, 1949
Oil and enamel on canvas mounted on masonite, 18 x 23"
Private collection

Jackson Pollock
Untitled, c. 1950
Ink on paper, 18 7/8 x 24 3/4"
The Museum of Modern Art, New York. The Joan and Lester Avnet Fund, 1983

Kazuo Shiraga
Dragons Emerging from the Forest, 1961
Oil on canvas, 51 1/2 x 51 1/4"
Roland Gibson Gallery, State University of New York at Potsdam

Yves Tanguy
Untitled, 1927
India ink on paper, 11 9/16 x 7 7/8"
Collection of Timothy Baum, New York

Jean Tinguely
Metamatic No. 9, 1958
Round rubber belt, steel rods, painted sheet metal, wire wooden pulleys, two clothes pins, and electric motor, 35 1/2 x 56 5/8 x 14 1/4"
Museum of Fine Arts, Houston. Gift of D. and J. de Menil

Jean Tinguely
Metamatic drawings from *Metamatic No. 9*, 1959
Seven ink on paper drawings, 12 3/4 x 9 3/4" each
Niki Charitable Art Foundation

GAMES AND SYSTEMS OF RANDOM ORDERING

Victor Brauner, Jacques Hérold, Violette Hérold, Yves Tanguy, and Raoul Ubac
Untitled "Cadavre exquis" ("Exquisite Corpse"), 1938
Graphite and collage on paper, 10 3/8 x 8 1/16"
Collection of Howard and Mauree Miller, Pennsylvania

Victor Brauner, Jacques Hérold, and Yves Tanguy
Exquisite Corpse, c. 1932
Graphite and collage on paper, 10 1/2 x 7 7/8"
Indiana University Art Museum: Partial gift of Mrs. William H. Conroy

George Brecht
Chance Painting, 1957
Ink-stained bed sheet, 70 7/8 x 86 5/8"
Collection of Gino Di Maggio, Milan

George Brecht
Chance-Imagery, 1957 / 1966
Artist's pamphlet, 8 3/8 x 5 5/16"
Private collection, St. Louis

André Breton, Jacqueline Lamba, Yves Tanguy
Untitled "Cadavre exquis" ("Exquisite Corpse"), 1938
Collage on graph paper, 10 15/16 x 5 1/2"
Collection of Timothy Baum, New York

John Cage
Score for *Music of Changes*, 1951
© Henmar Press Inc., 1961
Sheet music, 11 11/16 x 8 7/8"

John Cage
Score for *Fontana Mix*, 1958
© Henmar Press Inc., 1960
Sheet music on mylar, variable dimensions

Marcel Duchamp
Three Standard Stoppages, 1964 (replica of 1913–14 original)
Thread on canvas attached to glass, wood sticks, enclosed in wood croquet case, 51 x 11 1/8 x 9 (case)
Indiana University Art Museum: Partial gift of Mrs. William H. Conroy

Marcel Duchamp
La Mariée mise à nu par ses célibataires même (La Boîte verte) (The Bride Stripped Bare by Her Bachelors, Even [The Green Box]), 1934
Ninety-four facsimile documents in a green suede box, 13 1/16 x 11 1/8 x 1"
Yale University Art Gallery, Gift of Francis M. Naumann

Öyvind Fahlström
Sitting ... Dominoes, 1966
Color silkscreen on vinyl, magnets, metal, and Plexiglas, 40 3/8 x 28 1/4 x 11/16"
Private collection, New York

Öyvind Fahlström
C. I. A. Monopoly (small), 1971
Acrylic and india ink on magnets and vinyl, 25 3/8 x 35 1/2"
Private collection, New York

Ray Johnson
Year, c. 1960–61
Cardboard box with approximately 120 envelopes containing cut cardboard collage fragments, many with color and all perforated, 10 x 13 9/16 x 16 5/16"
Gilbert and Lila Silverman, Detroit
Photography, R. H. Hensleigh

Ellsworth Kelly
Spectrum Colors Arranged by Chance V, 1951
Collage on paper, 39 x 39"
Collection of the artist

Alison Knowles
A House of Dust, 1968
Ink on paper, variable dimensions
The Museum of Modern Art, New York.
The Museum of Modern Art Library
Research Library, The Getty Research Institute, Los Angeles, California (95-B3662)

George Maciunas

Fluxkit, 1966–67
Mixed media, 11 1/4 x 17 3/8 x 5 3/4"
Saint Louis Art Museum, Director's Discretionary Fund, Friends Fund, bequest of Helen K. Baer by exchange, the Contemporary Art Society, Donna Moog, Dorothy Moog, Mr. and Mrs. Charles F. Knight, and Museum Purchase by exchange

François Morellet

50 lignes au hasard, 1967
Adhesive on Plexiglas, 45 11/16 x 45 11/16"
Collection of the artist

François Morellet

40,000 carrés, 1971
Portfolio of eight serigraphs, edition Galerie Denise René, 31 1/2 x 31 1/2" each
Collection of the artist

Nam June Paik

Zen for Film, 1962–64 / 2009
Unexposed 16mm film, looped
Exhibition copy
Courtesy of Nam June Paik Studios, Inc.

Daniel Spoerri

Topographie anécdotée du hasard (An Anecdoted Topography of Chance), published 1962
Two copies of artist's book, 7 1/4 x 5 5/16" each
The Museum of Modern Art, New York.
The Museum of Modern Art Library.
The Gilbert and Lila Silverman Fluxus Collection Gift, 2008

Photography, R. H. Hensleigh

Ben Vautier

Flux Catalogue, 1960 / 1968
Dictionary with the concept for work handwritten by the artist on cover, 10 x 7 x 4" (approximate)
Prototype for proposed Fluxus Edition
The Museum of Modern Art, New York.
The Gilbert and Lila Silverman Fluxus Collection Gift, 2008

Photography, R. H. Hensleigh

La Monte Young (editor) and Georges Maciunas (designer)

An Anthology, 1963
Two copies of artist's book, 8 1/8 x 9 1/16" each
Published by Jackson Mac Low and La Monte Young, New York
The Museum of Modern Art, New York.
The Museum of Modern Art Library.
The Gilbert and Lila Silverman Fluxus Collection Gift, 2008

SUPPLEMENTAL ILLUSTRATIONS

Jean (Hans) Arp

Untitled (Collage with Squares Arranged according to the Laws of Chance), 1916–17
Torn-and-pasted paper and colored paper on paper, 19 1/8 x 13 5/8"
The Museum of Modern Art, New York. Purchase

George Brecht

Motor Vehicle Sundown (Event), 1960
Printed sheet, folded
Staatsgalerie Stuttgart, Archiv Sohm

Salvador Dalí

Paranoiac visage, 1931
Illustration published in *Le Surréalisme au service de la révolution*, 1931
Courtesy of the Division of Special Collections, Archives, and Rare Books, University of Missouri at Columbia

Robert Morris

Untitled (Threadwaste), 1968
Felt, asphalt, mirrors, wood, copper tubing, steel cable, and lead, dimensions variable

Jackson Pollock, 1950

Photograph by Hans Namuth
Courtesy of the Center for Creative Photography, University of Arizona

Richard Serra

Scatter Piece, 1967
Rubber latex, 12 x 12'

SELECTED BIBLIOGRAPHY

BOOKS

Ades, Dawn, ed. *The Dada Reader: A Critical Anthology*. Chicago: University of Chicago Press, 2006.

Andreotti, Libero, and Xavier Costa, eds. *Theory of the Dérive and other Situationist Writings on the City*. Barcelona: Museu d'Art Contemporani de Barcelona, 1996.

Arp, Jean (Hans). *Arp on Arp: Poems, Essays, Memories, by Jean Arp*. Ed. Marcel Jean. Trans. Joachim Neugroschel. New York: The Viking Press, 1972.

Baker, George. *The Artwork Caught by the Tail: Francis Picabia and Dada in Paris*. Cambridge, MA: MIT Press, 2007.

Ball, Hugo. *Flight Out of Time: A Dada Diary*. Ed. John Elderfield. Trans. Ann Raimes. Berkeley: University of California Press, 1996.

Barthes, Roland. *The Grain of the Voice: Interviews 1962–1980*. Trans. Linda Coverdale. Berkeley: University of California Press, 1981.

———. *Image, Music, Text*. Trans. Stephen Heath. New York: Hill and Wang, 1977.

Belgrad, Daniel. *The Culture of Spontaneity: Improvisation and the Arts in Postwar America*. Chicago: University of Chicago Press, 1998.

Bennett, Deborah J. *Randomness*. Cambridge, MA: Harvard University Press, 1998.

Benson, Timothy O. *Raoul Hausmann and Berlin Dada*. Ann Arbor, MI: UMI Research Press, 1987.

Berger, Maurice. *Labyrinths: Robert Morris, Minimalism, and the 1960s*. New York: Harper & Row, 1989.

Bois, Yve-Alain, and Rosalind E. Krauss. *Formless: A User's Guide*. New York: Zone Books, 1997.

Bourriaud, Nicolas, François Bon, and Kaira Marie Cabanas. *Villeglé: Jacques Villeglé*. Paris: Flammarion, 2007.

Brecht, George. *Chance-Imagery*. New York: Great Bear Pamphlet / Something Else Press, 1966.

Breton, André. *Conversations: The Autobiography of Surrealism*. Trans. Mark Polizzotti. New York: Paragon House, 1993. Originally published in 1969.

———. *Mad Love*. Trans. Mary Ann Caws. Lincoln: University of Nebraska Press, 1987.

———. *Manifestoes of Surrealism*. Trans. Richard Seaver and Helen R. Lane. Ann Arbor: University of Michigan Press, 1972.

———. *Nadja*. Trans. Richard Howard. New York: Grove Press, 1960.

Breton, André, and Philippe Soupalt. *Magnetic Fields* (1920). Trans. David Gascoyne. London: Atlas Press, 1985.

Breton, André, Paul Eluard, and Philippe Soupault. *The Automatic Message*. Trans. David Gascoyne, Antony Melville, and J. Graham. London: Atlas Press, 1997. Originally published in 1933.

Brotchie, Alastair. *A Book of Surrealist Games*. Ed. Mel Gooding. Boston: Shambhala Redstone Editions, 1995.

Buchloh, Benjamin H. D. *Neo-Avantgarde and Culture Industry: Essays on European and American Art from 1955 to 1975*. Cambridge, MA: MIT Press, 2000.

Bürger, Peter. *Theory of the Avant-Garde*. Trans. Michael Shaw. Minneapolis: University of Minnesota Press, 1984.

Buskirk, Martha. *The Contingent Object of Contemporary Art*. Cambridge, MA: MIT Press, 2003.

Cabanne, Pierre. *Dialogues with Marcel Duchamp*. Trans. Ron Padgett. New York: Da Capo Press, 1987.

Cage, John. *Silence*. Middletown, CT: Wesleyan University Press, 1961.

Caillois, Roger. *Man, Play, and Games* (1958). Trans. Meyer Barash. New York: Free Press of Glencoe, 1961.

Caws, Mary Ann, ed. *Surrealist Painters and Poets: An Anthology*. Cambridge, MA: MIT Press, 2001.

Dalí, Salvador. *Conquest of the Irrational*. Trans. David Gascoyne. New York: Julien Levy Gallery, 1935.

Diaz, Eva. "Chance and Design: Experimentation at Black Mountain College." PhD diss., Princeton University, 2008.

Dickerman, Leah, and Matthew S. Witkovsky, eds. *The Dada Seminars*. Washington, DC: National Gallery of Art, 2005.

Duchamp, Marcel. *The Writings of Marcel Duchamp*. Ed. Michel Sanouillet and Elmer Peterson. New York: Da Capo Press, 1989.

Eco, Umberto. *The Open Work*. Trans. Anna Cancogni. Cambridge, MA: Harvard University Press, 1989.

Ehrenzweig, Anton. *The Hidden Order of Art*. Berkeley: University of California Press, 1967.

Ernst, Max. *Beyond Painting and Other Writings by the Artist and His Friends*. Ed. Robert Motherwell. New York: Wittenborn, Schulze, 1948.

Foster, Hal. *Compulsive Beauty*. Cambridge, MA: MIT Press, 1993.

Foster, Stephen C., and Rudolf E. Kuenzli, eds. *Dada Spectrum: The Dialectics of Revolt*. Madison, WI: Coda Press Inc.; Iowa City: the University of Iowa, 1979.

Franzke, Andreas. *Jean Dubuffet: Petites statues de la vie précaire*. Berlin: Verlag Gachnang & Springer, 1988.

Gale, Matthew. *Dada & Surrealism*. London: Phaidon Press, 1997.

Gamboni, Dario. *Potential Images: Ambiguity and Indeterminacy in Modern Art*. Trans. Mark Treharne. London: Reaktion Books, 2001.

Gigerenzer, Gerd, et al. *The Empire of Chance: How Probability Changed Science and Everyday Life*. Cambridge: Cambridge University Press, 1989.

Hacking, Ian. *The Taming of Chance*. Cambridge: Cambridge University Press, 1990.

Hamilton, Ross. *Accident: A Philosophical and Literary History*. Chicago: University of Chicago Press, 2007.

Henderson, Linda Dalrymple. *Duchamp in Context: Science and Technology in the Large Glass and Related Works*. Princeton, NJ: Princeton University Press, 1998.

Hendricks, Jon. *Fluxus Codex*. Detroit: Gilbert and Lila Silverman Fluxus Collection; New York: Harry N. Abrams, 1988.

Higgins, Hannah. *Fluxus Experience*. Berkeley: University of California Press, 2002.

Huizinga, Johan. *Homo Ludens: A Study of the Play Element in Culture*. Boston: Beacon, 1955. Originally published in 1938.

James, Alison. *Constraining Chance: Georges Perec and the Oulipo*. Evanston, IL: Northwestern University Press, 2009.

Janet, Pierre. *L'Automatisme psychologique*. Paris: Éditions Odile Jacob, 1998. Originally published in 1889.

Joseph, Branden W. *Beyond the Dream Syndicate: Tony Conrad and the Arts after Cage (A "Minor" History)*. New York: Zone Books, 2008.

———. *Random Order: Robert Rauschenberg and the Neo-Avant-Garde*. Cambridge, MA: MIT Press, 2003.

Judovitz, Dalia. *Unpacking Duchamp: Art in Transit*. Berkeley: University of California Press, 1995.

Kahn, Douglas. *Noise, Water, Meat: A History of Sound in the Arts*. Cambridge, MA: MIT Press, 1999.

Kaprow, Allan. *Assemblage, Environments & Happenings*. New York: Harry N. Abrams, 1966.

———. *Essays on the Blurring of Art and Life*. Ed. Jeff Kelley. Berkeley: University of California Press, 1993.

Knabb, Ken, ed. *Situationist International Anthology*. Berkeley: Bureau of Public Secrets, 1981.

Kotz, Liz. *Words to be Looked At: Language in 1960s Art*. Cambridge, MA: MIT Press, 2007.

Krauss, Rosalind E. *The Optical Unconscious*. Cambridge, MA: MIT Press, 1993.

Landau, Ellen G., and Claude Cernuschi, eds. *Pollock Matters*. Chestnut Hill, MA: McMullen Museum of Art; Chicago: University of Chicago Press, 2007.

Lears, Jackson. *Something for Nothing: Luck in America*. New York: Penguin Books, 2003.

Lebel, Robert. *Marcel Duchamp*. New York: Grove Press, 1959.

Lefebvre, Henri. *Critique of Everyday Life*. Vol. 1. Trans. John Moore. London: Verso, 1991.

———. *Critique of Everyday Life*. Vol. 2. Trans. John Moore. London: Verso, 2002.

Leja, Michael. *Reframing Abstract Expressionism: Subjectivity and Painting in the 1940s*. New Haven, CT: Yale University Press, 1993.

Lemoin, Serge. *François Morellet*. Paris: Flammarion, 1996.

Lomas, David. *The Haunted Self: Surrealism, Psychoanalysis, Subjectivity*. New Haven, CT: Yale University Press, 2000.

Martin, Henry. *Arman; Or, Four and Twenty Blackbirds Baked in a Pie; or, Why Settle for Less When You Can Settle for More*. New York: Harry N. Abrams, 1973.

———. *An Introduction to George Brecht's Book of the Tumbler of Fire*. Milan: Multhipla Edizioni, 1978.

Masson, André. *Métamorphose de l'Artiste*. Geneva: Pierre Cailler, 1956.

Monod, Jacques. *Chance and Necessity: An Essay on the Natural Philosophy of Modern Biology*. Trans. Austryn Wainhouse. New York: Alfred A. Knopf, 1971.

Morris, Robert. *Continuous Project Altered Daily: The Writings of Robert Morris*. Cambridge, MA: MIT Press, 1993.

Motherwell, Robert. *The Collected Writings of Robert Motherwell*. Ed Stephanie Terenzio. Oxford: Oxford University Press, 1992.

Motherwell, Robert, ed. *The Dada Painters and Poets: An Anthology*. Second edition. Cambridge, MA: The Belknap Press of Harvard University Press, 1989. Originally published 1951.

Nöel, Emile, ed. *Le hasard aujourd'hui*. Paris: Seuil, 1991.

Parkinson, Gavin. *Surrealism, Art, and Modern Science: Relativity, Quantum Mechanics, Epistemology*. New Haven, CT: Yale University Press, 2008.

Patterson, David W., ed. *John Cage: Music, Philosophy, and Intention, 1933–1950*. New York: Routledge, 2002.

Poling, Clark V. *André Masson and the Surrealist Self*. New Haven, CT: Yale University Press, 2008.

Pollock, Jackson. *Jackson Pollock: Interviews, Articles, and Reviews*. Ed. Pepe Karmel. New York: Harry N. Abrams, 1999.

Restany, Pierre. *Les Nouveaux Réalistes*. Paris: Éditions Planète, 1968.

Richter, Hans. *Dada: Art and Anti-Art*. London: Thames and Hudson, 1965.

Robertson, Eric. *Arp: Painter, Poet, Sculptor*. New Haven, CT: Yale University Press, 2006.

Ross, Kristin. *Fast Cars, Clean Bodies: Decolonization and the Reordering of French Culture*. Cambridge, MA: MIT Press, 1995.

Roussel, Raymond. *How I Wrote Certain of My Books and Other Writings* (1932). Ed Trevor Winkfield.Trans. John Ashbery, Kenneth Koch, Harry Mathews, and Trevor Winkfield. Boston: Exact Change, 1995.

Scheunemann, Dietrich, ed. *Avant-Garde / Neo-Avant-Garde*. Amsterdam: Rodopi, 2005.

Schwarz, Arturo, ed. *Le Cadavre exquis, son exaltation*. Milan: Galleria Schwarz, 1975.

———. *The Complete Works of Marcel Duchamp*. New York: Harry N. Abrams, 1969.

Spoerri, Daniel, et al. *An Anecdoted Topography of Chance*. London: Atlas Press, 1995.

Stiles, Kristine, and Peter Selz, eds. *Theories and Documents of Contemporary Art: A Sourcebook of Artists' Writings*. Berkeley: University of California Press, 1996.

Tomkins, Calvin. *The Bride and the Bachelors: Five Masters of the Avant-Garde*. Middlesex, England: Penguin Books, 1976. Originally published in 1968.

Umland, Anne, and Adrian Sudhalter, eds. *Dada in the Collection of The Museum of Modern Art*. New York: Museum of Modern Art, 2008.

Watts, Alan. *The Way of Zen*. New York: Pantheon Books, 1957.

Watts, Harriett Ann. *Chance: A Perspective on Dada*. Ann Arbor, MI: UMI Research Press, 1975.

Young, La Monte, ed. *An Anthology of Chance Operations*. Second edition. New York: Heiner Friedrich, 1970. Originally published in 1963.

EXHIBITION CATALOGS

Andreotti, Libero, and Xavier Costa. *Situationists: Art, Politics, Urbanism*. Barcelona: Museu d'Art Contemporani de Barcelona, 1996.

Armstrong, Elizabeth, and Janet Jenkins, eds. *In the Spirit of Fluxus*. Minneapolis: Walker Art Center, 1993.

Ashbery, John, and Sidney Janis. *New Realists*. New York: Sidney Janis Gallery, 1962.

Bogle, Andrew. *Chance and Change: A Century of the Avant-garde*. Auckland, New Zealand: Auckland City Art Gallery, 1985.

Bois, Yve-Alain. *Ellsworth Kelly: The Early Drawings, 1948–1955*. Cambridge, MA: Harvard University Art Museum; Winterthur, Switzerland: Kunstmuseum Winterthur, 1999.

Bois, Yve-Alain, Jack Cowart, and Alfred Pacquement, eds. *Ellsworth Kelly: The Years in France, 1948–1954*. Washington, DC: National Gallery of Art, 1992.

Borja-Villel, Manuel, et al. *Öyvind Fahlström: Another Space for Painting*. Barcelona: Museu d'Art Contemporani de Barcelona, 2001.

Brett, Guy. *Force Fields: Phases of the Kinetic*. Barcelona: Museu d'Art Contemporani de Barcelona, 2000.

Buchloh, Benjamin H. D., and Judith F. Rodenbeck, eds. *Experiments in the Everyday: Allan Kaprow and Robert Watts—Events, Objects, Documents*. New York: Columbia University, Miriam and Ira D. Wallach Art Gallery, 1999.

Debray, Cécile, ed. *Le Nouveau Réalisme*. Paris: Galeries Nationales du Grand Palais, 2007.

De Salvo, Donna, and Catherine Gudis, eds. *Ray Johnson: Correspondences*. Columbus, OH: Wexner Center for the Arts; New York: Flammarion, 1999.

d'Harnoncourt, Anne, and Kynaston McShine, eds. *Marcel Duchamp*. New York: Museum of Modern Art; Philadelphia: Philadelphia Museum of Art, 1973.

Dickerman, Leah, ed. *Dada*. Washington, DC: National Gallery of Art, 2005.

Dobke, Dirk. *Roth Time: A Dieter Roth Retrospective*. New York: Museum of Modern Art, 2003.

Fischer, Alfred M., ed. *George Brecht Events. A Heterospective*. Cologne: Walther König, 2005.

Gumpert, Lynn, ed. *The Art of the Everyday: The Quotidian in Postwar French Culture*. New York: New York University Press, 1997.

Hapgood, Susan. *Neo-Dada: Redefining Art, 1958–1962*. New York: American Federation of Arts, 1994.

Haskell, Barbara. *Blam! The Explosion of Pop, Minimalism and Performance, 1958–1964*. New York: Museum of Modern Art; Philadelphia: Philadelphia Museum of Art, 1973.

Holeczek, Bernhard, and Lida von Mengden, eds. *Zufall als Prinzip: Spielwelt, Methode und System in der Kunst des 20. Jahrhunderts*. Ludwigshafen, Germany: Wilhelm-Hack-Museum, 1992.

Marter, Joan M., ed. *Off Limits: Rutgers University and the Avant-Garde, 1957–1963*. New Brunswick, NJ: Rutgers University Press, 1999.

McKenna, George L. *Art by Chance: Fortuitous Impressions*. Kansas City, MO: Nelson-Atkins Museum of Art, 1989.

Meyer-Hermann, Eva, Andrew Perchuk, and Stephanie Rosenthal, eds. *Allan Kaprow—Art as Life*. Los Angeles: Getty Research Institute, 2008.

Molesworth, Helen ed. *Work Ethic*. Baltimore: The Baltimore Museum of Art; University Park: Pennsylvania State University Press, 2003.

Mundy, Jennifer, and Dawn Ades, eds. *Surrealism: Desire Unbound*. London: Tate Modern; Princeton, NJ: Princeton University Press, 2001.

Munroe, Alexandra, ed. *Japanese Art After 1945: Scream against the Sky*. New York: Harry N. Abrams, 1994.

———. *The Third Mind: American Artists Contemplate Asia, 1860–1989*. New York: Solomon R. Guggenheim Museum, 2009.

Pincus-Witten, Robert. *Against Order: Chance and Art*. Philadelphia: Institute of Contemporary Art, 1970.

Rubin, William. *Dada, Surrealism, and Their Heritage*. New York: Museum of Modern Art, 1968.

Schimmel, Paul, ed. *Out of Actions: Between Performance and the Object, 1949–1979*. Los Angeles: Museum of Contemporary Art, 2000.

Seitz, William. *The Art of Assemblage*. New York: Museum of Modern Art, 1961.

Tucker, Maria, and James Monte, eds. *Anti-Illusion: Procedures / Materials*. New York: Whitney Museum of American Art, 1969.

Van der Marck, Jan. *François Morellet: Systems*. Buffalo, NY: Albright-Knox Art Gallery, 1984.

Zelevansky, Lynn, ed. *Beyond Geometry: Experiments in Form, 1940s–70s*. Los Angeles: Los Angeles County Museum of Art; Cambridge, MA: MIT Press, 2004.

ARTICLES AND ESSAYS

Adcock, Craig. "Marcel Duchamp's Gap Music: Operations in the Space between Art and Noise." In *Wireless Imagination: Sound, Radio, and the Avant-Garde*, ed. Douglas Kahn and Gregory Whitehead. Cambridge, MA: MIT Press, 1994.

Andreotti, Libero. "Play-tactics of the Internationale Situationniste." *October* 91 (Winter 2000): 37–58.

Arnheim, Rudolph. "Accident and the Necessity of Art." In *Toward a Psychology of Art*. Berkeley: University of California Press, 1966.

Bois, Yve-Alain. "François Morellet / Sol LeWitt: A Case Study." In *Artistic Exchange: Acts of the 28th International Congress of Art History, Berlin, July 15–20*. Berlin: Akademia Verlag, 1992.

Bryars, Gavin. "Notes on Marcel Duchamp's Music." *Studio International* 192, no. 984 (November / December 1976): 274–79.

Buchloh, Benjamin H.D. "Readymade, Objet Trouvé, Idée Reçue." In *Dissent: The Issue of Modern Art in Boston*. Boston: The Institute of Contemporary Art, 1985.

Carrick, Jill. "Phallic Victories? Niki de Saint Phalle's *Tirs*." *Art History* 26, no. 5 (November 2003): 700–729.

Challinor, Michael. "Chance and Structure: Randomness and Formalism in Art." *Leonardo* 4, no. 1 (Winter 1971): 1–11.

Dezeuze, Anna. "'Neo-Dada,' 'Junk Aesthetic,' and Spectator Participation." In *Neo-Avant-Garde*, ed. David Hopkins. Amsterdam: Rodopi, 2006.

———. "Origins of the Fluxus Score: From Indeterminacy to the 'Do-It-Yourself' Artwork." *Performance Research* 7, no. 3 (2002): 78–94.

Doris, David. "Zen Vaudeville: A Medi(t) ation in the Margins of Fluxus." In *The Fluxus Reader*, ed. Ken Friedman. New York: Academy Editions, 1998, 91–135.

Fer, Briony. "The Laws of Chance." In *On Abstract Art*. New Haven, CT: Yale University Press, 1997.

Foster, Hal. "What's Neo about the Neo-Avant-Garde?" *October* 70 (Fall 1994): 5–32.

Freud, Sigmund. "Parapraxes." In *The Everyday Life Reader*, ed. Ben Highmore. London: Routledge, 2002.

Gamboni, Dario. "'Fabrication of accidents': Factura and Chance in Nineteenth-Century Art." *Res: Journal of Anthropology and Aesthetics* 36 (Autumn 1999): 205–225.

———. "Stumbling Over / Upon Art." *Cabinet* 19 (Fall 2005): 58–61.

Gilbert-Rolfe, Jeremy. "Not By Chance Alone." In *Chance: The Catalogue*, ed. Sarah Gavlak and Chris Kraus. Santa Monica, CA: Smart Art Press, 1996.

Hamilton, Jaimey. "Arman's System of Objects." *Art Journal* 67, no.1 (Spring 2008): 55–67.

Hancock, Jane. "Arp's Chance Collages." In *Dada/Dimensions*, ed. Stephen C. Foster. Ann Arbor, MI: UMI Research Press, 1985.

Hopkins, David. "Questioning Dada's Potency: Picabia's *La Sainte Vierge* and the Dialogue with Duchamp." *Art History* 15, no. 3 (1992): 317–33.

Jenny, Laurent. "From Breton to Dali: The Adventures of Automatism." *October* 51 (Winter 1989): 105–14.

Joseph, Branden W. "Robert Morris and John Cage: Reconstructing a Dialogue." *October* 81 (Summer 1997): 59–69.

Kaprow, Allan. "The Legacy of Jackson Pollock." *ARTnews* 57, no. 6 (October 1958): 24–26, 55–57.

———. "Some Observations on Contemporary Art." In *New Forms—New Media I*. New York: Martha Jackson Gallery, 1960.

Kuo, Michelle. "9 *Evenings* in Reverse." In *9 Evenings Reconsidered: Art, Theatre, and Engineering, 1966*. Cambridge, MA: MIT List Visual Arts Center, 2006.

Kurczynski, Karen. "Ironic Gestures: Asger Jorn, Informel, and Abstract Expressionism." In *Abstract Expressionism: The International Context*, ed. Joan M. Marter. New Brunswick, NJ: Rutgers University Press, 2007.

Laxton, Susan. "The Guarantor of Chance: Surrealism's Ludic Practices." *Papers of Surrealism* 1 (Winter 2003), http://www.surrealismcentre.ac.uk/publications/papers/journal1/index.htm.

Lears, Jackson. "Out of Control: Art and Accident in a Managerial Age." In *Off Limits: Rutgers University and the Avant-Garde, 1957–1963*, ed. Joan M. Marter. New Brunswick, NJ: Rutgers University Press, 1999.

Lippard, Lucy, and John Chandler. "The Dematerialization of Art." *Art International* 12, no. 2 (February 1968): 31–36.

Molesworth, Helen. "From Dada to Neo-Dada and Back Again." *October* 105 (Summer 2003): 177–181.

Morellet, François. "The Choice in Present-Day Art." In *DATA: Directions in Art, Theory and Aesthetics*, ed. Anthony Hill. Greenwich, CT: New York Graphic Society, Ltd., 1969.

Potts, Alex. "Autonomy in Post-war Art, Quasi-heroic and Casual." *Oxford Art Journal* 27, no. 1 (2004): 43–59.

Robinson, Julia. "The Brechtian Event Score: A Structure in Fluxus." *Performance Research* 7, no. 3 (2002): 110–123.

———. "Maciunas as Producer: Performative Design in the Art of the 1960s." *Grey Room* 33 (Fall 2008): 56–83.

———. "The Sculpture of Indeterminacy: Alison Knowles's Beans and Variations." *Art Journal* 63, no. 4 (Winter 2004): 96–115.

Rose, Barbara. "Dada Then and Now." *Art International* 7, no. 1 (January 1963): 22–28.

Rosenberg, Harold. "The American Action Painters." *ARTnews* 51, no. 8 (December 1952): 22–23, 48–50.

Schapiro, Meyer. "The Liberating Quality of the Avant-Garde." *ARTnews* 56, no. 4 (Summer 1957): 36–42.

Spoerri, Daniel. "Trap Pictures." In *Zero*, ed. Otto Piene and Heinz Mack. Cambridge, MA: MIT Press, 1973. Originally published in 1961.

Zweig, Janet. "Ars Combinatoria: Mystical Systems, Procedural Art, and the Computer." *Art Journal* 56, no. 3 (Autumn 1997): 20–29.

INDEX

LENDERS TO THE EXHIBITION

Alan Koppel Gallery, Chicago
William Anastasi
Ashiya City Museum of Art & History*
Sharon Avery-Fahlström, The Öyvind Fahlström Foundation and Archives, Museu d'art contemporani de Barcelona (MACBA)*
Timothy Baum
Centre Pompidou, Musée national d'art moderne / Centre de création industrielle, Paris
Dedalus Foundation, Inc., New York
Gino Di Maggio
Dieter Roth Foundation, Hamburg
Fondazione Mimmo Rotella, Milan
The Getty Research Institute, Los Angeles
Indiana University Art Museum, Bloomington
Ellsworth Kelly
Knoedler & Company, New York
Leo Castelli Gallery, New York
Howard and Mauree Miller
François Morellet
Robert Morris
Museum of Fine Arts, Houston
The Museum of Modern Art, New York
Nam June Paik Studios, Inc., New York
Peter Namuth*
Niki Charitable Art Foundation*
Private collection, New York
Private collection, St. Louis
Private collections
Roland Gibson Gallery, State University of New York at Potsdam
Saint Louis Art Museum
San Francisco Museum of Modern Art
Gilbert and Lila Silverman
University of Michigan Museum of Art, Ann Arbor
Washington University Libraries, Department of Special Collections, St. Louis
Yale University Art Gallery, New Haven

* These lenders generously provided documentary materials for the exhibition

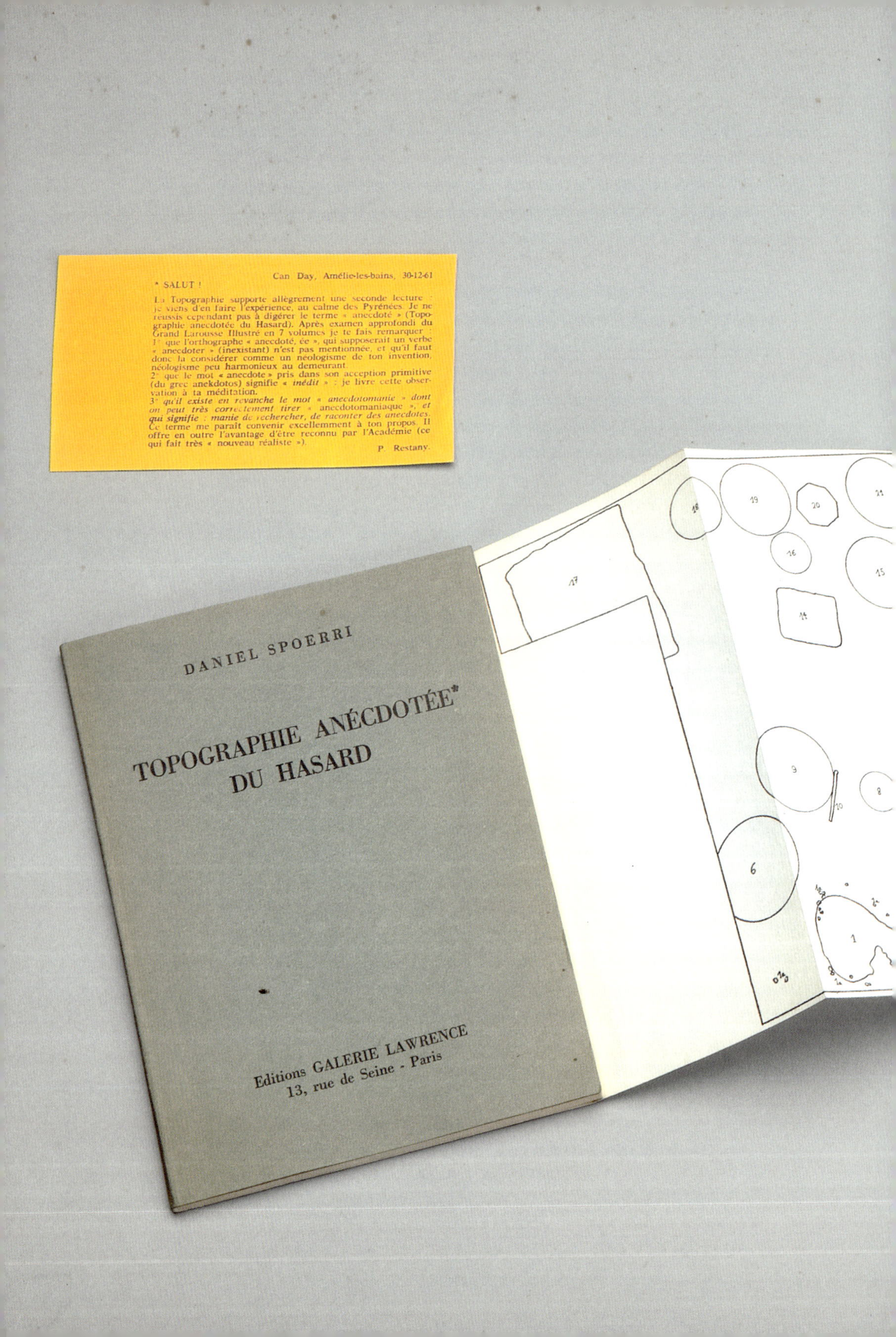
Can Day, Amélie-les-bains, 30-12-61
* SALUT !
La Topographie supporte allègrement une seconde lecture : je viens d'en faire l'expérience, au calme des Pyrénées. Je ne réussis cependant pas à digérer le terme « anecdoté » (Topographie anecdotée du Hasard). Après examen approfondi du Grand Larousse Illustré en 7 volumes je te fais remarquer :
1° que l'orthographe « anecdoté, ée », qui supposerait un verbe « anecdoter » (inexistant) n'est pas mentionnée, et qu'il faut donc la considérer comme un néologisme de ton invention, néologisme peu harmonieux au demeurant.
2° que le mot « anecdote » pris dans son acception primitive (du grec anekdotos) signifie « inédit » : je livre cette observation à ta méditation.
3° qu'il existe en revanche le mot « anecdotomanie » dont on peut très correctement tirer « anecdotomaniaque », et qui signifie : manie de rechercher, de raconter des anecdotes. Ce terme me paraît convenir excellemment à ton propos. Il offre en outre l'avantage d'être reconnu par l'Académie (ce qui fait très « nouveau réaliste »).
P. Restany.
DANIEL SPOERRI
TOPOGRAPHIE ANÉCDOTÉE*
DU HASARD
Editions GALERIE LAWRENCE
13, rue de Seine - Paris